"This original and compelling study of the phenomenon of sound in Christian worship invites its readers into a world much more complex than song, sermon, and vocalized prayer. Juliette Day's multi-disciplinary approach to the way worshippers hear and are themselves heard draws on the physics of sound as well as physiological, ritual, and architectural accounts of the way sound is created and received, as well as (most importantly) attending to the marking of sound by silence. Participating in the liturgy will not be the same again for those who let this book guide future listening and hearing."

— Bridget Nichols, author of *Lively Oracles of God*

"Contra Macbeth's view that life is full of sound and fury, signifying nothing, in worship sound—spoken, chanted, individual, or communal, as well as ritual gestures and silence—signify everything. In this widely-researched book, Juliette Day discusses contemporary understandings of sound and aurality, illustrated from different Christian traditions and from her wide knowledge of the history of liturgy. This study fills a glaring academic void, and it should be read and heeded by all those who study liturgy and those who both plan and lead worship."

— Bryan D. Spinks, Bishop F. Percy Goddard Professor Emeritus of Liturgical Studies and Pastoral Theology, Yale Institute of Sacred Music and Yale Divinity School

The Alcuin Club: Promoting the Study of Liturgy

Founded in 1897, the Alcuin Club seeks to promote the study of Christian liturgy and worship in general with special reference to worship in the Anglican Communion. The Club has published a series of annual Collections, including *A Companion to Common Worship*, volumes 1 and 2, edited by Paul F. Bradshaw; and a new completely revised 4th edition of R. C. D. Jasper and G. J. Cuming, *Prayers of the Eucharist: Early and Reformed*, edited by Paul F. Bradshaw and Maxwell E. Johnson (Liturgical Press Academic, 2019); also *Eucharistic Epicleses Ancient and Modern* by Anne McGowan (SPCK, 2014); *Dean Dwelly of Liverpool: Liturgical Genius* by Peter Kennerley (Carnegie Publishing, 2015); *Ancient Christian Worship* by Andrew B. McGowan (Baker Academic, 2016); *The Rise and Fall of the Incomparable Liturgy: The Book of Common Prayer 1559–1906* by Bryan D. Spinks (SPCK, 2017) and, by the same author, *Scottish Presbyterian Worship* (St Andrew Press, 2020); *The Pilgrimage of Egeria* by Anne McGowan and Paul F. Bradshaw (Liturgical Press Academic, 2018); *Lively Oracles of God: Perspectives on the Bible and Liturgy*, edited by Gordon Jeanes and Bridget Nichols (Liturgical Press Academic, 2022); and *Shaping the Assembly: How Our Buildings Form Us in Worship*, edited by Thomas O'Loughlin (Messenger Publications, 2023).

The Alcuin Liturgy Guide series aims to address the theology and practice of worship, and includes *The Use of Symbols in Worship*, edited by Christopher Irvine, two volumes covering the celebration of the Christian Year: *Celebrating Christ's Appearing: Advent to Christmas*; and *Celebrating Christ's Victory: Ash Wednesday to Trinity*, both by Benjamin Gordon-Taylor and Simon Jones, and most recently *Celebrating Christian Initiation* by Simon Jones.

The Club works in partnership with the Group for the Renewal of Worship (GROW) in the publication of the Joint Liturgical Studies series, with two studies being published each year.

In 2013 the Club also published a major new work of reference, *The Study of Liturgy and Worship: An Alcuin Guide*, edited by Juliette Day and Benjamin Gordon-Taylor (SPCK, 2013).

Members of the Club receive publications of the current year free and others at a reduced rate. The President of the Club is the Rt Revd Dr Stephen Platten, its Chairman is the Revd Canon Christopher Irvine, and the Secretary is the Revd Thomas McLean. For details of membership and the annual subscription, contact The Alcuin Club, 20 Burrows Close, Headington, Oxford OX3 8AN United Kingdom; email: publications@alcuinclub.org.uk; or visit the Alcuin Club website at: www.alcuinclub.org.uk.

Alcuin Club Collections 99

Hearing Our Prayers

An Exploration of Liturgical Listening

Juliette J. Day

**LITURGICAL PRESS
ACADEMIC**

Collegeville, Minnesota
litpress.org

Cover design by Laurie Ingram Art + Design.
Cover art courtesy of Wikimedia Commons.

Unless otherwise noted, Scripture quotations are from New Revised Standard Version Bible © 1989 National Council of the Churches of Christ in the United States of America. Used by permission. All rights reserved worldwide.

Excerpts from the English translation of *The General Instruction of the Roman Missal* © 2007, International Commission on English in the Liturgy Corporation. All rights reserved.

Excerpt from the English translation of the General Instruction from *The Liturgy of the Hours* © 1973, 1974, 1975, International Commission on English in the Liturgy Corporation (ICEL); excerpts from the General Instruction of the English translation of *The Roman Missal* © 2010, ICEL. All rights reserved.

© 2024 by Juliette J. Day
Published by Liturgical Press, Collegeville, Minnesota. All rights reserved. No part of this book may be used or reproduced in any manner whatsoever, except brief quotations in reviews, without written permission of Liturgical Press, Saint John's Abbey, PO Box 7500, Collegeville, MN 56321-7500.

Library of Congress Cataloging-in-Publication Data

Names: Day, Juliette, author.
Title: Hearing our prayers : an exploration of liturgical listening / Juliette J. Day.
Description: Collegeville, Minnesota : Liturgical Press Academic, [2024] | Series: Alcuin club collections ; 99 | Includes bibliographical references and index. | Summary: "In Hearing our Prayers, Juliette Day draws upon insights from a variety of disciplines to understand this one but often overlooked aspect of liturgical ritual, discover how acts of audition occur in Christian worship, learn what it means to listen liturgically, and to explore how it is foundational for the way in which we pray, think about God, the Church, and the world"—Provided by publisher.
Identifiers: LCCN 2023027976 (print) | LCCN 2023027977 (ebook) | ISBN 9780814669419 (trade paperback) | ISBN 9780814669426 (epub) | ISBN 9780814669433 (pdf)
Subjects: LCSH: Prayer—Christianity.
Classification: LCC BV220 .D37 2023 (print) | LCC BV220 (ebook) | DDC 248.3/2—dc23/eng/20231130
LC record available at https://lccn.loc.gov/2023027976
LC ebook record available at https://lccn.loc.gov/2023027977

Contents

List of Illustrations   vii

Acknowledgments   ix

Introduction   1

   Chapter 1
      Liturgical Soundscapes   9

   Chapter 2
      Hearing and Listening   31

   Chapter 3
      Ritual Listening   54

   Chapter 4
      Listening to Speech and Music   72

   Chapter 5
      Listening to Silence   97

   Chapter 6
      Hearing Noise   117

   Chapter 7
      Paying Attention   139

   Chapter 8
      Aural Architecture   158

Conclusion: Listening and Liturgical Listening   183

Bibliography   194

Index   213

List of Illustrations

Figure 1
William Hogarth, *The Sleeping Congregation* (1762). Etching and engraving. The Metropolitan Museum of Art, Acc. No. 91.1.1. Image courtesy of the Metropolitan Museum of Art, Creative Commons Zero (CC0) License.

Figure 2
William Hogarth, *Credulity, Superstition, and Fanaticism* (1762). Etching and engraving. The Metropolitan Museum of Art, Acc. No. 91.1.117. Image courtesy of the Metropolitan Museum of Art, Creative Commons Zero (CC0) License.

Figure 3
Jean Perrissin, *Le Temple de Paradis* (Lyon, France, 1569–1570). Oil on canvas. Bibliothèque de Genève, now in the Musée internationale de la Réforme, Geneva. Wikipedia Commons License CC-BY-SA 4.0.

Figure 4
The Broadway Tabernacle (New York, 1850). Print. The Miriam and Ira D. Wallach Division of Art, Prints and Photographs: Print Collection, The New York Public Library. "The Broadway Tabernacle," The New York Public Library Digital Collections. Accessed February 17, 2023. https://digitalcollections.nypl.org/items/510d47da-2381-a3d9-e040-e00a18064a99.

Figure 5
Interior View of the Metropolitan Tabernacle, depicting Charles H. Spurgeon preaching from pulpit. Image from Henry Davenport Northrop, *Life and Works of Rev. Charles H. Spurgeon* (Ontario: Bradley, Garretson, 1890), 200, plate.

Figure 6
The choir of San Clemente, Rome, with its double ambos. Photo: Dnalor 01, Wikipedia Commons License CC-BY-SA 3.0.

Figure 7
Sauvo parish church, southern Finland. Photo: Juliette Day.

Acknowledgments

I would particularly like to thank the Institute of Sacred Music at Yale University for awarding me a research fellowship in 2016–17. It was during this year that I enjoyed the freedom and resources to undertake the groundwork for this book, as well as to enjoy the numerous opportunities to share my thoughts with colleagues in a critical, yet supportive, environment.

Introduction

Worshippers go to church to hear Mass. In the late fourth century, catechumens were told by Bishop Cyril of Jerusalem that they are so-called because they "hear the Word of God echoing around" but do not understand it. In litany intercessions, God is asked, in his mercy, to "hear our prayer." The congregation might be invited to "listen to the Word of the Lord according to Saint Matthew." An Orthodox deacon will cry out, "Let us attend." In these various ways the liturgical activity of hearing is brought to the foreground, so it is curious that liturgical books and manuals to guide liturgical performance emphasize speech, rather than listening, as the dominant activity for the ministers and the people. The liturgical books prescribe who will say, or sing, what and when, and instructions may even be given about volume and performance. A rubric will often say, "The minister says," or, "The people say," but I have never encountered one which says, "The congregation listens." We could be forgiven, therefore, for presuming that the primary function of the liturgical assembly is to speak to God; however, the reality of the liturgical experience of the laity in most churches is that they spend a lot of time listening and not much being vocal. Victor Desarnaulds undertook a qualitative survey of the types of worship sounds and who makes them in a number of Swiss churches.[1] His results revealed that in Reformed churches, the people were passive for 80 percent of the time, and in Catholic churches for 45 percent of the time. Of course they were not exactly passive, but rather their participation was auditory and not by speaking, or singing, or making music.

[1] Victor Desarnaulds, "De l'acoustique des églises en Suisse—une approche pluridisciplinaire" (PhD diss., École Polytechnique Fédérale de Lausanne, 2002), 58–60.

The idea for this book originated with the enlightening statement of Gemma Corradi Fiumara that

> there could be no saying without hearing, no speaking which is not an integral part of listening, no speech which is not somehow received.[2]

That which we say or sing is not just an exclamation, but is directed to another whom we invite to hear it; it is only when the sound is received that the communicative act is complete. Speaking and hearing require relations between people, and between people and God, in order that the intention of the communication can be fulfilled. Corradi Fiumara continues: "in my opinion, something can speak if it is listened to, rather than there being something it might say, that one would subsequently attend to by listening."[3] Speech is not just completed by hearing, but it is constituted by it.

The relational aspect of speaking and hearing is essential in the church. Paul reminded the Corinthian congregation of their obligations as members of the Body of Christ (1 Cor. 12:12-31), and then immediately afterwards told them that without a relationship of love there can be no communication: "If I speak in the tongues of men or of angels, but do not have love, I am only a resounding gong or a clanging cymbal" (1 Cor 13:1). A gong or cymbal, sounded frivolously without regard for communication, is not a good model for our liturgical worship, but a relationship of love is. Such a relational model is proposed by Corradi Fiumara: all sonic communication requires reception in order for it to be completed, to achieve what it sets out to do.

The focus of much liturgical scholarship is on the words to be spoken or sung as presented in textual form, which are discussed as if the text itself revealed the auditory experience of the liturgical event. Paul Ricoeur wrote that "what is fixed by writing is a discourse which could be said but it is written precisely because it is not said."[4]

---

[2] Gemma Corradi Fiumara, *The Other Side of Language: A Philosophy of Listening* (London: Routledge, 1990), 1.
[3] Corradi Fiumara, *Other Side of Language*, 72.
[4] Paul Ricoeur, "What Is a Text?," in *From Text to Action: Essays in Hermeneutics II*, trans. Kathleen Blamey and John Thompson, 106 (London: Athlone Press, 1991).

For him, writing occurs where speech could have occurred and it may replace speech, or indeed be completely unrelated to speech. Texts offer us a mirage of stability over and against the ephemeral nature of sound. As Walter Ong so memorably put it, "When I pronounce the word 'permanence,' by the time I get to the '-nence,' the 'perma-' is gone and has to be gone."[5] What, then, is the value of text, speech, and audition in liturgical worship? Does it matter if our discourse of praise, petition, and anamnesis is conveyed audibly or textually? Most worshippers would want to assert that the act of worship is sonic (and multisensory), even while they read, silently or aloud, the carefully produced and comprehensive service sheet; most worshippers would not characterize their Sunday devotions as an hour spent reading to Jesus.

Augustine, though, reminded his congregation of the ephemeral nature of the text and that hearing in worship is preparatory for hearing (and seeing) in heaven:

> . . . and that you hear readings in the Church every day, is daily bread; and that you hear and sing hymns is daily bread. These are the things we need on our pilgrimage. But when we finally get there, do you imagine we shall be listening to a book? We shall be seeing the Word itself, listening to the Word itself, eating it, drinking it, as the angels do now. Do the angels need books, or lectures, or readers? Of course not. They read by seeing, since they see Truth itself.[6]

Sermon 57 is an explanation of the Lord's Prayer, a text normally experienced, in Hippo as now, orally and aurally. As a paradigmatic prayer, it offers many avenues of investigation, not least in relation to the aims of this book. Here is a prayer given by Christ for us to say to the Father. We hear ourselves speaking words which are God's and which we make our own; we assume God too hears his own words, and we too hear ourselves (not just one's self) saying them.

---

[5] Walter Ong, *Orality and Literacy: The Technologizing of the Word* (London: Routledge, 2002), 32.

[6] Augustine, *Sermon 57.7*, in *The Works of Saint Augustine*, ed. John E. Rotelle, vol. III/3, *Sermons (51–94) on the Old Testament*, trans. Edmund Hill, 112 (Hyde Park, NY: New City Press, 1991).

As we do this, we "hear-into-being" God's people in relationship with God and with each other. Thus the conditions for an authentic hearing are established: a speaking by God, through us, to God, whom we also hear. Thus, as Corradi Fiumara says, there can "be no saying without hearing, no speaking which is not an integral part of listening, no speech which is not somehow received."

This book sets out to explore how we *hear our prayers*. It offers neither a blueprint nor a model for congregational worship, but integrates reflections from theologians, philosophers, psychologists, historians, and, yes, liturgists too, about how acts of audition occur in Christian worship and what it might mean to "listen liturgically." Corrdi Fiumara proposed that "a philosophy of listening can be envisaged as an attempt to recover the neglected and perhaps deeper roots of what we call thinking, an activity which in some way gathers and synthesizes human endeavours."[7] This exploration of liturgical listening will gather and synthesize the auditory experience of worship, and indicate how it is foundational for the way in which we think about God, the church, and the world.

This book is more or less divided in to three main sections: in the first (chapters 1–3), I consider what the sonic environment of worship reveals and how we hear in it; in the second (chapters 4–6), the sounds of worship will be discussed in relation to their ritual significance and the listening strategies each sound-type requires; and the final section (chapters 7–8) investigates two factors which affect our ability to listen liturgically.

Soundscape is a useful catchall term for the totality of sounds available to be heard in an environment, because it takes account of the simultaneous presence of approved, disapproved, and ambient sounds and invites us to consider the criteria we apply when judging the value of a sound. Sounds do not just exist in the world to be heard, but are received and evaluated by listeners according to personal, social, and cultural preferences; in the church, theological and ecclesial differences have also been expressed in sonic terms. Chapter 1 concludes with proposing that the liturgical soundscape can be usefully explored in relation to three main sound-types: intentional sounds, unintentional sounds, and noise. What sorts of sounds belong

---

[7] Corradi Fiumara, *Other Side of Language*, 13.

in each category depends very much on the tradition and culture of each congregation, and using these as the components of the liturgical soundscape allows us to avoid prejudging the sounds of other communities.

Understanding how sounds are received and what it means to *hear* is discussed in chapter 2. Most languages have many words for *audition* that reveal the hearer's level of intent. It will be suggested that *listening* is a more appropriate word for the liturgical context. Philosophical and theological approaches to listening will be considered in relation to how listening, both physical and spiritual, contributes to and affects our sense of the world, ourselves, and God. The chapter concludes with a discussion of modes of listening which reflect nuances in the task of liturgical listening.

Chapter 3 will propose that listening is a ritual act to be considered alongside ritual speech, music, and gesture. Noting that ritual theorists have said very little about audition, ritual listening will be looked at as the "other side" of (ritual) language, following the suggestion of Corradi Fiumara. The category of *ritualized listening* is suggested for when a liturgical act is constituted, performed, and completed by an act of audition; examples will be offered from historic and contemporary worship.

The principal intentional sounds to be listened to in worship are speech and music, which can be placed in a sonic spectrum which starts from the spoken word, through cantillation, chant, and the singing of psalms and hymns, to instrumental music. Congregations attach different values to these sound-types, which often depend on the worship traditions of their denomination or of the wider culture. Although the physiological auditory system will function in the same way for all these sounds, contemporary psychological and cognitive studies have shown that we process them differently, and therefore make sense of their content in different ways. The chapter concludes by exploring listening to the intentional sounds of worship as embodied, as engaging the senses, and as creating social identities.

An overlooked "sound" in worship is silence; it is often intentional, even if those intentions are rarely clear. Silence, which has different qualities, is not the absence of sound but a space between sounds out of which the other intentional sounds are able to emerge. It will be argued that the structure and rhythm of worship is constituted by silences and not by the intentional or ritual sounds. Performing and hearing silence is also a ritual act; however, imprecise notions of its function can result in ritual failure when it may not be deployed in the most appropriate place nor for sufficient length of time. Silence, unlike the other intentional sounds of worship, must be performed by those who hear it, and it requires participants to be more acutely aware of being in the presence of God and of others.

If silence is overlooked, then "noise" certainly is not. Noise is sound to which the hearer reacts negatively, which the hearer considers not to belong in the context, and usually one which is made by others who are probably not listening correctly. It is considered as a theological and moral problem connected to sin and damnation, and the ecclesial consequences of noise during worship are viewed in light of poor adherence to the church community, and thus to Christ. Noise in worship manifests itself in different ways, from an unthinking distraction to deliberate disruption. Some behaviors persist in being considered as noise, whereas others are tolerated; but in any case, judgements about what sounds are noise are almost always subjective and contextual. Noise is certainly not an intentional sound, but it is part of the liturgical soundscape and it produces a response in the hearers which informs their experience of the worship event.

Listening requires attentiveness to the intentional sounds of worship as well as to the producers of those sounds. Paying attention is, however, rather difficult, and so understanding the physiological and psychological difficulties which lie behind inattentive listening will help contextualize the many complaints from preachers about behaviors which indicate a lack of attentiveness. Aural attentiveness has an ethical dimension to it when the listener enables the sonic participation of others, and there is also a spiritual dimension as the worshipper attends to the divine words pronounced in the liturgy. Because in spiritual discourse what enters the ear also enters the heart and the mind, the worshipper is expected to discipline their ears so that hearing God is not compromised. The complaints and the remedies from different ages reveal attitudes about the function of listening in worship more generally.

For most Christians, worship takes place in specially constructed spaces, and these have a direct effect on what is heard and how it is heard. Architectural styles and materials cause particular acoustical conditions by which the sound signal is modified before it reaches the ear of the listener; in some cases, the sound can be rendered unintelligible by the acoustic properties of the space. The intentional sounds of worship—speech, chant, singing, music, silence—each require a different optimal acoustic environment, and so liturgical listeners will necessarily be required to make compromises in their auditory experience. Listeners will often tolerate extreme compromises, such as unintelligible speech, because the sound signal correlates with the way in which a particular congregation hears itself before God. Specific changes to the design, materials, and arrangement of the space to enable better listening are evident in different historical periods; the most significant concerns the position of the pulpit in relation to the people, but this chapter will also look at some other strategies employed to enhance liturgical listening.

The final chapter, which acts as a review and conclusion of the book, considers how *liturgical listening* might be defined as an individual and communal auditory experience which constitutes a form of ritual participation.

Chapter 1

Liturgical Soundscapes

"Make a joyful noise to the Lord."
—Psalm 100:1

Every Christian community has decided for itself what a "joyful noise" consists of, based on its own particular theological, cultural, and historical responses to God. Imagine in your mind's ear what these worship events might sound like:

- Morning prayer among Benedictine monks;
- Greek Orthodox Divine Liturgy;
- A Pentecostal worship service;
- A Lutheran Service of the Word.

Even if you have never attended such worship, you would probably be able to have a reasonable guess at the style of worship and what sort of sounds you would hear, and be able to differentiate between the congregations on that basis. Of course, these examples function rather as caricatures, but they alert us already to the distinctive sonic environment of worship in different churches and congregations.

In the same way that literary genres can be distinguished by differences in their general characteristics, so too can worship genres and their soundscapes. The key differences might be determined by the type of music, the relationship between singing and speech, and the amount of silence. Each of these categories—music, speech, and silence—can be further subdivided: singing, instrumental music, the permitted instruments; who speaks and when; the language and style; the duration and function of silence. These reflect distinctive worship practices which are derived from the traditions of each denomination, and decisions at the local level about the style of worship that is appropriate and possible in each congregation.

The Soundscape

When R. Murray Schafer proposed the concept of the "soundscape" in his 1977 book, *Tuning the World* (reprinted in 1993 under the title *The Soundscape*[1]), he may not have been aware how ubiquitous the term would become, nor the variety of historical and contemporary musicological, anthropological, architectural, and theoretical studies it would inspire, nor even the interesting emphases of those who would develop and modify his concept. In the concept of "soundscape," he proposed an aural equivalent to "landscape," and by using historical and technologically driven research aimed to demonstrate the detrimental effect of post-industrial and urban noise in contrast to the auditory harmony of agrarian societies. Those planning cities and buildings, he argued, should take account of the negative effects of noise upon the psychological health of inhabitants, and if the type and level of harmful noise could be demonstrated, then noise-abatement processes could be initiated.[2]

It was, however, his methodological rather than his political concerns which have been most influential. He was concerned not just with how sound might be measured with scientific acoustical methods, but with the social impact of sounds and their significance. Schafer proposed a threefold classification of environmental sounds: the keynote, the signal, and the soundmark.[3] The keynote sound is the fundamental sound in, and created by, an environment; it is heard

---

[1] R. Murray Schafer, *The Tuning of the World* (New York: Alfred A. Knopf, 1977); *The Soundscape: Our Sonic Environment and the Tuning of the World* (Rochester, VT: Destiny Books, 1994).
[2] Schafer, *Tuning of the World*, 4.
[3] Schafer, 9–10.

but not remarked upon, and is the ground upon which other sounds emerge. Signals are foreground sounds which are consciously listened to; for example, alarms or warning sounds. The soundmark is analogous to a landmark; it is a characteristic sound which distinguishes communities or locations, and will be "especially regarded or noted by people in that community."[4] In pre-industrial communities, the keynote sound will come from natural features, such as water, wood, or cobblestones, and this allows the signal sound of church bells, for example, to be distinctly heard. In modern urban environments, the keynote may be traffic, and this "lo-fi" sound obscures and blends the signals such that it is difficult to separate signal from noise. He also noted how dominant sounds are linked to power in the community, and how an acoustic community is created by being within the range of the same sound. The important ideas to be taken from Schafer's book are that sound (a positive term) and noise (a negative term) are geographically, culturally, and socially determined. It is this which enables us to focus our ears to some of what we hear but take many other sounds for granted because of overfamiliarity, and how the anticipation of certain sounds and noises in a particular context renders them less bothersome, even if they may still be intrusive.

There have been numerous critiques and refinements of Schafer's ideas since 1977, and here we will mention a few of those which we consider to be particularly relevant to this present investigation. Mainly these expand the concept to include social and epistemological considerations. Ari Kelman critiqued Schafer's definition because of its reliance on an individual's evaluation of the sonic environment, while at the same time diminishing his or her agency for the sounds: "Differentiating sounds that matter from sounds that don't means that the soundscape only matters as a kind of background for a listener's adjudication of sonic experiences."[5] Kelman surveyed a number of key developments in soundscape studies and definitions, which we will summarize here.

In Kay Kaufman Shelemay's *Soundscapes*, she suggested that soundscape is not analogous to landscape, a static concept, but to the

---

[4] Schafer, 10.

[5] Ari Y. Kelman, "Rethinking the Soundscape: A Critical Genealogy of a Key Term in Sound Studies," *Senses and Society* 5, no. 2 (2010): 219.

constantly fluid "seascape," especially when considering music.[6] This is because seascape "provides a more flexible analogy to music's ability to both stay in place and to move in the world today, to absorb changes in its content and performance styles, and to continue to accrue new layers of meanings."[7] For liturgical historians, this should alert us to the manner in which certain traditional worship sounds have endured, or become popular only to recede over the centuries, or been replaced by new sounds which are deemed traditional even if they were introduced relatively recently. The aural caricatures with which I started this chapter may have ecclesial characteristics, but their soundscape will be different at every worship event, and the significance which listeners assign to them is just as fluid.

Kelman also positively referred to Alain Corbin's *Village Bells*.[8] Corbin neither referred to Schafer nor used the term *soundscape*, but in "auditory landscape" he emphasized the social use of sound and how a society and culture determine what sound means, whether it is acceptable or not, and the ideological basis for such judgements. As we progress in our study of liturgical listening, a key theme will be how each ecclesial community has made decisions of this nature concerning the sound which can or ought to be heard in worship; and, indeed, has often asserted what sound or noise is unacceptable, such as those from different communities. Sound and noise do not just exist in the world to be heard, but are interpreted and contested as ideological expressions of societal self-understanding.

This leads onto one of Kelman's key critiques of Schafer's agenda: the elimination of unhelpful "background noise." Kelman asserts, "To study sound means to attend to background noise not as something to be tuned out or silenced, but as a critical component of acoustic phenomena, and making informed distinctions about sound is a social process in which context plays a crucial role." Therefore, he concludes, "Background noise is not background at all."[9] Sound and noise lie on a hierarchy of significance, as ancient and contemporary liturgical texts demonstrate. Worship committees attend only to the

---

[6] Kay Kaufman Shelemay, *Soundscapes: Exploring Music in a Changing World* (New York: W. W. Norton, 2006).

[7] Shelemay, *Soundscapes*, xxxiv; in Kelman, "Rethinking the Soundscape," 224.

[8] Alain Corbin, *Village Bells: Sound and Meaning in the 19th-Century French Countryside* (New York: Columbia University Press, 1998).

[9] Kelman, "Rethinking the Soundscape," 230.

authorized sounds of words to be spoken and sung; church musicians attend to the instrumental and vocal music for worship; but worshippers worship in a much more varied and complex soundscape which includes sounds that are unintentional or theologically irrelevant to the task in hand. To what extent do these sounds contribute to the worship event? In chapter 6, we will argue that noises are significant ecclesiological, social, and cultural markers and, following Kelman, they are "not background at all."

Sound functions as communication, and this was the emphasis adopted by Barry Truax, who applied theories from communication studies to investigate the soundscape. Listening, he says, "is the primary interface between the individual and the environment. It is a path of information exchange, not just the auditory reaction to stimuli."[10] Thus, for him, "soundscape" refers to the way in which the listeners *understand* the acoustic environment through habits of attention and inattention. Sounds become meaningful in their context not just in their content, and hence what they communicate will differ between individuals and societies. Relationships are established between the sound, the listener, and the environment, and sound may also influence behavior. Truax restricts the meaning of soundscape by distinguishing it from "the sonic environment"; the latter refers to all the sound in an environment, whereas his soundscape refers to how that environment is understood by those in it, both those creating the sound and those listening.[11] What constitutes the "keynote sound" or noise is contextual and determined by the listener, admittedly based upon habitual and social or communal factors. Personal interpretations of sound include these social responses independently of the actual sound itself: who made the sound, whether it is acceptable or taboo, or if it is idealized in the memory.[12] Such a social interpretation also reflects the ordering of society and the power relations in it, and, Truax writes, "Those challenging the social order often do so by using sounds that are normally proscribed, or by making them at an improper time."[13]

---

[10] Barry Truax, *Acoustic Communication* (Westport, CT: Ablex Publishing, 2001), xviii.
[11] Truax, *Acoustic Communication*, 11.
[12] Truax, 29.
[13] Truax, 43.

Listening, therefore, constitutes the (acoustic) interface between the environment and the listener, but it works both ways because the listener is also a sound-maker as "even the sound of one's own voice comes back to the ear colored by the environment."[14] For Truax, the soundscape is "the entire system of the listener plus environment." When the system is well balanced, a high degree of communication can occur, and the listener is in an interactive relationship with the environment; "conversely an unbalanced environment is characterized by a high degree of redundancy and low amount of information exchange."[15]

Truax proposed the notion of an "acoustic community": a "soundscape where acoustic information plays a pervasive role in the lives of the inhabitants" and in which acoustic information is shared. Such a community is defined by positive sound rather than noise, which plays a significant role in community self-definition because of spatial, temporal, or cultural factors. The community is linked and defined by those sounds whose meaning is immediately accessible to them. Of the most important are "sound signals" which intentionally convey information, just like Schafer's use of bells and alarms, but even random sounds may be meaningful to members of the community as they bear particular or historical significance. Truax suggests that one might call these "soundmarks", whose significance may be unique to the community and may be preserved because of the long-term memories associated with it.[16] They may be the loudest sounds in the community, and thus have spatial characteristics which define the acoustic boundaries of the community and temporal ones to establish or define the community when they sound. Sound signals can bind the community together by gathering them or warning them to stay away, and they have psychological power. He suggests that these sounds are often acoustically rich, possibly musical, and become readily imprinted on the mind.

Although the sound signal conveys specific information to the community, it also accrues a symbolic or metaphorical meaning through long exposure: "The experience of a specific instance of a

---

[14] Truax, xviii.
[15] Truax, 65.
[16] Truax, 66–67.

sound may take on special significance when it touches or evokes such symbolic imagery."[17] Additionally, sounds may take on metaphorical meanings when the aural image is connected to other images, or objects, events, and ideas. The symbolic and metaphorical use of sound signals "suggest the layers of meaning that sound can have within the acoustic community."[18]

Three Liturgical Soundscapes

Theoretical approaches to soundscape have not been used as a conceptual and interpretative tool in liturgical and ritual studies, even though the term itself has been borrowed and used in a few studies to describe the sound of worship in different historical periods, or to survey the sonic history of a particular Christian community. The inherent problem with studying sound is that, unlike text, it is ephemeral; once sounded and heard it is lost. It is interesting to note that in today's media reports of newsworthy events it is the eyewitness who is cited, whereas in certain historical contexts, the earwitness was also called to testify. This shows that our language is more geared to explaining what we see, rather than what we hear. In what follows, I will present the results of three very different attempts to recover the soundscape of historical worship events in order that we might start to attend to liturgical sounds and how we might interpret them.

The Church of Hagia Sophia

Alexander Lingas's historical study of the sound of Byzantine worship focused on music. Borrowing Schafer's "soundscape," he explained it as the "acoustic ecology" of Byzantine liturgy, "encompassing every intentional and circumstantial aspect of its sonic environment."[19] We should note that, although he claims to use the term

---

[17] Truax, 80.
[18] Truax, 80–81.
[19] Alexander Lingas, "From Earth to Heaven: The Changing Musical Soundscape of Byzantine Liturgy," in *Experiencing Byzantium: Papers from the 44th Spring Symposium of Byzantine Studies*, ed. Claire Nesbitt and Mark Jackson, 314 (Farnham, UK: Ashgate, 2013).

soundscape in its broadest sense and does accept that "it would have embraced sonic elements that were incidental or otherwise not under the direct control of those responsible for planning and celebrating services: the ambient noise generated by crowds and nature as heard both inside churches and, during stational processions, in courtyards, monastic compounds and on city streets"[20], he does in fact restrict his study to the "acoustic design," to the intentional sounds which are prescribed in the manuscripts, which are normative, authorized, and hierarchically ordered. As a musicologist, Lingas is interested primarily in the musical performance in the liturgy, and, with reference to Shelemay, "to investigate how musical performance simultaneously shapes and reflects the belief systems of those who produce and consume it within a particular cultural setting."[21]

The distinctive feature of Byzantine worship is a "seamless musicality" executed by individual singers and choirs, without musical instruments. The acoustic design can be recovered from liturgical manuscripts, especially those retaining forms of musical notation, and very occasionally from descriptions in commentaries and homilies on the liturgy, from the few visual depictions of singers, and from modern methods for the acoustic measurement of Byzantine churches. Combined, these enable Lingas to reconstruct the sonic environment of the liturgy for the church of Hagia Sophia: the number, distinctions, and roles of the singers, their spatial arrangement, and the constant call and response of choirs, as well as "changes of mode, vocal register or timbre, and variations in the rate of interchange between spatially separated singers, from vigorous in litanies and ferial antiphons from the Constantinopolitan Psalter to glacial in melismatic responsorial chants."[22] For Byzantine musicologists, the description and performed reconstruction of one of the most complex chants in the repertoire, the final antiphon for the Kneeling Vespers of Pentecost, demonstrates the full texture and complexity of the soundscape and its potential effect on the listeners. In this chant, a conventional beginning moves into the most complex long main section (his recording lasts thirty-five minutes), in which the threefold alleluia loses any

---

[20] Lingas, "From Earth to Heaven," 314.
[21] Lingas, 314.
[22] Lingas, 322.

verbal intelligibility as the antiphon builds towards its climax. Of course the acoustic design of Byzantine worship from these Constantinopolitan sources required a highly trained group of choir monks and the vast space of Hagia Sophia with its distinctive reverberations; in parishes and lesser cathedrals such resources were not available, resulting in what Lingas calls "compromises," or even "the lowest common musical denominator of syllabic call-and-response led by a single cantor."[23] One might observe that what most Byzantines heard in the liturgy was the "compromises"!

Lingas's investigation into these historical soundscapes is enhanced by the *Icons of Sound* project at Stanford University, which is constructing a digital acoustic model for Hagia Sophia. This church has characteristic "wet" acoustics—that is, high reverberation—which "blur the intelligibility of the message, making words sound like an emanation, emerging from the depth of the sea."[24] The project involves performances of Byzantine music by the choir Capella Romana, directed by Lingas, which are subsequently digitally reworked to impose upon them the acoustic model of Hagia Sophia. The aim is to produce "auralizations" of that worship, which will enable further investigation into how they might have been perceived by participants.[25]

Counter-Reformation Bavaria

A quite different exploration of an historical soundscape was undertaken by Alexander Fisher on the religiously contested space of Counter-Reformation Munich, where Catholics, Jesuit-led and emboldened by Trent, encountered Lutheran detractors, and the ways in which the sounds of worship were instrumental in religious conflict.[26] Although Fisher refers to Schafer's terminology of signal, soundmark, and keynote sounds, and to Shelemay, his approach is

---

[23] Lingas, 356.

[24] Bissera V. Pentcheva, "Aesthetics and Acoustics of Hagia Sophia, Istanbul," *Icons of Sound*, accessed January 19, 2018, http://iconsofsound.stanford.edu/index.html.

[25] The project's website has a detailed explanation of the process, the acoustics, and sample recordings: https://ccrma.stanford.edu/groups/iconsofsound/

[26] Alexander J. Fisher, *Music, Piety, and Propaganda: The Soundscapes of Counter-Reformation Bavaria* (Oxford: Oxford University Press, 2014).

much closer to Truax's contextual and interpretative framework whereby the focus is upon how sounds are understood as meaningful by inhabitants of a particular acoustic environment. Fisher's working definition of soundscape is "the totality of perceived sounds in a given space and time, some of which command immediate attention, others of which are habitual sounds that are invested with cultural meaning, and still others which recede into the background as constant acoustic phenomena—signal, soundmark and keynote sounds, to again use Schafer's terminology."[27] As with Lingas, he notes that there is a "panoply of sounds" in any environment—that of weather, birds and animals, of human activity—but his focus is on those "deployed as acoustic communication, that is those which are intentional and essential to the construct of social identity."[28] Sound is communication, but it also creates the significance of the space in which it is heard.[29]

Fisher's research revealed how non-elite Lutherans interrupted Mass in the cathedral by singing Lutheran hymns in German and thereby prevented the Catholic preacher from starting his sermon. This demonstrates the contested function of vernacular singing in post-Tridentine Catholic liturgy. In the ducal chapel in Munich, however, some of the most elaborate polyphonic and polychoral music of the Counter-Reformation was being composed and performed by Orlando di Lasso (1532–1594). Out in the streets on the feast of Corpus Christi, the procession of the monstrance was accompanied by chanting and singing, and at each of the city's four gates the reading of the gospel was greeted by musket and cannon fire and the loud ringing of bells. These sounds were distinctively confessional and understood as such by the ecclesial and city authorities: "It stands to reason that Catholic authorities would deploy the loudest artificial sounds available to aurally mark these sites of stark confessional difference"[30], just as they also controlled the secular and popular noise which might interrupt authorized religious observances.[31]

---

[27] Fisher, *Music, Piety, and Propaganda*, 9.
[28] Fisher, 9.
[29] Fisher, 11.
[30] Fisher, 25.
[31] Fisher, 27.

Within the regular Mass, the soundscape included the performance of the liturgical texts by priests and a choir of men and boys "accompanied by the ambient sound of human activity in the nave." Interestingly, Fisher applies Schafer's keynote sound not to the noise of the laity, but to the liturgical texts recited and sung, upon which the signals of congregational song, polyphony, and elaborate music were placed to attract the attention of the laity.[32]

The Aruza Street Revival

David D. Daniels III undertook a most interesting "sonic exploration of earwitnesses to early Pentecostal sound in North America," in which he openly expressed his intention to reclaim the earwitness for history.[33] His sources were not musical notation or liturgical texts, but descriptions of early Pentecostal worship by participants, detractors, or journalists, and the recovery of the historical soundscape is sourced from these earwitnesses. Daniels follows Truax's idea of the soundscape as contextualized communication, and although he comments on Truax's taxonomy of sonic environment, soundscape, sound, soundways, and syntax, this does not really form the basis of the analysis.

Early Pentecostals forged a distinctive sound: it was loud, unpredictable, nonverbal, and multiracial, but it also displayed an original combination of sounds accompanied by bodily movements. Vocalization was extended beyond the intelligible, distinctively delivered reading of Scripture, preaching, testimony, and improvised prayer to the less intelligible glossolalia, "primal cries"—howls, shrieks, moans and groans, wailing, weeping, hollering, and ambient sounds such as "oh," "ah," and "mmm," which replicated those found in nature.[34] They broadened the musical repertoire from traditional and gospel hymnody to incorporate camp-meeting songs and spirituals, honky-tonk, blues, and jazz, as well as "up-beat rhythmic sounds, hard-beat intoxicating sounds, mournful, dirge-like sounds, and

---

[32] Fisher, 32–33.
[33] David D. Daniels III, "'Gotta Moan Sometime': A Sonic Exploration of Earwitnesses to Early Pentecostal Sound in North America," *Pneuma* 30 (2008): 5–32.
[34] Daniels, "'Gotta Moan Sometime,'" 11.

soothing, mellow sounds." These might be accompanied by bones, washboards, drums, violins, trumpets, stomping, and clapping.[35] Silence too had a place, as they "tarried" for the Spirit with a communal hush. Summarizing Grant Wacker's examination of contemporary written critiques of this worship, Daniels writes, "External accounts from Kansas to California to Oregon to Alabama to Iowa to Connecticut identified the early Pentecostal sounds as 'jabbering in a strange gibberish,' 'howlings of worshippers,' 'the rapid chattering of a frightened simian,' 'hideous noise,' 'moan, scream and speak unintelligible words,' 'chatter, scream, gnash their teeth,' 'laughing, high-trebled, piercing exclamations,' 'barking like dogs, hooting like owls,' and 'unearthly shrieks and groans.'"[36] Such "noise," so baffling and inappropriate to its detractors, was part of a different aesthetic which to the participants was the sweet, joyful, and simple sound of praising God. The sound signified the Pentecostals' religious identity and distinguished them from each other; so, too, within the congregation spiritual gifts could be discerned by the sounds each person produced. Daniels concluded that the early Pentecostals were engaged in a sonic world-making that transcended the world in which they lived in terms of race, gender, and class; for them, hearing was believing, as the Holy Spirit enabled them to "eavesdrop" on divine sound, replicate biblical sound, or imitate the heavenly choir.[37]

The three investigations of historical liturgical soundscapes attend primarily to the intentional sounds of the worship events, and from these three very distinctive Christian denominations it is easy to see how the sound of worship is directly connected to a sense of theological, ecclesiological, social, and cultural identity. Even when the sounds are contested or disapproved of by others, they still function as intentional and authorized within and by the community to which they belong.

---

[35] Daniels, 17–18.
[36] Daniels, 12.
[37] Daniels, 27.

An Approach to the Liturgical Soundscape

At the beginning of the chapter we explored how each definition of soundscape revealed a distinct taxonomy or hierarchy of sounds to be attended to in any one context. Although the writers acknowledge that the soundscape is all embracing, each implicitly considers that examining the foreground, or intentional, sound is what is most important and revelatory. This is problematic for the study of Christian liturgy, especially in churches whose formal liturgical texts have remained constant for centuries and which have been used in many different contexts. If we attend only to the intentional sounds in a worship event using, say, the 1662 Anglican Book of Common Prayer (BCP), then we could be misled into presuming that the soundscape of Anglican worship remained unchanged for nearly three hundred years; clearly this would be inaccurate. In each historical period, region, and even in each parish, the BCP has been performed in locally appropriate ways, be they determined by the space, musical and ministerial resources, or prevailing cultural expressions. Such ideas have become commonplace through the many studies of liturgical inculturation that investigate adaptations of the authorized liturgical forms in mainly non-European cultures, where authorized rites are inculturated by the inclusion of local ritual and musical forms.[38] Investigating the soundscape(s) of worship similarly forces us to look beyond the text to see how, sonically, the authorized texts are inculturated in each and every congregation as the sounds which are available to be heard change with the people, the place, the time of day, and other factors.

The liturgical soundscape may be investigated through three categories of sound:

- intentional sound,
- non-intentional sound, and
- noise.

---

[38] See Anscar Chupungco, *Cultural Adaptation of the Liturgy* (New York: Paulist Press, 1982), and *Liturgies of the Future: The Process and Methods of Inculturation* (New York: Paulist Press, 1989); and Phillip Tovey, *Inculturation of Christian Worship: Exploring the Eucharist* (Aldershot, UK: Ashgate, 2004).

Worshippers, in theory, attend to the intentional sounds; they tolerate or ignore the non-intentional sounds; and they disapprove of noise.

The intentional sounds have been the focus of two of the case studies we have just tried to hear, from Constantinople and Bavaria. These sounds form the content of the worship event; the event is constituted by these sounds, and the performance of the authorized text demarcates the start and end of the event. The sounds are written or printed; not just the words to be spoken or chanted, but also the musical notation which accompanies them, making the musical component of the soundscape as authoritative as the liturgical texts. In the historic liturgical churches, the intentional worship sounds transcend the individual community which uses them, even as each community employs them as their own. Intentional sounds are hierarchical and hierarchized. The sounds to be heard have been determined by an authorized person, council, or synod, or by the power of tradition, and where choices are presented, it is those in power who decide what is to be performed. In performance, too, those in positions of power dominate the production of the intentional sounds; it is their voices which are heard the most and for the longest duration. As we have already noted, Victor Desarnaulds's qualitative survey of sixteen Sunday services in Reformed and Catholic churches in Switzerland revealed that in Reformed churches the minister spoke for 80 percent of the time, and at Mass for 45 percent.[39]

The principal and dominant intentional sounds are verbal: the performance of the liturgical texts in speech or chant; psalmody or hymnody; the reading of Scripture and preaching. These sounds are semantically loaded and intelligible. Even if the ordinary worshipper may not understand the language in which they are spoken (Latin, Greek, Church Slavonic), there is a presumption that the sounds have a meaning which is pertinent to the event. Other intentional sounds may be spoken, such as ritual instructions or community notices, and these, too, are hierarchically determined and intelligible. Silence may also be an intentional sound. In chapter 5, I will argue that silence is not simply to be equated with the absence of sound, a hiatus in worship, but is itself a sound in the soundscape which contributes to the meaningfulness of the worship event.

---

[39] Desarnaulds, "De l'acoustique des églises en Suisse," 60.

In Pentecostal or charismatic worship the intentional sounds have a much broader range and, although it would be naive to consider that the soundscape was not determined to some extent hierarchically, the role of community tradition works equally powerfully. The repertoire of intentional sounds ranges from the semantically loaded preaching and reading of Scripture, community notices, and instructions about worship to include songs from a familiar repertoire deemed authoritative or relevant, even if not subject to any formal process of ecclesial authorization. However, these worshipping communities authorize and hold in esteem non-semantic sounds, such as glossolalia and nonverbal exclamations.

Instrumental music can be an intentional sound in the liturgical soundscape, but it is not immediately intelligible and reveals its meaning by association with the emotions. For these reasons some churches have deemed it entirely inappropriate or restricted its use to certain contexts. This will be discussed more fully in chapter 4, but here a few examples of the issues will be introduced. The Roman Catholic Instruction on Music in the Liturgy (*Musicam Sacram* [MS]) of 1967 reasserted the principles stated in the Constitution on Sacred Liturgy (*Sacrosanctum Concilium*) of 1963, and authorized the sound of particular instruments only. Musical instruments with secular associations were not authorized, but the pipe organ can "add a wonderful splendor to the Church's ceremonies and powerfully lift up men's minds to God and higher things." Any instrument "should be used in such a way that it meets the needs of the liturgical celebration, and is in the interests both of the beauty of worship and the edification of the faithful" (MS 63). It further insists that "The playing of these same instruments as solos is not permitted in Advent, Lent, during the Sacred Triduum and in the Offices and Masses of the Dead" (MS 66). But as no reason is given, the assumption must be that it is neither edifying nor conducive to praise in these seasons and liturgies. In the Lutheran Church, where the organ and hymn singing are a key part of the liturgical tradition, the rubrics of the 1978 minister's edition of the American *Book of Worship* suggest the use of an organ solo before the beginning of the liturgy, but conversely states that it is not appropriate at the end when people should be greeting each other: "Generally, however, loud postludes used merely to cover the sounds of the departing congregation are undesirable. Except on such somber occasions as the Holy Week services, it is appropriate for people to talk together as they leave church after the service."[40] Here, then, the post-worship chatter is intentional!

Notwithstanding the presence of organs in some American Orthodox churches, the use of such instruments does not form any part of the tradition and is generally viewed negatively. Johann von Gardner, in *Russian Church Singing*, argued that since the church fathers put forward reasons for not using instruments, mainly drawn from unfavorable comparisons with pagan and Jewish worship as well as secular entertainment, these views were held unquestioned by later Byzantine and Slavic churches such that the issue has never received a systematic treatment. Gardner offers some thoughts which support the emphasis I have given above to intelligible verbal sounds being the only unambiguously intentional sound:

> Only the word is capable of precisely expressing concrete, logically formulated ideas. Instrumental music, on the other hand, by its nature is incapable of such unambiguous expression; it can only express and evoke the emotional element, which is received subjectively by each individual listener, thus giving rise to a variety of interpretations. . . . The same musical form, whether a simple tune played on a fife, a complex piece of instrumental polyphony, or even a melody hummed without words by the human voice, can be supplied with texts of different content and character that will enable the same music to convey completely diverse ideas. Only the word can give musical sounds a definite, unambiguous meaning. And in worship only the word can clearly express the ideas contained in prayer, instruction, contemplation, etc. Thus, wordless instrumental music by itself is not suited for conveying the concrete verbal content of worship. It can only entertain and please the ear, evoke various emotions, and, to a certain extent, reflect the emotional content of ideas expressed by words. On the other hand, the word taken in conjunction with musical sounds can combine logical clarity and precision of meaning with the emotional response to verbal ideas.[41]

---

[40] Inter-Lutheran Commission on Worship, *Lutheran Book of Worship* (Minneapolis: Augsburg Fortress Press, 1978), 39.

[41] Johann von Gardner, *Russian Church Singing: Orthodox Worship and Hymnography*, trans. Vladimir Morosan, vol. 1, *Russian Church Singing* (Crestwood, NY: St. Vladimir's Seminary Press, 1980), 22–23.

I would also categorize *ritual sound* as an intentional sound. Ritual sound is nonverbal; however, it has a communicative function in the worship event and is not just sound produced as a by-product of a ritual action. We should distinguish the sound of a bell, which is an intentional communicative sound signal, from the sound of footsteps during a procession, which result from an intentional ritual act. Thus a bell might be rung to communicate the start of the liturgy: on hearing it, the people stand, the organ plays, and the ministers process. The sacring bell signals that the consecration of the bread and wine has been effected and invites a ritual response from the priest and people. But not every bell works like this. A church which has a mechanical clock striking the hours during the day may well strike ten times every morning, but as one waits on a Sunday morning for the liturgy to start, the ten o'clock bell is keenly anticipated, as indeed is the eleven o'clock bell. This bell is also a signal, but it is not an intentional ritual sound in the liturgical event.

The most consistent feature of the liturgical soundscape is the intentional words provided by authorized texts and by tradition, and it is, therefore, unsurprising that liturgical scholars have devoted most of their attention to these. Truax's idea of the soundscape being acoustic communication is useful here. The words are to be edifying and, normally, intelligible, as well as providing the means of effective communication between the congregation and God. Authorized music is also an intentional sound, even when some may not consider it to be edifying or appropriate, and it is intended to communicate as much as certain ritual sounds. But the limitations of focusing only on the intentional, communicative elements of the liturgical soundscape means that many other sounds which are present and heard are overlooked; these sounds do not have semantic or ritual significance but are nevertheless noticed by worshippers and contribute to their situatedness in the event. I call these sounds *non-intentional sounds*, and they could be further categorized as the sounds which accompany rituals and as ambient sounds. Although rarely remarked upon, these sounds do form a significant part of the worship experience.

Sounds which accompany rituals are to be distinguished from ritual sounds; here, what is meaningful is the ritual act, but in order to accomplish it a sound will be made. Thus, ritual movement may be accompanied by the sound of footsteps and the swishing of vestments. As the people stand and sit, wooden pews creak, kneelers shuffle about, or chairs scrape the floor. Vestments rustle in an imperfectly situated microphone. A thurible chinks against the chain as incense is wafted around the altar, sanctuary, and nave. The pages of a gospel book are turned ostentatiously as it is read. The ritual breaking of the eucharistic wafer may be picked up by a sensitive microphone on the altar during the fraction. Water is poured into the font during a baptism. In every case the sound draws attention to a ritual action; in many cases it would not be possible to perform the ritual action without making some sort of sound, but meaning is situated in the act and not the sound. Of course, through habit, the sound may function as a signal of the ritual action—particularly, say, at the fraction—such that the two become inseparably connected in the minds of worshippers.

The sounds which accompany rituals may well be associated with the meaning of that action in the mind of worshippers, but there are also sounds which carry no meaning but are tolerated as they convey information about the community and the place of worship. These are the ambient sounds, also known as background noise or, in Schafer's terminology, the "keynote." Liturgically, ambient sounds consist of the background sound or keynote of the locality in which the congregation is situated and the sounds of the building in which it worships. The keynote sound of modern urban life is ever present—motor traffic, trains, airplanes—and we are so accustomed to it that we barely notice; how special it is to hear the different keynote sound of birdsong when in a rural church! The church building may also have its own keynote sound from heating systems and organ bellows, for example. The congregation will produce sounds, and many of these are tolerated without causing a distraction to the intentional sounds of the worship event: thus the sounds of furniture, footsteps, page-turning, rummaging in bags and pockets for collection money, coughing. In all these cases, if we tune our ears to these sounds, we would become acutely aware of our situation in a particular town and church building and among a particular people. Each worshipping congregation has its own sound which is due to the non-intentional as much as the intentional sounds. These are the background sounds which, Kelman asserts, are not background at all.

My third category of sound in worship is *noise*, which will be examined in more detail in chapter 6. Briefly, noise is sound which does not belong, which distracts, and which is not tolerated. In this book I will make a distinction between "sound," a neutral term for any acoustic phenomenon or event, and "noise," which is a sound perceived negatively. Each congregation will have an understanding of what constitutes noise, usually implicit and based on social conventions, rather than made explicit in community decisions. Individuals generally employ subjective criteria in determining what is noise. The line between unintentional sounds and noise can be a fine one, and a whole range of personal and communal perceptions may intervene to allocate one sound to a tolerated and barely heard sound and another to a definitely heard and non-tolerated sound. Persuasion and legislation may be employed to reduce noise in worship, and we shall discuss some of these in later chapters, but it is not possible to eliminate all noises.

Studying the soundscape of worship needs to pay attention to the non-intentional sounds and noise, as well as the intentional sounds. It is the former which exist as the aural framework for all other activities. They tie the community to this particular place, and tie these people together in a shared perceptual experience of meaningful sounds and noise. The soundscape situates them in the world as the Body of Christ.

Conclusion

As this book continues its exploration of how and what we hear in worship, it is important to start by insisting that we attend to the total auditory environment, and that is what the notion of soundscape enables us to do. We must acknowledge that our ears receive more than the liturgical texts and music. The three historical case studies provided us with different approaches to investigating the distinctive soundscapes of different worshipping communities. Reconstructing the acoustic properties of the church of Hagia Sophia in Constantinople using the latest acoustical measurement techniques has enabled Lingas and his choir to imagine what sounds Byzantine worshippers might have perceived. The more traditional historiographical investigation of sixteenth-century Bavaria invites us to reread the records of religious conflict so that we attend to how sound functioned to create and sustain social and ecclesial boundaries. Historians can read the written texts, be they liturgical or homiletic, to find out what was said or sung, and how they reflect the theological and ecclesial conflicts. Fisher invites us to consider how liturgical sound and noise were also used in these religious conflicts. Daniels asks us to recover the earwitness to liturgical events and to think critically about the way in which we describe what we hear and the criteria we use when making value judgements about sound.

Whether we equate the soundscape with a landscape or a seascape, Schafer, Kelman, Shelemay, and Truax have usefully directed our attention to the totality of sounds which surround us at any one time, whether we consciously attend to them or not. For liturgical leaders, for worshippers, as well as for liturgical scholars, the concept of the soundscape is useful in forcing us to think beyond the performance of authorized texts as constituting the worship event, and to acknowledge more positively the totality of sound within and beyond the church building. However, the ways in which Schafer and Truax classified the sounds in their soundscapes does not work for our more focused study, and hence I took the liberty of creating my own categories of *intentional sounds*, *non-intentional sounds*, and *noise*. Intentional sounds and noise will receive more detailed examination in chapters 4, 5, and 6. Non-intentional or ambient sound will not be examined separately, given that it is highly contextual, but readers are invited to open their ears to these sounds next time they attend church.

Postscript: Visualizing the Liturgical Soundscape

In these satirical engravings by William Hogarth (1697–1764), he depicts two contrasting soundscapes, a rather dull Anglican sermon and an enthusiastic Methodist service, and neither come out of it unscathed. In *The Sleeping Congregation* (there are three editions with minor changes: 1728, 1736, and 1762) the preacher's text "Come unto me all ye who labour and are heavy laden and I will give you REST" has been taken up quite literally by the congregation who slumber and snore though the monotonous sermon. In his 1762 engraving, *Credulity, Superstition, and Fanaticism*, supposedly caricaturing an enthusiastic Methodist sermon, almost all figures appear to be responding noisily to the fiery sermon: not just the congregation, but even the relief figures on the pulpit are animated. The scene is admirably summed up in the inscription on the clerk's desk: "Continually do cry."

Figure 1
William Hogarth, *The Sleeping Congregation* (1762). Etching and engraving. The Metropolitan Museum of Art, Acc. No. 91.1.1. (Image courtesy of the Metropolitan Museum of Art, Creative Commons Zero (CC0) License.)

Figure 2

William Hogarth, *Credulity, Superstition, and Fanaticism* (1762). Etching and engraving. The Metropolitan Museum of Art, Acc. No. 91.1.117. (Image courtesy of the Metropolitan Museum of Art, Creative Commons Zero (CC0) License.)

Chapter 2

Hearing and Listening

The operation of our hearing system, the ears and the brain, have remained unchanged physiologically, but the way in which philosophers, theologians, and psychologists have understood how we hear, and how we make sense of what we hear, has indeed undergone considerable development over centuries.[1] We unconsciously accept our own culture's notions, often implicit, about how the senses operate to perceive and understand the world, but our forms of worship have been inherited from times when the sensorium was understood quite differently.[2] Although hearing was considered a superior sense along with sight (smell, taste, and touch were placed in a lower category), it was not presumed to be able to convey knowledge about the world in the same way as sight, and it was given much less attention in philosophical writings from the early and medieval periods. It was only in the early modern period and the Enlightenment that hearing was allowed more prominence. It remains to be explored whether significant changes in ritual text and performance occurred

---

[1] The first comprehensive history of the ear was published by Adam Politzer in 1907–13 in *Geschichte der Ohrenheilkunde*, and this was the standard treatment until Albert Mudry produced a revised history in 2015, *The History of Otology: A Tribute to Adam Politzer* (Amsterdam: Wayenborgh Publishing, 2015). A short summary of the history has also been provided by Jorge Hachmeister, "An Abbreviated History of the Ear: From Renaissance to Present," *Yale Journal of Biology and Medicine* 76, no. 2 (2003): 81–86.

[2] For a historical survey of changing ideas about the senses, see Robert Jütte, *A History of the Senses: From Antiquity to Cyberspace*, trans. James Lynn (Cambridge, UK: Polity, 2005).

in periods when there was a shift in intellectual and cultural attitudes to the senses.

It will be useful for us to start with a summary of how the ear enables us to hear. When we hear a sound, we identify it with the physical object or person who created it, and we do this even when we are unable to locate its source. We perceive *things*, but our ear receives intangible vibrations caused by the striking objects or vocal sounds. These are first received by the external ear, then channeled through the middle ear, in which three bones convey these vibrations to the cochlea, the spiral, "snail-shell" tube. The cochlea is filled with a liquid divided by a membrane and the organ of Corti, which vibrate in response to the moving liquid. The organ of Corti contains about sixteen thousand hair cells which convert the vibrations into electrical signals, or neurons, that are transmitted via nerves for processing in the brain. Recent research indicates that the membrane responds to different frequencies along its length and the hair cells move back and forth at different speeds according to the particular frequency they receive.[3] Those with partial hearing loss have impaired hair-cell response in particular locations along the membrane. A. James Hudspeth notes that this movement creates a distortion in the sound: "It turns out the ear is not just passively picking up sound and sending signals to the brain, but that the ear is actively interpreting the sound" by amplification and frequency tuning.[4] Hudspeth also notes that the ear itself produces sounds which are particular to each individual, to their left and right ears, and that these remain stable throughout one's life. So our ear contributes to the sound we hear, and is not simply a passive receptacle for the externally transmitted vibrations. What our brain does to process these signals is not yet fully understood, according to Hudspeth.

The language we use for auditory activity reveals cultural presuppositions, and so it is useful to consider these next. As I reflect upon my own everyday language, I find that I quite often use *hear* and *listen* as synonyms, but in specific situations I make the deliberate

---

[3] A helpful animation of this process can be found in a YouTube video, "Cochlea Animation," created by the Howard Hughes Medical Institute and available here: https://www.youtube.com/watch?v=dyenMluFaUw.

[4] A. James Hudspeth, "Where Listening Begins: The Inner Ear," in *What Now? The Politics of Listening*, ed. Anne Barlow, 9–15 (London: Black Dog Publishing, 2016).

choice to use one or the other, for example, "Can you hear me?" or "Are you listening to me?" The *Oxford English Dictionary* indicates that *hear* has a much wider application, used for any functioning of the ears: "To perceive, or have the sensation of, sound; to possess or exercise the faculty of audition, of which the specific organ is the ear. The proper verb to express this faculty or function."[5] *Hear* is an umbrella term for any act of audition. Interestingly, the editors note a specific religious and biblical use: "To listen to with compliance or assent; to accede to, grant (a request or prayer)."[6] *Listen*, by contrast, has the additional idea of attentive or intentional hearing. Thus, "To hear attentively; to give ear to; to pay attention to (a person speaking or what is said)" and "To give attention with the ear to some sound or utterance; to make an effort to hear something; to 'give ear'".[7] Whereas the editors indicate that *hear* might be used to mean "To listen to (a person or thing) with more or less attention or understanding," *listen* always implies an attitude of attentiveness.[8] *Hearken* is an archaic word which may be familiar to some readers from older translations of the Bible and the BCP. *Hearken* also implies an attentive and intentional listening, but can be used for covert listening or eavesdropping.[9] In the litany and other petitions, God is asked to "Hear our prayer" and not "Listen to our prayer," but surely the implication is that God will listen attentively, that is, he will "*Hearken* unto our prayer!"

Latin also distinguishes between the broader notion of *hear* and the more specific *listen*. *Audire* is the principal verb which comprises a range of meanings from any sound perception, through to the more attentive idea of "listen" and "heed," and even "obey." *Auscultare* is close to the English *listen*, as attentive and even covert listening.[10] The first line of the ancient Lenten hymn *Attende Domine* was translated for *The English Hymnal* (1906) as "Hear us, O Lord"; the petitions of the hymn ask for God's attentiveness to our suffering and need

---

[5] *Oxford English Dictionary (OED)*, s.v. "hear" (1), (Oxford: Oxford University Press, 2023), https://www.oed.com/.

[6] *OED*, s.v. "hear" (7.a).

[7] *OED*, s.v. "listen" (1.a and 2.a).

[8] *OED*, s.v. "hear" (4.b).

[9] *OED*, s.v. "hearken" (1 and 2).

[10] *Oxford Latin Dictionary*, s.v. "audio"; "ausculto" (ed. Charlton T. Lewis and Charles Short [Oxford: Oxford University Press, 1969]).

for pardon.[11] *Attendo* in Latin normally means to "turn towards," rather than to hear, but it clearly lies behind the English words *attend* and *attentive*.[12]

Spanish and French also distinguish between unspecific audition and attentive listening. In Spanish, the verb *oír* ("hear") is used generally, but listen is *escuchar*. Liturgical Spanish uses *escuchar* for the petition "Lord, hear our prayer": "*Señor, escucha nuestra oración.*" French has two principal words: *entendre* denotes auditory sense perception more generally, and as it is derived from *tendre* ("hold" or "keep"), it can also mean "understand"; *écouter* is used for more focused and attentive listening.[13] Musicologist Pierre Schaeffer (1910–1995), in *Traité des objects musicaux*, placed the verbs *écouter, entendre, comprendre,* and *oüir* in a hierarchy depending upon the listener's level of attentiveness. Thus, *oüir* is an inattentive audition in which the available sounds are unnoticed; *comprendre* relates to the reception and understanding of the utterance; and *écouter* pays attention to the sounds as signs of a sound-making object and/or location, and to the reception of sounds, but without necessarily any active reflection on their meanings. Lastly, *entendre* is intentional listening: "What I hear [*j'entends*], what is manifested to me, is a function of this intention [*intention*]."[14] In the latter, only the sounds are attended to without reference to their spatial location and identity, nor even with attention to their signification. Even if his use of *entendre* is unusual, the hierarchy suggests an interesting framework for considering the various ways in which sounds are perceived. Clearly, our ears are always open and thus receive sounds whether we attend to them or not. More focused listening can be subdivided depending on what the listener does with the sounds they receive: does the listener only take the meaning and nothing else? Or is the focus on the source of the sound, or simply on the sound itself?

---

[11] *The English Hymnal* (London: Oxford University Press and A. R. Mowbray, 1906), 736. *The Lent Prose*.

[12] *Oxford Latin Dictionary*, s.v. "attendo."

[13] *Le Grand Robert* (2001), s.v. "entendre" (B.1); "écouter" (1).

[14] Pierre Schaeffer, *Traité des objets musicaux: essai interdisciplines* (Paris: Éditions du Seuil, 1966), 104. See Brian Kane, "Jean-Luc Nancy and the Listening Subject," *Contemporary Music Review* 31, no. 5–6 (2012): 441.

Some Philosophical Reflections

There are a number of useful philosophical and theological reflections on hearing and listening which relate to human self-understanding and our place in the world, and before God. Phenomenologists such as Martin Heidegger, Maurice Merleau-Ponty, Jean-Luc Nancy, and Gemma Corradi Fiumara ground their philosophy on the human experience of the world as the source of knowledge, which is received via the senses. These thinkers have all engaged with audition and its function in human understanding.

Martin Heidegger (1889–1976) proposed a new way of considering what it means to speak which has significant implications for the way we hear and make sense through a reflection on the Greek word λέγειν (= speak, say, or tell), which has an earlier meaning in the sense of "laying down" or "laying before such that it can be gathered."[15] If λέγειν means "to lay," then this has implications for the way in which we understand λέγειν as "say" or "tell"; it is the mystery of revealing that which was concealed, of making it present: "Saying is a letting-lie-together-before which gathers and is gathered. If such is the essence of speaking, then what is hearing?" Hearing, Heidegger observed, is not "the activation of the body's audio equipment" or sensory perception, nor the invasion of verbal sounds, but rather it is a gathering of oneself to what has been said or laid before us. Proper hearing (*das eigentliche Hören*) is hearkening (*Horchsamen*) and heeding (*Gehorsams*). Thus, λέγειν is ὁμολογεῖν. Ὁμολογεῖν usually means "to confess," but here the emphasis is upon ὁμόν (= same), and so a gathering of ourselves into that which has been let-lie-before us, that which already belongs to us by virtue of its sameness: "We have heard (*gehört*) when we *belong to* (*gehören*) the matter addressed." Proper hearing is not a casual reception by the ears but an attitude of "hearkening attunement" (*horchsamen Gehören*). If we reflect liturgically on this, we might recalibrate our understanding of what it is when we speak and listen in worship such that they are not two separate

---

[15] Martin Heidegger, "*Logos* (Heraclitus, Fragment B 50)," in *Early Greek Thinking: The Dawn of Western Philosophy*, trans. David Farrell Krell and Frank A. Capuzzi, 59–78 (San Francisco: Harper & Row, 1984). Quotations on this page from pp. 64–66. German: *Vorträge und Aufsätze*, Teil III (Tübingen: Neske, 1967), 3–25.

activities of active and passive participation, but that speaking is a laying down of that which is to be gathered by the hearers; the hearers are those to whom the speech belongs, and who receive it into themselves. Perhaps "hearkening attunement" is an apt expression for fulfilled liturgical listening?

Jean-Luc Nancy (1940–2021) used sonority and audition to construct a philosophy of the self, beginning with an investigation into *entendre* and *écouter* and the expressions which contain them.[16] From *écouter* comes *être à l'écoute*, "to be all ears," that is, to be "tuned in" or listening; but *l'écoute*, a spy, is derived from *être aux écoutes* and carries the sense of listening secretly, of eavesdropping. Nancy asks "what secret is at stake when one truly listens" to the sonority rather than the message? *Écouter*, from *auscultare*, implies listening with intention and attention; it is the quasi-physical "*tendre l'oreille*," "stretching an ear."[17] But audition is related not just to sensory perception but also to sense as meaning, such that *entendre* "also means *comprendre*, 'to understand,' as if 'hearing' were above all 'hearing say' <*entendre dire*> (rather than 'hearing sound' <*entendre bruire*>), or rather, as if in all 'hearing' there had to be a 'hearing say,' regardless of whether the sound perceived was a word or not."[18] For Nancy, listening is a straining towards meaning; it is to be at the extremity or fringe of meaning. Sense (*sens*) and sound (*son*) share a common space of referral (*renvoi*); they become apparent in the totality of their resonances (or reverberations) and their shared space is the self.[19] This self is reflexive and relational, a resonating subject which goes out and is heard within: "To be listening is, thus, to enter into tension and to be on the look out for a relation to *self*."[20] The connection between sound and self is not metaphorical for Nancy, but it reveals reality; as sound is not fixed at a temporal and spatial point, neither is the self: it is always coming, passing, extending, and penetrating.[21]

---

[16] Jean-Luc Nancy, *Listening*, trans. Charlotte Mandell (New York: Fordham University Press, 2007). French: *À l'écoute* (Paris: Éditions Galilée, 2002).
[17] Nancy, *Listening*, 5.
[18] Nancy, 6.
[19] Nancy, 7–8.
[20] Nancy, 11.
[21] Nancy, 14.

The inspiration for this book began with Gemma Corradi Fiumara's observation that "perhaps we could start out by admitting that there could be no saying without hearing, no speaking which is not also an integral part of listening, no speech which is not somehow received."[22] Her words force us to shift the focus of our investigation away from the intentional sounds we make—be they verbal or musical—towards the reception of those sounds. Corradi Fiumara wants to challenge a world where in many spheres of life there is much saying without listening, and where rationality is expressed by the assertion of propositions expressed in abstractions uprooted from their original relationships and contexts. Thus, she suggests, "a philosophy of listening can be envisaged as an attempt to recover the neglected and perhaps deeper roots of what we call thinking, an activity which in some way gathers and synthesizes human endeavours."[23] Her philosophy of listening builds from Heidegger, Hans-Georg Gadamer, and Richard Rorty. From Heidegger she uses his interpretation of *legein*; from Gadamer, the hermeneutical task which requires openness to what is set before us, to a bringing into relation that which is before us; and from Rorty, that what we do not understand must needs be interpreted. She comments that "Listening, in fact, faces all difficulties unarmed and lets unfold what must happen," which requires an openness to all its potentials.[24] She wishes to reclaim a more authentic form of listening which is attentive, alert, interpretative, and is critical of much listening in the world which hears in order to respond or rebut, or is overwhelmed by other views, leading to what she calls "benumbment" or torpor. Silence in listening should not be numb or mute or rejecting, but the sign of an active "listening silence," a fully present hearing of the other.

Some Theological Reflections

Theologians have rarely been interested in exploring hearing and the auditory ideas that permeate both the Old and New Testaments.

[22] Gemma Corradi Fiumara, *The Other Side of Language: A Philosophy of Listening*, trans. Charles Lambert (London: Routledge, 1990), 1.
[23] Corradi Fiumara, *Other Side of Language*, 13.
[24] Corradi Fiumara, 61.

Imploring God to hear the people, or prophetic demands that the people listen to God, can be found throughout the Old Testament. It is in the psalms that such ideas are encountered in Christian liturgy, although it is primarily God who is expected to do the listening. In Psalm 17, as in many others, we find such statements as this:

> Hear me, Lord, my plea is just;
>   listen to my cry.
>   Hear my prayer—
> . . .
> I call on you, my God, for you will answer me;
>   turn your ear to me and hear my prayer. (Pss 17:1; 17:6)

The trust that God does indeed hear us is based upon the human sensorium:

> Does he who fashioned the ear not hear?
> Does he who formed the eye not see? (Ps 94:9)

And it is this which distinguishes God from idols in Psalm 115:4-6:

> But their idols are silver and gold,
> made by human hands.
> They have mouths, but cannot speak,
> eyes, but cannot see.
> They have ears, but cannot hear,
> noses, but cannot smell.

The New Testament shows a shift in responsibility for hearing to God's people. Audition is explicitly linked to faith, and "right hearing" is fulfilled by repentance. Not only is Christ designated as the Word in John's Gospel, but at his baptism, the voice from heaven declares, "This is my Son, whom I love. Listen to him!" (Mark 9:7; Matt 17:5; Luke 9:35). Jesus's addresses to the crowd are often prefaced with "Listen," and listening is the sign of the believer: "My sheep listen to my voice; I know them, and they follow me" (John 10:37). Models of good and bad listening are the theme of a number of parables, such as the parable of the sower (Matt 13:1-24; Mark 4:1-20; Luke 8:1-15) and the teaching on the wise and foolish builders (Matt 7:24-29; Luke 6:46-49). Additionally, Jesus's teaching is concluded on several occasions with "Whoever has ears to hear, let them hear" (e.g., Luke 14:34).

In the book of Acts, listening to the apostolic preaching usually results in conversion, and thus hearing is presented as foundational for Christian faith. It is only when people have heard the preaching that they can declare "Jesus is Lord," and Paul asserts that "faith comes by hearing, and hearing by the word of God" (Rom 10:17 King James Version).[25] Although early Christian commentators linked this verse directly to hearing Christ preached, it was primarily among Reformation theologians that it received greater prominence.[26]

Among some early and medieval theologians, the emphasis moved away from the physical senses to the spiritual senses as the only proper way to perceive God. In his biblical exegesis, Origen interpreted physical, sensory language in a spiritual way, referring to the "divine senses of the inner man": every physical sense also has an inner spiritual counterpart, thus the spiritual or inner ears.[27] With these inner ears the believer can perceive God, and hearing in this context is equated with understanding rather than the act of audition. Medieval mystical theologians had similar ideas and separated the intellectual apprehension of God from the affective. Sarah Coakley and Paul Gavrilyuk note that Alexander of Hales, Thomas Gallus, and Bonaventure "aligned 'spiritual' sight and hearing with

---

[25] There are some significant variations in the modern English translations of Romans 10:17. The Greek, Latin, and modern English translations have Christ instead of God, thus "*Ergo fides ex auditu, auditus autem per verbum Christi.*" The Greek is ἄρα ἡ πίστις ἐξ ἀκοῆς, ἡ δὲ ἀκοὴ διὰ ῥήματος Χριστοῦ. The problematic word is τό ῥῆμα, which can be anything which is spoken (*Greek-English Lexicon*, ed. Henry G. Liddell and Robert Scott [Oxford: Oxford University Press, 1996], s.v. ῥήμα), and translators have tried to clarify what it is that is to be heard. The New Revised Standard Version has "So faith comes from what is heard, and what is heard comes through the word of Christ," and the Revised Standard Version is even more specific: "Faith comes from what is heard, and what is heard comes by the preaching of Christ."

[26] See Francis Russo, "Sonic Piety in Early New England," *The New England Quarterly* 95, no. 4 (2022): 610–44, and Jennifer Rae McDermott, "'The Melodie of Heaven': Sermonizing the Open Ear in Early Modern England," in *Religion and the Senses Early Modern Europe*, ed. Wietse De Boer and Christine Göttler, 177–97 (Leiden: Brill, 2012).

[27] Mark J. McInroy, "Origen of Alexandria," in *The Spiritual Senses: Perceiving God in Western Christianity*, ed. Paul L. Gavrilyuk and Sarah Coakley, 21 (Cambridge: Cambridge University Press, 2011).

the intellect (*intellectus*), and the remaining three spiritual senses with affectivity (*affectus*)"; however, for these theologians spiritual touch was the highest sense.[28] Alexander of Hales considered that the *corpus mysticum* was central, as Boyd Taylor Coolman explains: "the explicit condition for the possibility of spiritually sensuous perception of God was participation in this mystical body. Only if 'made sensate by their Head' (*sensificentur a capite*) could members of the ecclesia perceive the divine nature."[29] Christ possesses all the spiritual senses which are passed to the people via the church. The ability to sense spiritually is made possible at baptism, particularly with the anointing by which the ears are opened. The spiritual senses are not at all the same as the physical, they are superior, and when activated enable perception of non-physical realties and understanding. Coolman cites Alexander's *Glossa* on the *Sentences* of Peter Lombard: "in so far as God sounds (*sonat*) in the ears of the perfect, God is audible (*auditus*)."[30]

For seventeenth-century Protestants, especially, physical hearing was the means to encounter God and was a sense to be developed for appropriate spiritual ends but not spiritualized in itself. It was a commonplace for Protestants like Ralph Brownrig to assert, "Popery is a religion for the eye; ours for the ear," which meant prioritizing hearing as the source of faith and as a spiritual discipline.[31] Following St. Paul's statement that faith came by hearing, Protestant preachers could use hearing as a metaphor for faith itself: "Right Hearing" was akin to right believing and essential for salvation. Francis Russo has called this a "sonic piety," which was alert to the fact that any sound could carry signs of God even if produced outside the meeting house, so long as one knew how to hear them correctly.[32] To this end, numer-

---

[28] Paul L. Gavrilyuk and Sarah Coakley, "Introduction," in *The Spiritual Senses: Perceiving God in Western Christianity*, 5, 9 (Cambridge: Cambridge University Press, 2011).

[29] Boyd Taylor Coolman, "Alexander of Hales," in *The Spiritual Senses: Perceiving God in Western Christianity*, ed. Paul L. Gavrilyuk and Sarah Coakley, 122 (Cambridge: Cambridge University Press, 2011).

[30] Coolman, "Alexander of Hales," 132.

[31] Ralph Brownrig, *Twenty-Five Sermons by the Right Reverend Father in God, Ralph Brownrig, Late Lord Bishop of Exeter* (Cambridge: W. Martyn, 1664), 117. Cited in McDermott, "'Melodie of Heaven,'" 179.

[32] Russo, "Sonic Piety," 610–44.

ous treatises and published sermons from the early seventeenth century in England established a genre of writing to cultivate Right Hearing. Their names are revealing: Henry Smith's *The art of hearing* (1592); Robert Wilkinson's *A sermon of hearing, or Iewell for the eare: Wherein is contained a preparatiue to the hearing of the word, with sundry lessons of instruction for the eare, which who so hath not learned and digested, can neither enter into Gods temple with reuerence, nor depart with profit* (1593); and Stephen Egerton's *The boring of the eare: contayning a plaine and profitable discourse by way of dialogue: concerning 1. Our preparation before hearing, 2. Our demeanour in hearing, 3. Our exercise after we haue heard the Word of God* (1623).[33] Jennifer Rae McDermott made a connection between the Protestant imperative to have an "open Eare" with the discovery of the Eustachian tube connecting the ear and throat. This revealed that the ear was permeable, and preachers exploited the idea to speak about the ear as the route to the heart, or having ears open to God but closed to evil, and that, through the ears, Christ could enter the believers.[34] As Robert Wilkinson wrote, "God never commeth so neere a mans soule as when he entreth in by the doore of the eare."[35]

The spiritual senses received renewed attention from the twentieth-century Roman Catholic theologians Karl Rahner (1904–1984) and Hans Urs von Balthasar (1905–1988). Here we will consider the ideas of Balthasar as he specifically applied his notion of spiritual hearing to the liturgy. As Mark McInroy asserts, for Balthasar "our perceptual faculties must become 'spiritualized' if we are to perceive the splendour (*Glanz*) of the form through which God is revealed."[36] In his 1961 essay "Seeing, Hearing, and Reading within the Church," Balthasar noted the immateriality of hearing, and how it sets up a

---

[33] See Arnold Hunt, *The Art of Hearing: English Preachers and Their Audiences, 1590–1640* (Cambridge: Cambridge University Press 2010). Hunt reviews this literature in chapter 2.

[34] McDermott, "'Melodie of Heaven,'" 181, with reference to Eustachio, *De auditus organis* (1564).

[35] Robert Wilkinson, *A Jewell for the Eare* (London, 1593), 11. Cited in McDermott, "'Melodie of Heaven,'" 186.

[36] Mark McInroy, *Balthasar on the Spiritual Senses: Perceiving Splendour* (Oxford: Oxford University Press, 2014), 2.

relationship of defenselessness on one side and communication on the other. What is communicated is the sound itself, and not the concealed speaker or singer who is in a position of power over the hearer. Hearing, together with the other sensual modes, "play[s] a role both in the analogous natural knowledge of God on man's part and in the supernatural revelation of God to man."[37] The sensual modes are spiritualized in order to receive spiritual things. From his understanding of the role of hearing in normal communication exchange, Balthasar proposed an analogous way in which God communicates through hearing. In hearing, God is removed from the act of communication and "The Creator himself makes use of the defenseless and needy openness of our finite spirit, which does not bear its own object in itself but must await this passively from outside itself, in order to make himself heard by the listening ear of our spirit."[38] God is heard particularly through the revelation of the Word, and it is the church's service to listen obediently. Balthasar writes, "And when she herself speaks as one who teaches and proclaims, she herself listens while she speaks the word in the commission that she has received from the Word."[39] Hearing is the "decisive attitude of the Church," because, as Saint Paul says, "Faith comes from hearing." In the article Balthasar goes on to consider the liturgical implications for priest and people: in the readings and preaching there is to be an awareness that this communication is "the direct continuation of the sending of the Son by the Father", which requires the ears to be attuned to receive it.[40]

Modes of Listening

Researchers have investigated specific listening contexts which can be differentiated by either the position and attitude of the source of the sound, or by the attitude of the listener. The examples here are

---

[37] Hans Urs von Balthasar, "Seeing, Hearing, and Reading within the Church," in *Explorations in Theology*, trans. A. V. Littledale and Alexander Dru, vol. 2, *Spouse of the Word*, 477 (San Francisco: Ignatius Press, 1991). German: *Sponsa Verbi: Skizzen Zur Theologie* II (Einsiedeln: Johannes Verlag, 1961).
[38] Balthasar, "Seeing, Hearing, and Reading," 480.
[39] Balthasar, 480.
[40] Balthasar, 488.

not exhaustive, but will illustrate the variety of listening conditions and listening roles in worship.

Listeners as Producers of the Sound

Our society has a somewhat negative attitude to speaking aloud to oneself, although not singing to oneself or generating other sounds, and it also condemns those who like the sound of their own voice. By contrast, in the liturgy, worshippers hear themselves speaking to God. Even daily prayers conducted privately may be recited aloud. Indeed, such listening was encouraged by *Sacrosanctum Concilium* (Constitution for the Sacred Liturgy) for the recitation of the Divine Office: "The divine office, because it is the public prayer of the Church, is a source of piety, and nourishment for personal prayer. And therefore priests and all others who take part in the divine office are earnestly exhorted in the Lord to attune their minds to their voices when praying it" (90).

As I speak the words, I hear myself simultaneously from within, through bodily resonance, and from without, via my ears, and together these establish me temporally, spatially, but also with an inner sense of self as the speaking subject. Usually in worship, the source of the sound is visible or identifiable, but when I hear myself speak I do not see myself producing sound, and, as we know from voicemail, I do not hear myself as others do. In contrast, too, to other communication contexts, I do not speak for or to others, but I speak to myself, to God and *with* fellow worshippers. This simultaneous act of speaking and listening is fundamental to my liturgical participation, and this is the case even if all I say is "Amen." In communal prayer, the congregation speaks as a single subject to and before God with a combined voice, which is most evident when singing hymns or reciting a text which uses the first-person pronoun. We do not hear each individual, but the congregation as a whole.

Listeners as Audience

An audience is a group of listeners constituted by a relationship to the speaker/performer in which they assent to their role by attentive listening. If one considers that the content of the message functions as a transaction between both parties, as Antonio Gramsci suggested, then quite clearly the audience cannot be merely a passive recipient.[41] Alessandro Duranti has explained that in a situation of speech communication, the audience interprets the speaker's words regardless of the latter's intentions, and he suggests that the audience are therefore co-authors in the production: "Speakers and audience are equals . . . because every act of speaking is directed to and must be ratified by an audience."[42] Listening is not a passive act in which the listeners try to detect the speaker's intentions, but the audience make sense of it for themselves by linking it to a world or context which they already know.

In the Graeco-Roman culture where Christian liturgical forms first developed, the educated, among whom we must include bishops, were highly trained in rhetoric, which prioritized the composition of formal speech such that it would be received according to the intentions and meaning of the speaker. Rhetoric was not just verbal display, but display with the aim of producing a desired effect upon the audience. Aristotle's definition of three types of rhetoric—deliberative, judicial, and epideictic—was based on three types of hearer—decision-maker, juryman, and observer; book 2 of his *Rhetoric* was on the emotions which a speaker could generate.[43] Later writers on rhetoric, such as Cicero and Quintilian, modified these categories but still emphasized rhetoric as a means of persuading the audience. Carol Harrison showed how early Christian writers, such as Gregory Nazianzen and Augustine, both highly educated and accomplished in rhetoric, combined the traditional genres with Scripture in an attempt to work out a Christian rhetoric. Augustine spent much of his episcopal career writing and revising his *De doctrina Christiana* (between 396 and 426), and Gregory reflected on these matters in his *Oration VIII: On Gorgonia* (c. 374).[44] For Christian preachers, the truth

---

[41] Graham Furniss, *Orality: The Power of the Spoken Word* (Basingstoke, UK: Palgrave Macmillan 2004), 123.

[42] Alessandro Duranti, "The Audience as Co-Author: An Introduction," *Text* 6, no. 3 (1986): 239–347, here at 243.

[43] Malcolm Heath, "Codifications of Rhetoric," in *The Cambridge Companion to Ancient Rhetoric*, ed. Erik Gunderson, 63 (Cambridge: Cambridge University Press, 2009).

[44] Carol Harrison, *The Art of Listening in the Early Church* (Oxford: Oxford University Press, 2013), 37–60.

took precedence because of the authorizing force of Scripture. The audience heard Scripture read and then the text preached upon, and thus, as Gregory said, "No place will be given here simply to what delights the ear, even if we should wish to do so; for the listener stands here, like a skilled umpire, between my speech and the truth, giving no praise to words that are undeserved, but demanding what is deserved—and that is only just. . . . So we shall take the truth as our norm, and look to it alone, not regarding any other considerations that might sound attractive to the lowly crowd."[45] The audience's role as "skilled umpire" gives it more responsibility than simply listening attentively and being persuaded by what they hear; they are ratifiers of the message, as Duranti indicated. In book four of *De doctrina*, Augustine presents a Christian rhetoric based upon the requirement to teach, delight, and sway the audience so that the speaker is listened to with understanding, enjoyment, and obedience. The preacher is to be alert to the audience's response: Are they bored because they know this already? Do they not understand? Is the applause merely because they enjoyed the eloquence? Have their emotions been roused sufficiently or even unsustainably? Have they been convinced by the desired course of action? Ultimately, believers who listen obediently listen "not to any mere human being, but to the Lord himself. . . ."[46] The preacher himself had also first listened to Christ and had prepared by prayer, and the audience was "not just passive hearers but participants in his attempt to convey the truth of Scripture to them; they were encouraged to relate it to themselves, reflect on it, take it to heart, and allow it to transform their lives."[47]

Graham Furniss observed that societies have different audience cultures which determine the behavior of speaker and listeners. In a highly participative "congregationalist" culture, the speaker will employ a strategy of call-and-response in which an active, often spoken, response is expected; more reserved cultures will have more passive mechanisms by which the audience affirms what it has

---

[45] Gregory Nazianzen, *Oration* 8.1, in *Gregory of Nazianzus*, trans. Brian Daley, 64 (London: Taylor & Francis, 2006).
[46] Augustine, *De doctrina Christiana* 4.27, 59, in *The Works of Saint Augustine*, vol. 1/11, trans. Edmund Hill and John E. Rotelle, 238 (Charlottesville, VA: InteLex Corporation, 2014).
[47] Harrison, *Art of Listening*, 153.

heard.[48] Regardless of any observed response in the listeners, they are still actively engaged in meaning-making in the liturgical event and do so by connecting past experiences and prior knowledge to interpret what they hear. At the Easter Vigil, the people hear these words from Isaiah 55, which aptly mirror the ideas in this section:

> Listen carefully to me, and eat what is good,
> and delight yourselves in rich food.
> Incline your ear, and come to me;
> listen, so that you may live. . . .
>
> so shall my word be that goes out from my mouth;
> it shall not return to me empty,
> but it shall accomplish that which I purpose, and succeed in the
>   thing for which I sent it. (Isa 55:1-3, 11)

Listener as Earwitness

An earwitness remembers a past sound event so that it can be told again as a relevant contribution to a new and quite different situation. Theories about what an earwitness is and does vary according to the mode in which that memory is preserved or conveyed, be it in writing or orally, and about the faithfulness of the report to the past event. It is not always necessary for the listener to have actively participated in the event; they simply need to have been present and are able to recall and recount the sonic event when required. The sound event is important, but without the memory of it, it ceases to have relevance. The memory is an embodied one because it involves recall of a sense perception, and it is performative when the sound is described or re-created in the present.

It is possible to see how worshippers can function as earwitnesses, especially because of the importance of memory, of anamnesis, in liturgical worship. Not only are biblical events recalled through hearing the Scriptures read, but prayers constantly recall these words and events. The anamnesis of the eucharistic prayer has just this function: a sonic memory of the history of salvation in which the congregation participates as they hear it prayed. Using earwitness in relation to

---

[48] Furniss, *Orality*, 87–88.

liturgical participation shows how different it is from other historical and forensic uses: the worshipper witnesses with their ears in the present to a past which is constantly re-presented in the Mass, and which is always simultaneously present in the heavenly liturgy.[49]

Listener as Eavesdropper

The term *eavesdropper* is, as Anne Gaylin explained, derived from the placement of a listener under the eaves drop, where the water runs off the roof. Private space is transgressed so that, deliberately or inadvertently, the listener overhears information which is not intended for him.[50] It suggests spatial positioning at the margins or boundaries, real and metaphorical liminality. As walls and doors are no longer the sole location for spying on the private world of others, the notion has expanded to include all "surreptitious observation as a technique for the sampling of the intimate experiences of others," which can involve any sensory activity, not just hearing.[51] However, once the information has been heard, then the hearer's role changes; what is heard comes into the ownership of the listener; they become participants in it and engage in interpretation unfettered by the original context. This new interpretation then forms the basis for the retelling of what was heard based upon how the eavesdropper has combined the content with other heard and known information. Thus eavesdropping is transgressional in two ways—in relation to the spatial positioning of the listener and in relation to what the listener does to and with the information received.[52] The act may also impact the listener's sense of self by changing power relations or arousing emotional responses such as guilt or shame. Unlikely as it may seem, there are a number of features of liturgical listening which can be illuminated by considering eavesdropping: these are the status of the

---

[49] See Nathan P. Chase, "The Ascent into Heaven: An Answer to the Problem of Time in Liturgical Anamnesis," *Studia Liturgica* online (2022), n.p.

[50] Ann Gaylin, *Eavesdropping in the Novel from Austen to Proust* (Cambridge: Cambridge University Press, 2002), 2.

[51] John L. Locke, *Eavesdropping: An Intimate History* (Oxford: Oxford University Press, 2010), 4, 17.

[52] See Gaylin, *Eavesdropping*, 10–14.

listener in relation to what is heard, the spatial positioning of the listener, and the interpretative autonomy of the listener.

In Cyril of Jerusalem's *Procatechesis*, delivered at the beginning of Lent in 351 to those enrolling for baptism, he uses a rich array of metaphors drawn from eavesdropping to explain the status change resulting from enrollment. Previously they were eavesdroppers (he does not use this term): "Up till now have been called a catechumen, one who hears from the outside. You heard hope, but you didn't know it. You heard mysteries, but didn't understand them. You heard the Scriptures, but you didn't understand their depth. But now you are not hearing a sound outside you but one within, for now the Spirit lives in you and makes your mind God's home."[53] But they have been allowed to enter: "We had the responsibility of doorkeepers, but we left the door open"; however, they have not yet fully entered: "You are already outside the outer hall of the palace; I pray that the king may lead you inside."[54] And they are warned not to use the period of pre-baptismal catechesis to eavesdrop upon the faithful: "Let no one come here saying: 'Come on, let's see what the Faithful do. Let me go in and watch, so as to learn what goes on.' Do you expect to see without being seen? Do you think that you can be curious about what is going on without God being curious about your heart?"[55] Whereas before they were free to interpret what they heard in church, out of ignorance of its full implications, they will now be enlightened by the Holy Spirit through the pre-baptismal instruction. And whereas an eavesdropper is, in theory, an unseen earwitness, the newly enrolled have never been secret listeners, as God is always the ultimate witness to what is going on in their heart.

Cyril uses boundary and door as metaphors here, but there is plenty of evidence of the operation of physical boundaries in liturgical space that assign the role of eavesdropper to particular members of the congregation. Most barriers which demarcate liturgical space are porous rather than solid, and even the most formidable rarely prevent sound leaving the enclosed space. Iconostasis, veil, and

---

[53] Cyril of Jerusalem, *Procatechesis* 6–9, in *Cyril of Jerusalem*, trans. Edward J. Yarnold, SJ, 81 (London: Taylor & Francis, 2000).

[54] Cyril of Jerusalem, *Procatechesis* 4 and 1, in *Cyril of Jerusalem*, 79–80.

[55] Cyril of Jerusalem, *Procatechesis* 2–3, in *Cyril of Jerusalem*, 79.

screen separate the privileged listener and can turn others into eavesdroppers. The door of the church is another liminal space and has long formed a symbolic and real barrier to liturgical participation. Evidence from the early and medieval church shows that certain people, catechumens and penitents, were excluded from the Eucharist and placed behind closed doors, which did not necessarily exclude the sound reaching them, as Ivan Foletti and Katarína Kravčíková have shown.[56] Medieval handbooks of penance showed that different categories of penitents were placed in "tiers of decreasing distance from the altar according to their penitential station." Those furthest away, the "weepers" outside the door and the "hearers" in the vestibule, would have only just heard the priest. As Mary Hayes comments, "The boundary between these two communities, both labelled by sound-orientated terms, served to define the church as a sound-orientated arena by demarcating its acoustic horizon, the point past which the priest's voice could no longer be heard."[57]

Carol Harrison presents a more positive view of eavesdropping by the congregation on the priest or preacher in worship, although she prefers the term "overhearer," which carries less social stigma.[58] Preaching, she suggests, is a form of "prayerful overhearing," in which the congregation heard the preacher's personal conversation with God. This prayerful overhearing also applies to the prayers: "communal prayer should, first of all, be understood as a form of communal listening, or, more precisely, communal overhearing."[59] This arises from the complicated relationship between speaker and listener in worship when what is heard is God's own speech returning to him; such is the case when the Lord's Prayer is recited. Harrison describes the "polyphony of speaking and hearing" in which "God speaks to Himself; the individual and the congregation speak to God; God hears His own words and those of the faithful; the faithful hear

---

[56] Ivan Foletti and Katarína Kravčíková, "Closed Doors as Bearers and Constructors of Images," *Convivium Supplementum* (2019): 24–45. See also Juliette Day, "The Status and Role of Doorkeepers in the Early Medieval West," *Studies in Late Antiquity* 6, no. 1 (2022): 148–73.

[57] Mary Hayes, *Divine Ventriloquism in Medieval English Literature: Power, Anxiety, Subversion* (New York: Palgrave Macmillan, 2011), 88.

[58] Harrison, *Art of Listening*, 183–228.

[59] Harrison, 199.

what they pray, overhear the words of their neighbour as they pray with them, and, above all, overhear God's own words." Clearly if God is the intended hearer of the entire liturgy, then all participants are, by default, eavesdroppers. Harrison goes on to explain how being an eavesdropper frees the listener to participate on their own terms, to hear without needing to respond, to explain why early Christian preachers frequently addressed God directly in their sermons or dialogued with an imaginary interlocutor. In both cases, the congregation is complicit in overhearing conversations in which they do not participate and in which they are not addressed.[60]

I certainly agree that, at some points in worship, the congregation do become eavesdroppers or overhearers, but I am not sure that it is for the reasons Harrison suggests. Formally, from the content of these sermons and prayers, it could be said that the congregation overhear, but in the context of their performance they are also the intended co-hearers of the prayers and sermons. The passivity of these overhearers should also be questioned: as Mary Cunningham and Pauline Allen show, many preachers were only too well aware of the audience's active response, "including applause, laughter or grumbling; there is evidence that on many occasions a preacher might alter his discourse in response to reactions from the audience or again, that he might choose not to alter it."[61] Hayes shows that for early medieval preachers there was encouragement to hear themselves speak the sermon, to become co-listeners with the congregation; again, this does not seem to establish the congregation as eavesdroppers on a private homiletic conversation with God.[62]

There are some rather select moments when worshippers can become eavesdroppers, such as when a prayer of preparation for a particular ministry is performed audibly: for example, prayers to accompany the priest's ablution before the eucharistic prayer. Other situations where the congregation might be said to eavesdrop or overhear are during the "silent" or concealed recitation of the eucharistic prayer; during the words to administer baptism, confirmation, and ordination; and during the committal prayer at burial. However,

---

[60] Harrison, 202–4.
[61] Mary Cunningham and Pauline Allen, *Preacher and Audience: Studies in Early Christian and Byzantine Homiletics* (Leiden: Brill, 2017), 18.
[62] Hayes, *Divine Ventriloquism*, 102.

in each of these cases the liturgical action requires the presence of the people, and thus their listening is quite unlike eavesdropping.

Listening to Invisible Sound Sources

In this section I wish to combine two rather separate aspects of auditory displacement: ventriloquism and concealment.

Although ventriloquism is a mode of speaking, it does require a particular form of listening in which the perceived sound source is not the actual sound source. Mary Hayes suggested this was a useful term to interpret the English medieval liturgical experience when "the divine voice was ventriloquized by the clergy" which "galvanized the normative relationship between priest and people, making them his subservient listeners."[63] When the priest speaks in God's voice, the listener must relocate the source from the human to the divine participants. In the Mass this was particularly the case when the priest repeated Christ's words in the institution narrative, but because of a fear of misappropriation by acts of improper ventriloquism by the laity, this was recited silently.[64] One function of the silence was to situate the speaking of these sacred words away from human ears and mouths. If speech denotes the presence of a speaker, then in the Mass the speaker is Christ who is truly present in the consecrated bread and wine, and thus the priest, too, is to hear Christ even as he articulates silently the sacred words.

Liturgists are familiar with the practice of visually concealing certain ritual objects with veils or screens for symbolic or sacramental reasons. Concealment of the sound source has also been used in liturgical performance, primarily in the situation of singers and choirs. Among the liturgical instructions contained in Ælfric's *Letter to the Monks of Eynsham* (between 1005 and 1010) is a description of the blessing of palms on Palm Sunday:

> And after the processional collect, the deacon shall read the gospel "A great multitude," up to the words "Behold, the whole world is gone after him." When this has been done, the blessing of the palms shall follow: they are to be sprinkled with holy

---

[63] Hayes, 2.
[64] Hayes, 7.

water, censed and divided up while the boys begin the antiphons "The Hebrew children" [and the rest]. At the end of the procession they shall stop before the church where, from within, boys shall sing "All glory, laud and honour" with its verses, while the rest respond in the usual way. When these things have been done, they shall enter the church while the cantor begins the responsory "As the Lord entered [the holy city]" . . . ."[65]

Brian Kane describes a seventeenth-century practice of positioning the choir, especially of girls or nuns, away from view. Initially this was necessitated by the Council of Trent's decision to confine nuns to the convent, but by placing these choirs behind grilles or in hidden places, they could produce the sensation of hearing an angelic choir. The church in the Convent of Santi Domenico e Sisto in Rome had an extremely high altar "with grated windows above to the left and right, and, high up near the vaults, a series of grated openings that circled the church. The voices emanating from these high grates were juxtaposed against the frescoed ceilings depicting images of the heavenly host. The architectural space reinforced the fantasy: The listeners were encouraged to identify the vocalic body, heard in the nuns' voices, with the celestial figures floating above their heads."[66]

These forms of ritualization of unseen sound sources indicate the power of hearing in religious experience, and that it is hearing rather than sight which validates the experience. They are also a physical and sensorial ritualization of the spiritual and heavenly realm which cannot be perceived directly by sensory means. Hearing the voice of God or of the saints is found frequently in the reports of mystics and early Puritans, and was interpreted as a sign of favor and salvation. The liturgical performance of this type of listening brings direct spiritual communication into the realm of the possible while at the same time establishing the physical boundary between the world and the longed-for immediate presence of God.

---

[65] Ælfric, *Letter to the Monks of Eynsham* 32, in Christopher A. Jones, *Ælfric's Letter to the Monks of Eynsham*, 125 (Cambridge: Cambridge University Press, 1999).

[66] Brian Kane, *Sound Unseen: Acousmatic Sound in Theory and Practice* (New York: Oxford University Press, 2014), 109.

Conclusion

In this chapter, we have considered how the act of audition is transformed depending on the role the hearers adopt, their relationship to the sound source, and the way in which the sound signal is made meaningful. *Hearing* is what we do anyway, with our ears always open to receive sound signals, but worship demands the more attentive and purposeful *listening* or *hearkening*. The connection made in French with waiting or anticipation indicates how listeners are alert for meaningful communication, but their task does not end there. Any meaning derived from the signal is based on memories and the context of hearing, which the listeners apply in collaboration with the speaker or producer of the sound. A listener can never be a passive recipient of sound because it is their task to complete the communication, which also entails letting the other speak and being open to the potential of what is said. A listener needs to be truly present to the other, and to the sound, in order for this to happen. In Christian theology, God speaks and hears in the act of worship; it is God who both initiates the communication and who completes it. Worshippers collaborate with God in that process by themselves speaking and hearing, and are open to the transformative potential of that which they hear and make sense of. The liturgy presents to the worshipper a paradigm for authentic and fulfilled human hearing.

Chapter 3

Ritual Listening

In the previous chapter, we explored the difference between hearing and more focused listening, and this chapter will develop those ideas to reflect on listening as a mode of ritual participation and performance. Despite extensive research into ritual theory and practice, only very few scholars have attended to the auditory, and none of them in any extended way. This is curious given that many features of religious ritual performance require audition for their completion, either by the divine or the human participants. If it is indeed the case that there can be no speaking without listening—to which we could also add, no making of music—then clearly acts of audition are necessary to complete a ritual act which involves both speech and music. In this chapter I shall first present and discuss some useful and relevant ideas from ritual and sensory studies to see how they might help us move towards an understanding of *ritual listening*, and then, in an investigation of examples drawn from Christian worship, I shall suggest the further category of *ritualized* listening.

Ritual and Ritual Listening

Listening as an intentional and purposeful act of audition is obviously to be preferred to *hearing* when considering ritual. Ritual frames the activities which constitute it by separating them from similar activities in everyday life, and a distinction is clearly made between ritual and non-ritual; ritual is an intentional act and requires intentional audition. In the Mass, the frame is constituted by the opening words, "The Lord be with you", and the closing words, "Go, the Mass is ended"; what happens within these words is set aside from the mundane, the everyday activities, and shifts the participants from one reality into another.[1] In Erving Goffman's theory of frames, he proposed the notion of "keying": "the set of conventions by which a given activity . . . is transformed into something patterned on this activity but seen by the participants to be something quite else."[2] Frames change over time and they may constitute a hard or a fuzzy boundary between ritual and non-ritual. By speaking of the boundaries between ritual and non-ritual as a frame, we provide a focusing device to reflect upon the added value given to ritual activities compared to the same or similar activities outside ritual. Although we can presume that the operation of the senses remains physiologically the same, the cultural value applied to their operation will differ; thus, in religious ritual, the senses are attuned to the immanence of the divine participants. The senses themselves and what is perceived by them will be imbued with specific, heightened, or symbolic meaning. We have already seen how early Protestants developed a theology of listening in relation to the sermon which they distinguished from ordinary hearing.

In *Ritual and Religion in the Making of Humanity*, Roy Rappaport defined ritual as "the performance of more or less invariant sequences of formal acts and utterances not entirely encoded by the performers."[3] The verbal messages, as with the gestures and music, usually do not change much from one ritual performance to the next, they do not originate with the performers, and they may not necessarily express the current state of those uttering them—indeed, they are unlikely to. He refers to the Roman Catholic Mass as a particular conveyor of what he calls "canonical" messages, which are meaningful, not informational.[4] In public rituals as well as private devotion

---

[1] See Don Handelman, "Framing," in *Theorizing Rituals*, ed. Jens Kreinath, J. A. M. Snoek, and Michael Stausberg, vol. 1, *Issues, Topics, Approaches, Concepts*, 572 (Leiden: Brill, 2018).

[2] Erving Goffman, *Frame Analysis: An Essay on the Organization of Experience* (Boston: Northeastern University Press, 1974), 43–44.

[3] Roy A. Rappaport, *Ritual and Religion in the Making of Humanity* (Cambridge: Cambridge University Press, 1999), 24.

[4] Rappaport, *Ritual and Religion*, 52, 109.

there occurs "auto-communication," that is the *"transmitters of ritual's messages are always among their most important receivers"* [his italics].[5] What is conveyed by words and what by gestures is complementary but also to be distinguished: the gestures enable the performer to embody or incarnate the canonical meanings.[6] Meaning is conveyed not just by the words spoken, but also by the gestures accompanying them, and is created by the transmitters and receivers, who are, in fact, identical. It is interesting that, although he emphasizes the verbal aspect of ritual and the role of transmitters and receivers, he does not specifically address listening, which is surely essential for the appropriation of the ritual's meaning(s). In fact, the terms *audition*, *hearing*, and *listening* are entirely absent from the index. I find Rappaport provides one of the more cogent treatments of ritual, but he is certainly not alone in overlooking listening as a key component of ritual performance.

In chapter 1, we explored the soundscape of worship and suggested that it was composed of intentional sounds, non-intentional sounds, and noise. Most theories of ritual emphasize the intentional sounds, which correspond to those that are "not entirely encoded by the performers." These are the most stable and can be easily isolated for investigation. The ritual performance is constituted by these intentional sounds (and gestures), but within each performance there will also be non-intentional, ambient sounds and noise; however, as these sounds are not "framed" by the ritual event, we will leave them to one side for now.

Ritual Language

Despite the lack of an explicit scholarly treatment of ritual listening, it should be possible to infer acts of audition from discussions about ritual language and ritual music, as these necessitate listening for their completion and for the discernment of meaning. Liturgists, linguists, and anthropologists have investigated ritual language as the content and performance of the verbal aspects of a ritual event, and ritual discourse/speech as the way in which language contributes

---

[5] Rappaport, 51.
[6] Rappaport, 153.

to the functioning of ritual. It is noticeable that language is contrasted with other symbolic systems, and thus hearing nonverbal sounds in worship is either not discussed or placed among gesture, movement, etc. And, as we have seen with Rappaport's analysis, the act of listening to any sound is almost never explicitly mentioned; at best we must assume it is implied in the analysis of speaking, even though ritual's effects are presumed to arise from speech rather than audition. In this section we shall present a number of theories of ritual language and speech and indicate what sort of model of ritual listening they imply.

In everyday, ordinary dialogue situations the speaker and listener collaborate to ensure that meaning is successfully conveyed through visual and verbal prompts, and through a feedback system whereby understanding is checked and reinforced. Wade Wheelock noted the limitations of such a model of language in ritual contexts, because it presumes that the function of speech is to convey information.[7] In analyzing liturgical language, all too often it is investigated without regard to the mode in which that language is conveyed. There is deemed to be no difference between speech and written language, nor how the deployment of metaphors and other language forms, as well as their presentation/performance, might influence meaning.

Roy Rappaport summarizes some of the characteristics of ritual language: "It is virtually definitive of ritual speech that it is stereotyped and stylized, composed of specified sequences of words that are often archaic, is repeated under particular, usually well-established circumstances, and great stress is often laid upon its precise enunciation."[8] He refers to Maurice Bloch's observation that the ritual components of speech are immutable, and to Gregory Bateson's suggestion that meaning is fused such that individual speech-language elements are subsumed under the whole ritual performance and they lose their individual meanings. Flexibility and subtilty of language are eschewed in favor of clarity. But the words need gestures as well as further words because "ritual words by themselves lack the ability

---

[7] Wade T. Wheelock, "The Problem of Ritual Language: From Information to Situation," *Journal of the American Academy of Religion* 50, no. 1 (1982): 49–72.

[8] Rappaport, *Ritual and Religion*, 151.

to substantiate the messages they transmit."[9] The physical and the verbal must combine for the presentation and generation of meaning: "in the successful conjunction of word and act there may be, or seem to be, a unification of first, the physical, affective and cognitive processes constituting the self; of second, the unified self with its visible representation; and, finally, of the self and its representation with the canon in which it participates."[10] Clearly the words alone do not constitute the meaning of the ritual, requiring gestures too, but what is the place of listening in the unification of the processes which constitute the self in the ritual? Is listening to be classed as physical, or as affective, or as cognitive? Or is it, perhaps, that the unification takes place and is most evident in ritual listening? It is clear, though, that if there is repetition of the ritual words, and that these words do not substantiate what they propose, then the mode of listening is not for the reception of new information, but is the means for the creation of a new situation in which a reality that is not perceptible is in fact perceived.

Interest in the performative aspect of speech over its informative role was sparked by John L. Austin's notion of "speech acts" which he set out in *How to Do Things with Words*, and which was influentially modified by John Searle.[11] They showed how a verbal construct may establish a new situation: the speech effects what it says, and thus quite clearly the listeners are essential to complete performative act, although neither Austin nor Searle in fact mention them. Austin's classic example of a speech act was "I declare you man and wife." At the moment of speaking this declaration, the listener is not intended to be informed, but clearly after the event they act in relation to the new situation brought about by the speech act.

Wheelock and others have noted that ritual language serves the accomplishment of the aim of the ritual performance as a whole; the words alone do not by themselves constitute it. He describes such language's characteristics as "choppiness," the succession of short

---

[9] Rappaport, 152.
[10] Rappaport, 153.
[11] John L. Austin, *How to Do Things with Words: The William James Lectures Delivered at Harvard University in 1955* (Oxford: Clarendon Press, 1962). John R. Searle, *Expression and Meaning: Studies in the Theory of Speech Acts* (Cambridge: Cambridge University Press, 1979).

items imprecisely connected to each other by verbal means and interspersed with ritual action; the "constant oscillation" between ritual words and instructions for the ritual; and disconnectedness and a lack of cohesion in the narrative and argument. The use of first-person pronouns without explanation indicates implicit knowledge of who the referents are. Participants use predetermined language, and not their own, which usually employs metaphors that rely upon prior understanding of the symbolic system. Ritual language interacts with other symbolic systems of gesture, movement, and ritual objects, clarifying and augmenting them; language is not sufficient on its own, but neither is it entirely explained by the other symbolic systems.[12] In distinguishing ritual from ordinary language, Wheelock asserts that there is no immediate hearer of ritual language:

> While much of this could be interpreted as intended for the ears of invisible spiritual beings, a close scrutiny of the language of specific liturgies (my own familiarity with Vedic rituals in particular bears out this point) shows that just as often no second-person addressee is given or implied in such instances. Perhaps more typical is the case where all the participants in the ritual form a global first-person plural, a "we" that speaks in unison to itself and not to any audience—for example, the recitation of the creed in the Mass, where all references to the Trinity are in the third person with no indication of any second-person addressee.[13]

The text is known already; there is no information exchange, and even the invisible spiritual beings are presumed to know the words beforehand. This leads Wheelock to propose the category of "situational speech" as a counterpart to ordinary language. He wrote, "Because the text precedes the actual enactment of a ritual situation . . . an indicative utterance does not represent the speaker's perception of a past or present state of affairs. The speaking of the text presents the situation."[14] Even more, it brings about the state of affairs by the fact of its being spoken and can do so repeatedly.

---

[12] Wheelock, "Problem of Ritual Language," 50, 57.
[13] Wheelock, 58.
[14] Wheelock, 60.

Ritual language, then, enables participation in a situation; it engenders a state of being rather than of knowing. Wheelock concludes:

> It is largely through the utterances of the liturgy that the ritual participants can create and enact the roles and relationships of an idealized situation and partake of the value traditionally assigned to them. The actual utterance of the words of the liturgy, which will include such very personal elements as expressions of attitudes and intentions, causes one to take on the identity of a cultural ideal. The formalized role is put into your mouth to speak and comes out as your own responsible perception of and involvement in the situation. The first person of the ritual text comes to life as the "I" or "we" of the participants who speak the liturgy and who then proceed to fashion around themselves a whole world made of language.[15]

Wheelock points out the transformative effect of ritual participation, and how the speaking of ritual words creates a situation where the speaker takes on the identity presumed by the words. He assumes, though, that this is an effect of the speaking alone, and not of the hearing. I would argue that unless the ritual participants hear themselves uttering the ritual words, then they cannot possibly "fashion themselves" in relation to what that language proposes.

John W. Du Bois, in his summary of the characteristics and effects of ritual language, identified a number of universal features connected to the content, structure, and performance of ritual speech, and although he did not actively reflect upon the role of the listener, he does imply that they do have a performative role. It is the listeners who act as constrainers upon the expressive freedom of the speaker, and so they act as witness and bearers of ritual traditions. And, in order for the ritual to be successfully achieved, they need to identify the real source of the speech as the divine being, for whom the speaker is simply a medium. This requires the "attenuation of the directness of ordinary speaker-hearer interaction," and indicates a different type of auditory activity from that outside the ritual context.[16]

---

[15] Wheelock, 65.
[16] John W. Du Bois, "Ritual Language," in *The International Encyclopedia of Linguistics*, vol. 3, ed. William J. Frawley, 463–65 (New York: Oxford University Press, 2003).

Mostly, ritual language is investigated for is stylistic and performative features such as vocabulary, metaphor, vocalization, intentionality, etc.[17] John W. Du Bois is somewhat rare in suggesting a role for the hearer too. This focus on the speakers, by which is often meant the ritual leaders, gives them the authority to select from the verbal repertoire and to determine its performance. But the human listeners are required to complete the act of speaking and not just the divine listeners; they act as witnesses and verifiers of the effective performance of the ritual, and in many cases they are also the direct addressees of the ritual speech.

Ritualized Listening

In Christian worship, there are certain rituals which are constituted by, performed by, and completed by an act of audition; that is, listening itself is ritualized. This has two elements: first, where the ritual includes explicit injunctions to listen within discrete subsections or units; and second, where the very act of listening is ritualized—that is, within the ritual frame—a specific act of listening becomes paradigmatic of ideal forms of listening. What is important in *ritualized listening* is not only what is heard, but the act of listening itself. In this section I shall discuss a number of examples drawn from different styles of Christian worship.

Acclamations and instructions often function as a call to heightened attentiveness. One obvious example is in the Orthodox Divine Liturgy, when the deacon cries, "Wisdom, let us attend!" during the Little Entrance as the gospel book is processed into the sanctuary.[18] This ritual entrance was originally the procession of the clergy and

---

[17] See also Gail Ramshaw, *Reviving Sacred Speech: The Meaning of Liturgical Language; Second Thoughts on Christ in Sacred Speech* (Franklin, NJ: OSL Publications, 2000); Robert A. Yelle, "Ritual and Religious Language," in *The Encyclopedia of Language & Linguistics*, 2nd ed., ed. E. K. Brown and Anne Anderson, 633–40 (Amsterdam: Elsevier, 2006).

[18] See Robert F. Taft, "Little Entrance," in *The Oxford Dictionary of Byzantium*, ed. Alexander P. Kazhdan, n.p. (Oxford: Oxford University Press, 1991); Juan Mateos, *La célébration de la parole dans la liturgie byzantine: étude historique*, Orientalia Christiana Analecta, vol. 191 (Rome: Pont. Institutum Studiorum Orientalium, 1971); Robert F. Taft, "How Liturgies Grow: The Evolution of the Byzantine 'Divine Liturgy,'" *Orientalia Christiana Periodica* 53 (1977): 8–30.

people into church, and thus the call to attentiveness applied to the entire liturgy; now it forms the opening of the Liturgy of the Word and focuses attention on the reading of Scripture which is to follow, although not immediately. The Roman Catholic General Instruction on the Roman Missal (GIRM) also connects the rituals at the start of Mass with listening. Concerning the introductory rites (entrance, veneration of the altar, act of penance, *Kyrie Eleison*, Gloria, and collect), it states: "Their purpose is to ensure that the faithful, who come together as one, establish communion and dispose themselves properly to listen to the Word of God and to celebrate the Eucharist worthily" (GIRM 46). The acclamation "Let us pray" is commonly a call for the congregation to listen silently while another prays on their behalf. Such is the case with the ritual introduction to the collect for the day, where "Let us pray" is followed by a short period of silence which functions to call the congregation into an attentive listening mode.

Dialogue constitutes a key component of liturgical worship, alongside poetry and prose texts, and it calls for both an engaged listening and an active response. As Julia T. Wood has summarized, "central to dialogue is the idea that any utterance or act is always responding to and anticipating other utterances and acts. Genuine dialogue depends less on self-expression and other transmissional aspects of communication than upon responsiveness."[19] If responsiveness is the key characteristic of dialogue, then it implies a relationship of mutual listening between participants. In liturgical worship, dialogues are scripted exchanges which can take three forms: versicle/response, litany, and interrogatory. There are also unscripted dialogues in, for example, spontaneous exchanges in sermons. The performance of dialogue is a collaborative task with participants alternately taking on the role of speaker and listener; they are mutually dependent upon each other to ensure the successful completion of the ritual exchange and for the creation of a new state of being or new information.

---

[19] Julia T. Wood, "Foreword," in *Dialogue: Theorizing Difference in Communication Studies*, ed. Rob Anderson, Leslie A. Baxter, and Kenneth N. Cissna, xvi (Thousand Oaks, CA: Sage Publications, 2003).

Versicles and responses most clearly establish the collaborative listening relationship between the speaker and listener, and between the respondent and listener. The most frequently used, "The Lord be with you / And also with you", calls the minister and congregation to renewed attentiveness to each other at several points during the Mass: at the start, before the gospel, before the Canon, and the final blessing. I suggest that, in practice, this reconstitutes the congregation into a single listening body by refocusing their collective attention on the minister and the words and actions to follow. Rupert of Deutz (c.1075–c.1129), in his commentary on the Mass, asserted that "*Dominus vobiscum*" before the gospel was a call for attentive listening because "the highest reverence is indeed owed to listening to the gospel."[20] This versicle and response often functions as a transitional device, indicating to the responsive listener that the liturgy is about to move to a different phase, mood, or activity. Michael Anderson's work on the sung performance of this exchange in medieval liturgy, especially in the Liturgy of the Hours, indicates how the performance of the response requires a rather special level of attentiveness. In the Book of Hours, this exchange was almost never given any musical notation; first, because it was so familiar; and second, because the officiant was able to elaborate the versicle according to the solemnity of the feast. The performance of the versicle primes the listener's response, as Anderson explains: "The congregation listens to its degree of elaboration and responds by mirroring the precise formula established by the prompt with its assigned text."[21]

In other scripted versicle/response dialogues, both parties cooperate in the creation and completion of meaningful statements. This is the case in the *Sursum corda* and the Suffrages, the intercessory prayers in Morning and Evening Prayer in the BCP. In the liturgical books and in performance, they appear to be the same as other versicle/response units, but what differentiates them is that the meaningful utterance is divided between the versicle and response, so that the

---

[20] Rupert of Deutz, *De divinis officiis* 1.36, in *Readers and Hearers of the Word: The Cantillation of Scripture in the Middle Ages*, trans. Joseph Dyer, Ritus Et Artes 10, 25 (Turnhout: Brepols, 2022).

[21] Michael Alan Anderson, *Music and Performance in the Book of Hours* (New York: Routledge, 2022), 105.

roles of speaker and listener are constantly being exchanged. Thus, for example:

Priest. O Lord, shew thy mercy upon us.

Answer. And grant us thy salvation.

Priest. O Lord, save the King.

Answer. And mercifully hear us when we call upon thee.

Priest. Endue thy Ministers with righteousness.

Answer. And make thy chosen people joyful.[22]

These scripted exchanges require an attentive listening from both minister and congregation for their successful completion, and so, to a certain extent, does the litany; however, because the congregation's response requires considerably less effort, they are able to listen more intently to the petition. As Anderson commented with regard to the Litany of the Saints, "The format of the Litany is characterized by a cantor-prompted 'roll call' of holy personages, invocations, and supplications, which produces a musical response by a choir or community gathered. The full significance of the ritual materializes only when these two parts coordinate, the assembly answering the cantor's brief intention."[23] Again, the role of the listener-as-respondent is required to provide the correct response to the cantor's appeals and thereby complete the petition. The key difference is that whereas the cantor's versicles exhibited great variability, the relative invariance of the responses created "a dynamic and mesmerizing sound experience" for all present.[24] The litany enables a meditative listening by the participants.

The rituals surrounding the gospel reading in Orthodox, Roman Catholic, and some Anglican churches are customarily discussed in relation to the *proclamation* of the gospel; however, within the immediate context of congregational worship, these rituals call the worshippers into a differentiated listening mode. GIRM makes this clear:

---

[22] BCP: Suffrages at Morning and Evening Prayer.
[23] Anderson, *Music and Performance*, 142.
[24] Anderson, 152.

> The reading of the Gospel constitutes the high point of the Liturgy of the Word. The Liturgy itself teaches the great reverence that is to be shown to this reading by setting it off from the other readings with special marks of honor, by the fact of which minister is appointed to proclaim it and by the blessing or prayer with which he prepares himself; and also by the fact that through their acclamations the faithful acknowledge and confess that Christ is present and is speaking to them and stand as they listen to the reading; and by the mere fact of the marks of reverence that are given to the *Book of the Gospels*. (GIRM 60)

When the Church of England revised her liturgy in *Common Worship* (2000), the introduction to the gospel became "Hear the Gospel of our Lord Jesus Christ according to N."[25] Such a change establishes and emphasizes listening as the principal ritual activity at that point.

In *Common Worship*, the rubric suggests, "An acclamation may herald the Gospel reading," and the Roman Catholic GIRM refers to "marks of reverence that are given to the *Book of the Gospels*." This leads us to consider the means by which this act of listening is differentiated, enhanced, and prepared for by a range of other ritual actions and sounds. Listening to the gospel may be further ritualized when, in some congregations, the gospel book is carried in procession to the middle of the people who turn to face the reader. There is more historical precedence for processing to and reading the gospel from the ambo, a specially built platform raised above the congregation, often placed between the sanctuary and nave and sometimes highly decorated (see chapter 8).[26] And there is also a long history of other ritual embellishments such as chants, candles, incense, and even highly decorated covers for the book; the ritualization of the reading has its counterpart in a ritualization of listening when these other sensory perceptions are added. Conversely, if the people follow the proclamation of the gospel from Bibles or pew sheets, there is a de-ritualization of listening, when the people retreat into an interiorized

---

[25] Church of England, *Common Worship: Services and Prayers for the Church of England* (London: Church House Publishing, 2000), 171.

[26] Laskarina Bouras and Robert F. Taft, "Ambo," in *Oxford Dictionary of Byzantium*, n.p.

and private reading. It is interesting to find that in some seventeenth-century Protestant groups, bringing Bibles to church was discouraged so as not to distract from listening; at the least, the people were not to look up every passage referred to in the sermon.[27]

There are, though, occasions when listening is the primary mode of ritual participation of the entire liturgical event; that is, in liturgies composed mainly or entirely of extensive biblical readings in which the sermon does not form the central act. Two examples spring to mind: Anglican Evensong and the Easter Vigil. One might also suggest that the laity's role during the eucharistic prayer is to listen, in churches where the ritual performance permits them to do so. As we have already argued, they are not "eavesdroppers," but their participation is by this act of ritual listening, and this is made clear in GIRM 78: "The Eucharistic Prayer requires that everybody listens to it with reverence and in silence."

There are two elements of the Easter Vigil which also seem to fulfill the criteria of ritual listening: the *Exsultet* and the Scripture readings. Here the worshippers are to attend in silence to the words sung and spoken by others. *On Preparing and Celebrating the Paschal Feasts* (1988) directs:

> 85. The readings from Sacred Scripture constitute the second part of the Vigil. They give the account of the outstanding deeds of the history of salvation, which the faithful are helped to meditate calmly upon by the singing of the responsorial psalm, by a silent pause, and by the celebrant's prayer.
>
> The restored order for the Vigil has seven readings from the Old Testament, . . . and two readings from the New Testament, namely, from the apostles and from the gospel. Thus, the Church, "beginning with Moses and all the prophets," explains Christ's paschal mystery. Consequently, wherever this is possible, all the readings should be read in order so that the character of the

---

[27] Nicholas Bownde, *The Doctrine of the Sabbath* (1595) 2Div: "least in the meane season some other most necessarie doctrine overslip us, and we not marking what went before, and followed after, cannot tel to what ende the place was alleaged, and so we lose the profit of it." Quoted in Arnold Hunt, *The Art of Hearing: English Preachers and Their Audiences, 1590–1640* (Cambridge: Cambridge University Press, 2010), 69.

Easter Vigil, which demands that it be somewhat prolonged, be respected at all costs.[28]

At the Easter Vigil in a Roman Catholic church, the deacon invites the congregation to hear the story of salvation. This is presented in a patterned and ritualized form of units of Scripture, psalm, and collect prayer. The community is gathered in order to *listen to* the story: the readings are not the basis for preaching, but the hearing of them is a witness to God's saving acts that continue right up to the reading of the gospel of the resurrection—at which point the congregation, minister, and people move out of a listening mode in to a more active speaking/response mode.

English and American Puritan writers of the seventeenth and eighteenth centuries who wrote treatises about listening, emphasized "right hearing" of the preacher. The preacher was to be listened to as Christ, and the congregation were not only to listen with their ears, but to display their listening through their physical behavior.[29] Treatises on how to listen in worship, particularly to the sermon, recommended memory skills and note-taking (see chapter 7), but an effective preacher would expect his congregation to demonstrate their close listening by displaying the desired emotional response, normally contrition. Preachers aimed to "stir up godly emotions," and, as Hunt put it, the "tears of the people are the minister's praise."[30] Tears may then be understood as the performance of right listening. In Henry Mason's 1656 treatise, he has a chapter entitled "Duties required in the time of hearing." Most of these concern the individual's inner disposition; however, he also discusses the "dutifull behaviour in the outer man."[31] Maintaining eye contact with the preacher and decorum constitute a commonly agreed-upon set of behaviors which are particular to the context; with a broad definition

---

[28] Roman Catholic Church, *Paschale Solemnitatis* (On Preparing and Celebrating the Paschal Feasts), 1988, accessed February 7, 2018, http://www.liturgyoffice.org.uk/Calendar/Seasons/Documents/TriduumPF.shtml#Vigil.

[29] Hunt, *Art of Hearing*, 66–67.

[30] Hunt, 91.

[31] Henry Mason, *Hearing and Doing the Ready Way to Blessednesse: With an Appendix Containing Rules of Right Hearing Gods Word* (London: John Clark, 1656), chap. 13.11 (p. 649).

of ritual, it would be possible to consider these also as a ritual performance of listening.

Contemporary Pentecostal and charismatic worship can extend our notions of ritual and ritualized listening because of the unscripted, although patterned, exchanges between minister and people. As Daniel Albrecht, Bohdan Szuchewycz, and others have shown, the verbal components of charismatic worship display ritual characteristics even though they would not fulfill Rappaport's definition.[32] There are two characteristics of this type of ritual speech which are specifically pertinent to our study. First, that the speakers, although displaying some autonomy, assert that they are speaking from authoritative, divine inspiration—this implies a hearing which may not be physical. Second, in the unscripted sequences there are coherence strategies—prayers and personal narratives follow clearly identifiable and explicitly stated themes which indicate an attentiveness to what others have said.

Thomas J. Csordas's detailed analysis of certain Catholic charismatic groups confirmed that prophecy is a key component of their worship and community life; not just the utterance of prophecy, but of equal importance is its reception.[33] For the listener, it is a primary means of direct experience of the sacred. During prophecy, the speaker's agency is subjugated to God as author of the message and to the listener as recipient and validator.[34] However, Csordas comments that, as there are no rules or instructions for declaring a prophecy valid, it is the listener's role to adjudicate. He found them more disposed to a positive response when the prophecy had a general application, or was regarded as "innocuous," but they would test further one that was overly specific or detrimental, all the while acknowledging that "the same lines of prophecy carry different messages for

---

[32] Daniel E. Albrecht, *Rites in the Spirit: A Ritual Approach to Pentecostal/Charismatic Spirituality* (Sheffield, UK: Sheffield Academic Press, 1999); Bohdan Szuchewycz, "Evidentiality in Ritual Discourse: The Social Construction of Religious Meaning," *Language in Society* 23 (1994): 389–410. See also Mark Cartledge, *Testimony in the Spirit: Rescripting Ordinary Pentecostal Theology* (Farnham, UK: Ashgate, 2010), chap. 3.

[33] Thomas J. Csordas, *Language, Charisma, and Creativity: The Ritual Life of a Religious Movement* (Berkeley and Los Angeles: University of California Press, 1997), chap. 7.

[34] Csordas, *Language, Charisma, and Creativity*, 205.

different individuals."[35] Csordas comments that "the hearer's interpretative intentions are as much at issue as the communicative intentions of the human/divine speaker. At least for the ideally 'mature' hearer, being experientially moved and spiritually tuned in to a divine wavelength is not the sole source of validation."[36]. In chapter 2 we noted Alessandro Duranti's important article on "The Audience as Co-Author"[37], and Csordas also refers to it when emphasizing the fundamental role of the listener in the successful performance of prophecy. Critical and evaluative listening is therefore a key component to the ritual performance of prophecy; it is a ritual listening.

Dialogue can be studied as a rhetorical device used by the preacher to engage his audience, but it also necessarily functions to ensure the congregation are listening, or to facilitate their listening. Mary Cunningham's exploration of dialogue in Byzantine preaching starts with two important observations: first, that *homilia* means "conversation"; and second, that the form may have come into the church via its purely rhetorical use in poetry and hymnography. Cunningham usefully brings to our attention a distinction in homiletics proposed by Ingunn Lunde: the "intra-textual" and the "extra-textual" dialogue. In the first, the dialogue is invented speech by the preacher, and the second, of more interest to us, is between preacher and congregation. This extra-textual dialogue may be initiated by preachers as "exclamations, questions and other interjections to the audience . . . to engage their attention," but they also enhance the preachers' role as "mediators of the divine Word as they seek to involve their listeners in the events so dramatically described."[38]

In Pentecostal and charismatic worship, we can clearly see how the minister and people should be considered as co-authors of the sermon. The minister relies on the responses of the listeners to indicate that they follow the train of thought, that they approve of it, that they are being led where the minister leads them. The responses like

---

[35] Csordas, 233.
[36] Csordas, 234.
[37] Alessandro Duranti, "The Audience as Co-Author: An Introduction," *Text* 6, no. 3 (1986): 239–347.
[38] Mary Cunningham, "Dramatic Device or Didactic Tool? The Function of Dialogue in Byzantine Preaching," in *Rhetoric in Byzantium*, ed. Elizabeth Jeffreys, 103, 105 (Aldershot, UK: Ashgate, 2003).

"Amen" are ritually determined, as Albrecht has suggested. And Mark Cartledge also noted the ways in which the congregational acclamations link the units within worship as well as contribute to the sermons. They are fixed and formalized, even in the absence of a script, and fulfil the definition of ritual language. In these instances, ritual listening leads to ritual speech, and to an extent this replicates normal dialogic conventions.

In *Testimony in the Spirit*, Mark Cartledge presents a description of worship in a particular British Pentecostal congregation and repeats the comments on it made by a focus group of worshippers. Following Albrecht's categorization of ritual in this type of congregation, Cartledge identifies a ritual structure within which particular language acts occur, but without subjecting them to any specific analysis. Despite the lack of fixity in much Pentecostal/charismatic ritual speech, there are, nevertheless, acts of ritualized listening, demonstrated particularly when there is call-and-response between the leader or preacher and the other participants. "Brian" commented in the focus group, "Okay, when you've got a good worship leader, like Pastor Angela, then they encourage you with certain practices. So often at the start of the service it will be, you know, 'Look are you ready to worship? Have you got the correct mindset?' . . . . And sometimes when there's tongues or interpretation and prophecy and things like that we'll stop and respond and say, 'Look, God is speaking to us now in worship . . ., as we worship God is speaking. We must respond.' "[39] Cartledge reported another contributor discussing the preacher: "Occasionally, during the sermon, a member of the congregation may shout out: 'Praise the Lord' or 'Thank you, Jesus.' Most often the preacher punctuates the sermon with 'Amen,' which usually means 'Are you still with me?,' and the congregation reply 'Amen,' with varying degrees of enthusiasm.' "[40] These ritual exchanges, in which participants engage self-reflectively, serve to recollect the congregation into a listening mode such that they listen more attentively. They remind the congregation that at that particular point their participation is effected by a self-conscious and contextual listening activity which we have characterized as *ritualized listening*.

---

[39] Cartledge, *Testimony in the Spirit*, 35.
[40] Cartledge, 31.

Lastly, we should add that silence has its place among the repertoire of ritualized listening practices. As we shall see in chapter 5, liturgical silence is more than a keeping quiet while something else happens; rather, it is something which is to be heard and attended to. As a repetitive and purposed activity not encoded by the participants, it is certainly a ritual act, for which the appropriate participation is a ritualized listening during which the congregation *inhabits* the silence. David D. Daniels, whose work we presented in chapter 1, referred to early Pentecostals "tarrying for the Lord," a communal silence of expectation in the presence of God.[41] Similarly, at the end of the eucharistic prayer in Roman Catholic and some Anglican churches, after Christ has been made present in the sacrament, a silence is kept—a communal and ritual silence.

Conclusion

In liturgical worship as in other rituals, the act of listening is differentiated by being framed, set aside, from listening in the world. It is more than the physical operation of the auditory system that is active while other ritual acts take place. I have used the term *ritual listening* to highlight the particular way in which worshippers are intended to hear the ritual sounds—sounds whose ultimate hearer is God, sounds which they themselves make or are made on their behalf. Ritual listening is what is required when there is ritual speech, or even ritual music. It denotes a particular attentiveness to the divine and to the aim of the ritual event, whose words and outcomes are already known. Worshippers are not necessarily in a situation of information exchange; they are witnesses to what is heard and an audience who co-authors what is heard. Additionally, I have suggested that the successful completion of certain ritual acts involves a *ritualization* of listening, when participants model, by auditory and physical means, the ideal of attentive listening to God.

---

[41] Daniels, "'Gotta Moan Sometime,'" 15.

Chapter 4

Listening to Speech and Music

In chapter 1, I presented a threefold categorization of the sounds of worship: intentional, non-intentional, and noise. In this chapter I will consider the two most significant intentional sounds, namely speech and music. These are not mutually distinct but, as I shall show, can be placed on a sonic spectrum from natural speech to instrumental music. Not only do these require different performance capabilities but they also require different listening strategies for comprehension as well as participation. Isidore of Seville (c. 560–636) demonstrated an awareness of this when he related the performance of liturgical texts by speech and by singing to the different effects produced in the listener: "Readers (*lector*) are named from reading and psalmists (*psalmista*) from singing psalms, for the former pronounce to the people what they should follow, and the latter sing to kindle the spirits of their audience to compunction—although some readers also declaim in so heart-rending a way that they drive some people to sorrow and lamentation."[1]

Speech and music dominate the sound of worship but, despite some of the arguments for and against which is most appropriate for worship, they should not be considered as two distinct performances in opposition to each other. Instead, they should be placed on a spectrum from natural speech to instrumental music, via communal reci-

---

[1] Isidore of Seville, *Etymologies* VII.24, in *The Etymologies of Isidore of Seville*, trans. Stephen A. Barney et al., 171 (Cambridge: Cambridge University Press, 2006).

tation, chant, and hymns.[2] Just as each of these require different performance strategies so, too, do they necessitate different listening strategies. The decision to say, chant, or sing a text, and whether to have any instrumental music, is generally seen as either a cultural or pragmatic choice, the latter based upon the resources of the congregation. But theologians as well as churches in their official pronouncements have placed speech, song, and music into a hierarchy of what is appropriate for liturgical worship. As these become embedded in particular churches and their liturgical traditions, they constitute the sonic identity of that community. It is no surprise that such statements draw upon biblical material but also refer to the perceived effect of each sound-type on the worshippers. What they do not do is consider just what it is about each sound-type, their inherent perceptual qualities, that make them (in)appropriate.

This chapter will examine in turn each element of the sonic spectrum of worship: speech; choral recitation; chant; psalms and hymns; and instrumental music. We will consider how, for each one, the listener engages with different auditory strategies and investigate whether they are used to provoke particular responses.

Listening to Speech

Little attention is normally paid to the way speech happens in worship because it is often seen as an extension of ordinary, everyday speech. Of course there may be moments when ordinary speech intervenes, but this is often in a moment of ritual hiatus; for example, in the community notices given by the minister, or even in conversation between worshippers (see chapters 6 and 7). Liturgical speech is "framed" by the ritual context so that it creates the conditions for communication with God. Gail Ramshaw has noted how context is all important: "It is more accurate to think of liturgy as speech than as words, for in the liturgy words find their meaning in the context of the sentence, the hymn, the prayer, the whole rite, and the assembly."[3] In worship, both speaker and hearer are to interpret the words

---

[2] In this chapter, "speech" means spoken language and not discourse, as here I wish to distinguish saying words from singing them.

[3] Gail Ramshaw, *Reviving Sacred Speech: The Meaning of Liturgical Language: Second Thoughts on Christ in Sacred Speech* (Franklin, NJ: OSL Publications, 2000), 1.

in the context of the whole ritual event in which the performance of the text brings into existence that which it proposes.[4]

There is something of a paradox in the attitude to liturgical speech. On the one hand, its significance as a mode of liturgical sound-making has often been inadvertently diminished in relation to a musical performance. A Mass without music is a "Low Mass"; spoken Evening Prayer in an Anglican cathedral is "Said Evensong" to distinguish it from the supposedly normative sung office. In these performances, texts which could be chanted or sung are spoken, and this mode of performance affects the way that the words are received; it is invariably quicker, there is little or no repetition, intonation is often unchanging, as is too the emotional tone. On the other hand, in a religion whose focus of worship is on God incarnate who is described as the Word, it is not surprising that the coherent delivery of spoken language should have been considered to reflect divine immanence. Nor should it be a surprise that hearing is used as a physical, theological, and metaphorical term for faith.

St. Paul wrote to the Romans that "faith comes by what is heard and what is heard comes through the Word of Christ" (Rom 10:17). Thus, going against both ancient and modern physiology, the ear is connected to the heart, mind, and spirit; as the Word penetrates the heart, the response to God, in faith, is initiated. John Calvin (1509–1564), in dismissing the noise and pomp of musical instruments in worship, praised the spoken voice: "Paul allows us to bless God in the public assembly of the saints only in a known tongue (1 Cor 14:16). The voice of man, although not understood by the generality, assuredly excels all inanimate instruments of music. . . ."[5] The clear articulation of scripture in speech had also been a key aspect of the initial worship pattern proposed by Ulrich Zwingli (1484–1531), even if his heirs, like Calvin's, did permit singing of biblical texts.[6]

---

[4] John Austin's Speech Act Theory has been considered particularly useful in examining how words function in liturgical worship. I discussed this in my *Reading the Liturgy: An Exploration of Texts in Christian Worship* (London: Bloomsbury/T&T Clark, 2014), 106–9.

[5] John Calvin, Psalm 33.2, *John Calvin: Commentary on the Book of Psalms*, vol. 2, trans. James Anderson (Edinburgh: Calvin Translation Society, 1845–49).

[6] See Francisca Loetz, "Giving the Reformation a Voice: The Practice of Psalm Singing in Zurich," in *The Cultural History of the Reformations: Theories and Applications*,

In the late eighteenth and nineteenth centuries in England, there was a keen interest in how to perform the Book of Common Prayer in a manner to attract and maintain the listening attention of the people through the science of elocution. The actor, playwright, and theatre manager David Garrick (1717–1779) produced a printed performance of the BCP complete with instructions on how and when to visually engage the congregation. There are also many nineteenth-century tracts with revelatory titles such as these:

> John Henry Howlett, *Instructions in Reading the Liturgy of the United Church of England and Ireland; Offered to the Attention of the Younger Clergy and Candidates for Holy Orders: With an Appendix on Pronunciation* (England: C. & J. Rivington, 1826).
>
> Benjamin Humphrey Smart, *The Theory of Elocution, to Which Are Now Added Practical Aids for Reading the Liturgy* (England: J. Richardson, 1826).

Howlett set out the problems listeners have with poorly spoken liturgy. Indeed, his words seem strangely relevant today: "monotonous solemnity of tone will inevitably prevent emotion, deaden attention and produce drowsiness"; a "peculiarity" of speech "not unfrequently excited the smiles of the giddy . . . and painful regret in the minds of the serious and devout."[7] Good reading will excite serious and devout feelings, which must clearly be the aim of the minister.

These authors understood that speech is fulfilled when the meaning of that which is conveyed is received by the listener, not just when the auditory signals are heard. This is not the place to rehearse the debate about vernacular, liturgical, or even sacred language in worship, but simply to remark that the listening strategy for comprehension (of the words and syntax) is only part of the auditory task of worshippers. Meaning lies also in the appropriation of the signals given by the ritual performance: who speaks, from where, in what context, with what rituals. These are parts of the communication which are evident regardless of whether the listener understands the

---

ed. Susan C. Karant-Nunn and Ute Lotz-Heumann, 105–13 (Wiesbaden: Harrassowitz Verlag, 2021).

[7] John Henry Howlett, *Instructions in Reading the Liturgy of the United Church of England and Ireland; Offered to the Attention of the Younger Clergy and Candidates for Holy Orders: With an Appendix on Pronunciation* (England: C. & J. Rivington, 1826), ix.

language, or even attends to it. However, for the Protestant reformers, clear and comprehensible articulation of Scripture and the words of the liturgy were key, as Zwingli and Calvin emphasized.

The words and performance of them combine in the listener's appropriation of what is heard to enable them to discern the different speaking situations. In some cases, the speaker performs acts of "ventriloquism" where they speak for God, through Scripture or, say, the institution narrative of the eucharistic prayer. In other cases, they speak before God, representatively on behalf of the congregation, as in intercessory prayer. In yet others, the speaker directly addresses the listeners in sermons and testimony. For each situation, the listeners' strategy changes. In the first they should, in theory, be attentive to the unseen yet ever-present God whose presence is signaled by this very speech; listening is then a form of divine-human encounter. In the second, by listening the worshipper participates in the speech event offered on their behalf, and this is often signaled by invitations to assent to what is said by "Amen." In the last, the listeners are in a situation of information exchange in which situational listening is demonstrated by an attentive attitude, whereas effective (successful) listening may be delayed until any subsequent changes in lifestyle or spirituality are enjoined by the speaker.

Speech is supposed to provide clarity despite the different vocal styles we all have. Robert Remez described speech signals as highly unstable, varied, and rapid. The rhythm consists of a rapid stop/start of sharp consonants and long vowels, interspersed with silences of varied lengths, which makes following speech a complex activity, especially when there are competing sound sources.[8] The sounds are short lived and must be grasped immediately if one is to combine them with neighboring sounds to construct meaningful sentences or utterances.

Jacqueline Vaissière focused on how intonation is used to present and interpret the syntactical structure of what is said, as well as conveying the emotion and attitudes of the speaker. By following the intonation, the listener can separate the sequence of sounds into

---

[8] Robert E. Remez, "Perceptual Organization of Speech," in *The Handbook of Speech Perception*, ed. David B. Pisoni and Robert E. Remez, 32–33 (Malden, MA: Blackwell Publishing, 2005).

meaningful units. Intonation shows a departure from neutral speech delivery by pauses, loudness, voice quality, and length of the sound. With more intonation, as Garrick tried to show in his rather dramatic rendering of the BCP, the listener is given clues about how to follow the rapid sequence of sounds. Speech sounds, including intonation, are also connected to exhalation. When the speaker wishes to make a long statement, which therefore requires an extended focus from the listener, s/he will take in more air, and this results in increased volume at the start. Listeners are alert to loudness, which is perceived from the vocal effort being made by the speaker. Similarly, pitch is interpreted in relation to the level of emotion or arousal of the speaker: a higher pitch signaling increased excitement, whereas a lower and slower rate of delivery may indicate detachment or passivity. Vaissière reports on a variety of experiments for the interpretation of different pitches: small variation in pitch was associated with disgust, anger, fear, and boredom, and large pitch variation with more positive responses of happiness, pleasantness, activity, and surprise.[9] Intonation functions, therefore, as vocal gesturing.

Listening to Choral Speech

The choral recitation of prayer texts, especially the Lord's Prayer, or prose texts such as the Creed, as well as the psalms and canticles, is not uncommon. This performance method is like ordinary speech in that it preserves natural rhythms and natural stress patterns, but is like chant in that intonation is flatter and delivery is slower; often is it used for texts which could be chanted. Choral recitation in the liturgy is rarely accompanied by ritual gesture and movement, so we can consider that the ritual act is constituted and completed by sound alone. The hierarchy implied by solo speaking diminishes, to be replaced by a communal voice, sometimes demonstrated by frequently using "we" or "our." The listening experience is twofold: we listen to ourselves from without via our ears and from within by physical resonance, but we also listen to ourselves, to the communal voice, from without.

---

[9] Jacqueline Vaissière, "Perception of Intonation," in *Handbook of Speech Perception*, chap. 10.

Education theorists have commented on how communal reading can generate communal interpretations of the text. In Mark Pike's article on aesthetic reading in the classroom, he cited Wolfgang Iser and others on how the reader fills the gaps in meaning left by the text.[10] It is these gaps which provide scope for the reader to make an aesthetic response; indeed, they are the start of a transaction in meaning between reader and text. We combine this with the insights from Ann Trousdale, Jacqueline Bach, and Elizabeth Willis's research into children's choral reading of poetry, which revealed that "the understanding of the poem is more visceral, more direct, more immediate. The negotiation of meaning does not necessarily use the language of literary conventions but occurs through the child's entering the poem in a holistic way. In choral reading, children understand poetry by doing poetry."[11] Consequently, in choral recitation, I suggest the "gap," that is, the meaning, is not filled by the individual reader alone, but by the community who collectively reflects on the content in light of their communal lives. Unlike the chorus in Greek theatre, liturgical choral recitation often minimizes the intonational effects to approximate a single speaking and heard voice, but also to exhibit a communal cohesion which may spill over outside the liturgical event. Medieval monastic rules often include punishments for those who disturb this cohesion by making mistakes in the Offices, but what was considered an infringement differed from one congregation to the next, indicating how each community heard itself uniquely in the way the Offices were performed. The choral reading or recitation moves the interpretation of the text away from the individual and it enhances communal cohesion, and listening becomes a communal listening and not an individual affair.

---

[10] Mark A. Pike, "From Personal to Social Transaction: A Model of Aesthetic Reading in the Classroom," *Journal of Aesthetic Education* 37, no. 3 (2003): 61–72. Wolfgang Iser, "Indeterminacy and the Reader's Response in Prose Fiction," in *Aspects of Narrative*, ed. J. Hillis Miller, 2–45 (New York: Columbia University Press, 1971).

[11] Ann Trousdale, Jacqueline Bach, and Elizabeth Willis, "Freedom, Physicality, Friendship and Feeling: Aspects of Children's Spirituality Expressed through the Choral Reading of Poetry," *International Journal of Children's Spirituality* 15, no. 4 (2010): 317–29.

Listening to Chant

Almost paralleling solo speech and choral recitation, but now with a singing voice, is chant. Chant can take many forms, from a single recitation note performed by a cantor, *cantillation*, to elaborate polyphony performed by a choir, and between this we can find more or less complex chants for congregational use.[12] Chant is a way of performing the liturgical text, not simply an embellishment of it, and the text remains significant whether the words can be determined or not. In its origin, chant increased the intelligibility of liturgical texts in highly resonant church buildings (see chapter 8).

In this discussion, I will distinguish cantillation as a subset of chant. Joseph Dyer provided this definition of cantillation: "a semi-improvisatory recitative falling between speaking and song, most frequently employed in reference to the chanting of liturgical texts (especially the Bible) among the Jews."[13] It sits, therefore, between speaking and singing, and is characterized by being used for prose texts. It uses a restricted range of pitches for recitation, so that the rhythm of the text is preserved, and ornamentation is used as a way of indicating punctuation rather than as an enhancement of the text.[14] Late antique and medieval writers tended not to distinguish between speech, cantillation, and singing by using *dicere* ("to say") and *canere* ("to sing") interchangeably; however, context reveals that more often than not cantillation was presumed.[15] The principal texts to receive this treatment in the medieval Mass were the epistle and gospel, but it could also be used for prayer texts such as the collect, blessings, or prose readings in a monastic context. The recitation note was on a higher pitch than when speaking, and the syllables were lengthened to follow the normal stress pattern and rhythm of the words; Dyer

---

[12] For a survey of the history and development of plainchant in the West, see Kenneth Levy et al., "Plainchant," in *Grove Music Online* (New York: Oxford University Press, 2001), n.p.

[13] Joseph Dyer, trans., *Readers and Hearers of the Word: The Cantillation of Scripture in the Middle Ages*, Ritus Et Artes 10 (Turnhout: Brepols, 2022), 63. See also Gordon E. Trutt, "Cantillation," in *Worship Music: A Concise Dictionary*, ed. Edward Foley, 53 (Collegeville, MN: Liturgical Press, 2000).

[14] Dyer, *Readers and Hearers*, 63, citing Solange Corbin, "La cantillation des rituels chrétiens," *Revue de musicologie* 47 (1962): 3–36.

[15] Dyer, *Readers and Hearers*, 66.

contrasts with the "Solesmes" style of Gregorian, or plainchant, which gives each syllable an equal value. The medieval instructions for lectors show that they should aim to read or cantillate with understanding, such that the meaning of the text was conveyed to the listener without undue haste, gesticulation, or idiosyncrasy. The changes in pace and pauses functioned as "aural punctuation" and served to enable the hearers to "sense where they were in a sentence."[16]

Martin Luther gave instructions for the cantillation of scripture in his *Deutsche Messe* of 1526: the gospel was to be differentiated from the epistle by a more elaborate recitation, and the lector should differentiate between the biblical narrative, the voice of Jesus, and the voices of other participants.[17] An accomplished reader may, according to Isidore of Seville, "declaim in so heart-rending a way that they drive some people to sorrow and lamentation." He should "pay attention to the ears and the heart, not the eyes," in order to "move the minds and senses of all to understanding."[18] Of primary importance, however, was the intelligibility of the text. Dyer contrasts the medieval consensus over the performance and intent of cantillation with modern tastes which discourage interpretation of the text in performance, as well as any emotional emphases, which are to be left to the listener to create.[19]

Whereas cantillation is used to denote a chanted interpretation of longer prose texts by a single cantor, plainchant (*cantus planus*) refers to the inflexible, according to the text, although musically variable, according to the day or the feast, chant for other texts of the Mass and the Offices. Plainchant may be one of three styles—syllabic, neumatic, and melismatic—according to the level of embellishment of the text. It is also distinguished by eight modes, in evidence by the eleventh century, which are determined according to the melodies used for the final syllables of each line of text. These modes pay no attention to the interpretation of the text being sung, nor to natural stresses and speech rhythm, but are based solely on the syllable count of each line. Performance of the chant is also highly varied: "antiphonal

[16] Dyer, 66.
[17] Dyer, 87.
[18] Isidore of Seville, *Etymologiae* 7.12.24, in *Etymologies*, 171. Isidore of Seville, *De ecclesiasticis Officiis* 2.11.5, in *De ecclesiasticis Officiis*, trans. Thomas L. Knoebel, 82–83 (New York: Newman Press, 2008).
[19] Dyer, *Readers and Hearers*, 94–95.

chants, sung by two alternating groups of singers; responsorial chants, sung by a soloist (or soloists) in alternation with the choir; chants sung entirely by the celebrant, the soloist or the choir."[20] These modes of performance would often indicate to the listener what type of text was being sung, as well as the emotional and theological significance of the liturgy or the day. A simple syllabic form was often for congregational texts whose principal function lies in the semantic meaning, whereas the *Sanctus*, for example, as a hymn of praise, required an elaboration of the chant; embellishment can go even further in something like a festal alleluia, whose power comes from the exclamation and elaboration of the chant and not its semantic meaning.

The most complex melismatic chants entirely lose the semantic meaning of the words; examples are certain Byzantine chants and late medieval polyphony. Some listeners would have known the texts by heart; such was the case with medieval monks and the psalms, and so the elaborate chant could then refocus attention on the meaning of and appropriate response to the text. Alexander Lingas's study of the thirty-five-minute-long, and unintelligible, alleluia for Vespers at Pentecost in the Byzantine rite shows how an "over-the-top" performance reinforces the significance of the feast.[21]

Insistence on the clear articulation of Scripture, as well as on understanding and participation, caused a shift in the Reformed churches, although, as we have seen, many of the ideas were familiar to Isidore and other early commentators. Hence, we noted already, Luther's concern with the appropriate cantillation of Scripture in the Deutsche Messe. In England in 1550, Thomas Cranmer instructed John Merbecke to provide suitable chants for the BCP with the proviso that there should be "for every syllable a note." Although Merbecke's *Book of Common Prayer Noted* had a short shelf life, the principle of providing chants for congregational texts based on simplified forms of the Latin chants, was developed in later centuries and came to be known as Anglican Chant.[22]

---

[20] Kenneth Levy et al., "Plainchant 5.iv Performance," in *Grove Music Online*, n.p.
[21] Alexander Lingas, "From Earth to Heaven: The Changing Musical Soundscape of Byzantine Liturgy," in *Experiencing Byzantium*, ed. Claire Nesbitt and Mark Jackson, 311–58 (Farnham, UK: Ashgate, 2013). See also the previous discussion in chapter 1.
[22] See Peter Le Huray and John Harper, "Anglican Chant," in *Grove Music Online*, n.p.

Because chanting is such a varied feature of Christian worship, it is not possible to propose a single model of reception by the listener. Clearly, cantillation predates speech as a way of performing biblical texts in liturgical worship, and as the performance is intended to convey the meaning of the text, then we could suggest a similar listening strategy as we have already suggested for speech. The listener is attentive to the meaning of the words, and the slowness of the chant more easily facilitates the appropriation of that meaning. In some instances, the music may reflect the content: Tim Carter noted the common example of "He came down from heaven" being sung to a falling line.[23] When the persons in the biblical narrative are distinguished in the chant, then the listener is invited to place himself imaginatively in the narrative through the sound. The singer may also identify with the writer of the biblical text, and this is particularly likely with the psalms, where, as Christopher Page suggested, "A monastic or clerical singer of the Middle Ages helped David bare his soul one hundred and fifty times a week."[24]

Many medieval commentators did refer to the way in which chant produced strong emotions. Christopher Page explored the emotional expectations of medieval chant in his article "To Chant in a Vale of Tears," in which he showed that medievals considered that "music could evoke feelings of piety and contrition in those who found themselves unmoved by the words of Scripture alone" which challenged "the supremacy of the rational powers embodied in language and grammar."[25] The singers were listeners rather than performers. Page says that "they heard but did not exactly listen," inhabiting the sound from within rather than from without.[26] Words and music combined to produce compunction (*compunctio*), a spiritually valued, emotional response of being moved to tears out of a sense of contrition for sin. Among Page's collection of examples of *compunctio* is this revealing extract from Grimlaicus's *Regula solitariorum* (*Rule for Solitaries*) of c. 900: "Unflagging chanting of the psalms consoles sad hearts, makes

---

[23] Tim Carter, "Word-Painting," in *Grove Music Online*, n.p.

[24] Christopher Page, "To Chant in a Vale of Tears," in *Chant, Liturgy, and the Inheritance of Rome: Essays in Honour of Joseph Dyer*, ed. Daniel J. DiCenso and Rebecca Maloy, 440 (Woodbridge, UK: Boydell & Brewer, Henry Bradshaw Society, 2017).

[25] Page, "To Chant in a Vale of Tears," 432.

[26] Page, 433.

minds more well-disposed, delights those who feel disgust, puts new life into the lifeless, and invites sinners to lament. Even though our hearts are hard, nevertheless, as soon as we hear the sweetness of the psalms begin sounding, it attunes our whole self to make progress in piety."[27]

The research of Christina Vanden Bosch der Nederlanden and others explored the way that comprehension is affected by listening to either speech or song.[28] When listening to speech, the brain synchronizes with the speed of input and uses the oscillations to separate the sounds into intelligible units, which is further aided by sharp breaks between syllables. The rhythm of the speech is determined by each syllable or phenome, and the listener's brain needs to be sufficiently agile to follow and separate them. Their research focused on why some people find it hard to follow speech but have no difficulties when the same words are sung. They noted that language and music are similar in that they both unfold in time and are composed of discreet units; however, temporally, they unfold in different ways. In song, the rhythm is determined by the duration of the notes, which are inevitably longer than each short, sharp syllable of spoken language, which additionally has an irregular rhythm and the rapid delivery of syllables. Song, by contrast, has a slower transition between notes and pitches, which enables the brain to more easily lock onto the syllables. The listener may also use her prior knowledge of melodies and harmonies to predict when the next syllable will arrive and when the unit of meaning will end. They conclude that "These findings provide some of the first evidence that, under difficult listening conditions, the brain can track low-frequency information in the speech stream better when that utterance is sung compared to spoken."[29] Their research seems to corroborate why chant may be a more effective way of enabling people to hear liturgical texts than speech.

---

[27] Grimlaicus, *Regula solitariorum* (*Rule for Solitaries*) 35, in *Grimlaicus: Rule for Solitaries*, trans. Andrew L. Thornton, 104 (Collegeville, MN: Cistercian Publications, 2011). The *Regula* was written for monks who remained in their cell but participated in the monastery's liturgy through a window into the church.

[28] Christina M. Vanden Bosch der Nederlanden, Marc F. Joanisse, and Jessica A. Grahn, "Music as a Scaffold for Listening to Speech: Better Neural Phase-Locking to Song than Speech," *NeuroImage* 214 (2020): 116767.

[29] Vanden Bosch der Nederlanden et al., "Music as a Scaffold," 7.

Listening to Psalms and Hymns

The Psalms were, and in some traditions remain, the foundational hymn book of the church. Although in the early and medieval church they were chanted, I have placed them with hymns because of the distinction which Isidore among others make between "reading," or cantillation, and singing: "psalmists (*psalmista*) [are named] from singing psalms, for . . . [they] sing to kindle the spirits of their audience to compunction."[30] The *psalmista* "is to be clear and illustrious in his voice and skill, so that he may incite the soul of the hearers by the delight of sweetness."[31] Metrical psalms were known in late antiquity and the medieval church; however, it was the Protestant reformers who particularly developed this form for congregational singing in the vernacular. John Calvin was particularly active in producing verse forms of the psalms and insisted on monophonic congregational singing of biblical texts only. In his preface to the 1542 Psalter, he differentiated between praying in words alone and with singing: "in truth we know by experience that singing has great force and vigor to move and inflame the hearts of men to invoke and praise God with a more vehement and ardent zeal. Care must be taken that the song be neither light nor frivolous: but that it have weight and majesty . . ." Charles Carside made an important observation on Calvin's attitude expressed in this preface: he distinguished between music "at table" and in church, and that in church, "before God and his angels," only the psalms were acceptable.[32] In 1562 the complete Calvinist Psalter was published, which provided 125 different tunes for monophonic singing, many taken from popular songs. Unlike chanted psalms using the eight modes, certain psalms would become associated with particular tunes.

Hymns are liturgical poetry in which the metrical lines are sung to a melody repeating every four or six lines. The meaning of the text is essential to its function in the liturgical event because it supports the theology of the feast and reinforces the content of scriptural readings or the sermon. The regularly repeating melody provides struc-

---

[30] Isidore of Seville, *Etymologiae* VII.12.24 and 26, in *Etymologies*, 177.
[31] Isidore of Seville, *De ecclesiasticis officiis* 2.12.2, in *De ecclesiasticis officiis*, 83.
[32] Charles Carside, "Calvin's Preface to the Psalter: A Re-Appraisal," *The Music Quarterly* 37 (1951): 569.

ture to the unfolding of the meaning through the hymn's narrative, and the regular structure and rhyme of the verses aid memory. The latter has been frequently commented upon throughout Christian history: Arius had successfully taught his hymns to the Alexandrian dockworkers who sang them while loading and unloading ships, much to the disgust of Athanasius.[33] Ambrose of Milan composed staunchly Nicene hymns for his congregation to sing in a standoff with the Arian imperial family.[34] Martin Luther composed hymns for congregational use that functioned as a form of catechesis.[35] In hymns, the words carry the theological meaning while the music carries the intended emotional response, and it is no surprise that the combination has been seen as so effective in many Christian traditions, especially in situations of mission or persecution. As hymns are a popular form of liturgical music, those who sing are also those who are intended to listen; as they perform the message and emotion of the hymn, they also hear and appropriate it as their own. Because the meter and melody are memorable, hymns are one of the few liturgical texts to be performed outside of the liturgical event. When hearing them sung, even when by oneself, the meaning and emotional import remain stable despite being recontextualized.

Listening to Instrumental Music

At the far end of my spectrum, I place instrumental music. Once again, I turn to Robert Taft's perceptive observation about the "soft points" of the liturgy; those moments when a ritual action takes place for which there is no explicit sonic accompaniment.[36] In his case, he referred to the filling of this space with words, but we can apply it

---

[33] Philostorgius, *Church History* II.2: "Once Arius left the church . . . he wrote songs for sailing, grinding, traveling, and so on, set them to the music he thought suitable to each, and through the pleasure given by the music stole away the simpler folk for his own heresy." *Philostorgius: Church History*, trans. Philip R. Amidon (Atlanta: Society of Biblical Literature, 2007), 16.

[34] See Paulinus, *Life of St. Ambrose* 13, in *Ambrose*, trans. Boniface Ramsey (London: Routledge, 1997), 200.

[35] See Robin A. Leaver, *Luther's Liturgical Music: Principles and Implications* (Grand Rapids, MI: Eerdmans, 2007).

[36] Robert F. Taft, "How Liturgies Grow: The Evolution of the Byzantine 'Divine Liturgy,'" *Orientalia Christiana Periodica* 53 (1977): 8–30.

equally to much of the use of instrumental music in liturgy. In many Western church traditions, the organ is played to mask ambient sound as worshippers arrive and depart, and to cover certain ritual actions within the liturgy (e.g., offertory processions). What is played (and heard) is very much dependent upon the musicians' choice of music and their skills at improvisation. On the one hand, the wordless music leaves space for the listener's own unrestricted response and interpretation, but on the other that response has already been determined by whatever it is the organist decides to play. New musical idioms, especially using electronic and amplified sounds, aim to some extent to align the sounds heard in church with contemporary culture. The Eastern churches traditionally ban instrumental music, although organs can be found in some Orthodox churches in North America due, presumably, to influences from other churches.

Instrumental music seems to have been the most controversial sound. The few early Christian writers who express an opinion about music in church tend to forbid it because of its connection with non-Christian entertainment and Jewish and pagan worship. The use of instruments was a key feature of Byzantine public life, especially in the theatre and in public ceremonies; however, it was exactly these connotations which rendered it unsuitable for Christian worship. It is not the instruments themselves which are the problem, but the association made in the minds of listeners to these morally and spiritually harmful contexts. Writing in the third century, Clement of Alexandria discussed the harmful effect of music at banquets: "The exciting rhythm of flutes and harps, choruses and dances, Egyptian castanets and other entertainments get out of control and become indecent and burlesque, especially when they are re-enforced by cymbals and drums and accompanied by the noise of all these instruments of deception."[37] This music is reminiscent of idol worship, and more suited to wild beasts than rational humans. Such ideas are common in relation to the other contexts in which musical instruments are used: Tertullian railed against the theatre, as did many fourth-century writers such as John Chrysostom and Gregory of

---

[37] Clement of Alexandria, *Paedagogus (Christ the Educator)* II.4.40, trans. Simon P. Wood, in *Clement of Alexandria: Christ the Educator*, Fathers of the Church, vol. 23, 130 (Washington, DC: Catholic University of America Press, 1954).

Nyssa. Of course, Christians who regularly prayed with the psalms, where instruments are frequently mentioned, had to explain why they were acceptable there but not in worship. Clement reinterprets Psalm 150 in an anthropological way so that the words of the psalm are fulfilled, but without the sin-inducing effect of hearing each instrument:

> . . . "praise Him with harp," for the tongue is a harp of the Lord; "and with the lute, praise Him," understanding the mouth as a lute moved by the Spirit as the lute is by the plectrum; "praise Him with timbal and choir," that is, the Church awaiting the resurrection of the body in the flesh which is its echo; "praise Him with strings and organ," calling our bodies an organ and its sinews strings, for from them the body derives its co-ordinated movement, and when touched by the Spirit, gives forth human sounds; "praise Him on high-sounding cymbals," which mean the tongue of the mouth, which, with the movement of the lips, produces words. Then, to all mankind He calls out: "Let every spirit praise the Lord," because He rules over every spirit He has made. In reality, man is an instrument made for peace, but these other things, if anyone concerns himself overmuch with them, become instruments of conflict, for they either enkindle desires or inflame the passions.[38]

The other argument against instruments was their use in the Temple and contemporary Jewish worship. Some forms of Jewish music were attractive to late antique Christians; for example, the *Sanctus* came to be incorporated into Christian worship as a result, but the instruments were not. Theodoret of Cyrus said that God permitted instruments not because he liked the sound but to prevent idolatry, and Chrysostom considered it a concession to weakness.[39]

The Eastern church retained its ban on instrumental music, but the medieval Western church adopted the organ where resources

---

[38] Clement of Alexandria, *Paedagogus* II.4.41-2, in *Clement of Alexandria*, 131.

[39] Theodoret of Cyrus, *Graecarum affectionum curatio (A Cure for Pagan Maladies), On Sacrifices*, 21, in *Theodoret of Cyrus: A Cure for Pagan Maladies*, trans. Thomas P. Halton (New York: Newman Press, 2013). John Chrysostom, *Homily on Psalm 150*, in *St. John Chrysostom: Commentary on the Psalms*, trans. Robert C. Hill (Brookline, MA: Holy Cross Orthodox Press, 1998). See Egon Wellesz, *A History of Byzantine Music and Hymnography* (Oxford: Oxford University Press, 1961), 93–94.

permitted, and it was only among some Protestant reformers that the value of instruments in worship was again questioned. John Calvin did not approve of musical instruments in worship, as he made clear in his *Commentary on Psalm 33*:

> *Praise Jehovah upon the harp.* It is evident that the Psalmist here expresses the vehement and ardent affection which the faithful ought to have in praising God, when he enjoins musical instruments to be employed for this purpose. . . . There is a distinction, however, to be observed here, that we may not indiscriminately consider as applicable to ourselves, every thing which was formerly enjoined upon the Jews. I have no doubt that playing upon cymbals, touching the harp and the viol, and all that kind of music, which is so frequently mentioned in the Psalms, was a part of . . . the stated service of the temple. . . . But when they [believers] frequent their sacred assemblies, musical instruments in celebrating the praises of God would be no more suitable than the burning of incense, the lighting up of lamps, and the restoration of the other shadows of the law. The Papists, therefore, have foolishly borrowed this, as well as many other things, from the Jews. Men who are fond of outward pomp may delight in that noise; but the simplicity which God recommends to us by the apostle is far more pleasing to him. Paul allows us to bless God in the public assembly of the saints only in a known tongue (1 Cor 14:16). . . ."[40]

Of course some Calvinist congregations would, later on, adopt the organ for worship in imitation of other Protestant churches. Zwingli also considered the organ to be inappropriate for worship on the basis of Scripture, its connection with the images and vestments of Roman Catholicism, and from his ideal of spiritual worship.[41] Zwinglian congregations also eventually departed from their founder's ideals.

Luther greatly valued music, writing positively about it himself, as did later Lutheran theologians. In the seventeenth century, there was the phenomenon of the "organ sermon" in which the organ was

---

[40] Calvin, *Commentary on Psalms* 33.2, in *John Calvin: Commentary*.

[41] See Gottfried W. Locher, *Zwingli's Thought: New Perspectives* (Leiden: Brill, 1981), 61–62.

the central theme, following inspiration from Praetorius's *Syntagma Musica*, which was frequently cited. Praetorius collected material and citations from many works, among them this from Girolamo Diruta's *Il Transilvano*: "Furthermore, just as beautiful, skilful paintings attract the eye of the beholder, the lovely, sweet harmony penetrates the secret thoughts and feelings of the listeners as it strikes their ears. Enraptured, so to speak, by the sound, they will follow the sermons more attentively, and the lovely sound will persuade and move them to join in the praise sung to the High and Divine Majesty."[42] Johann Sebastian Bach's organ works contribute to the high esteem in which solo organ music is held in the Lutheran churches.

In the modern era, the Roman Catholic church has produced many documents on music in the liturgy, and these have been discussed fully elsewhere.[43] It is sufficient here to reiterate the points about *Musicam Sacram* which I made in a previous chapter. In this document, the organ is the supreme instrument for liturgy because it "adds a wonderful splendour to the Church's ceremonies and powerfully lifts up the spirit to God and to higher things" (MS 62, cf. *Sacrosanctum Concilium* 120), but solo playing is not permitted in the more somber periods of the church year, Advent and Lent, the Triduum and at Masses for the Dead (MS 66). Other instruments are permitted if they have an appropriate cultural significance; however, "instruments that are generally associated and used only with worldly music are to be absolutely barred from liturgical services and religious devotions" (MS 63). The criteria applied to instrumental music here are appropriateness for liturgy and the edification of the faithful.

Don Idhe considered that listening to wordless music may require a different type of listening than when words are included, although he was less than specific on how this listening differs.[44] Clearly, the physical operation of the ear does not change, but what differs is how the listener makes sense of what is heard. Music is "opaque," that is,

---

[42] Quoted by Lucinde Braun in "The *Syntagma musicum* in Lutheran Organ Sermons of the Seventeenth and the Eighteenth Centuries," *De musica disserenda* 15 (2019): 186.

[43] See Jan Michael Joncas, *From Sacred Song to Ritual Music: Twentieth-Century Understandings of Roman Catholic Worship Music* (Collegeville, MN: Liturgical Press, 1997).

[44] Don Ihde, *Listening and Voice: Phenomenologies of Sound* (Albany: State University of New York Press, 2007), 155.

it does not refer to the world in a direct way. Any comprehension comes about through a physical participation which he likens to dance, as the sound fills, surrounds, and penetrates space, just as it does the listener. What dominates is the sounding: music requires us to be attentive to the sound just as speech requires us to be attentive to the meaning. It can therefore be considered a special sort of listening: Idhe refers to musical sound as "set-aside sound," and thus he suggests it requires "set-aside listening," a special mode of attentiveness.[45]

Music fills space, and hence the listener is placed in a more intimate physical connection to it. Lawrence M. Zbikowski is not alone in suggesting that, as we sense it physically, not just aurally, listening to music is a form of bodily, and hence ritual, participation.[46] Its symbolic system is anagogical. It conveys dynamic processes such that "sequences of sound . . . represent a wide range of visual, kinesthetic, and psychological phenomena."[47] Zbikowski continues, "Where language is predicated on the illusion that concepts are firm, stable, and unchanging, music celebrates all that is changeable and transitory. And so when music listens to itself, it does not hear meaningless sounds arranged in artful patterns but sonic analogs for the psychological and physiological processes associated with the emotions, for the gestures that shape our thought, for the patterned movements of dance, and for the prosody that vivifies language."[48]

Ihde and Zbikowski are phenomenological philosophers who see music and spoken language requiring different sense-making strategies, which necessarily imply different listening strategies; however, Aniruddh D. Patel and others working in cognitive science have tended to minimize these differences. The sound itself may be organized differently (nouns and verbs versus pitch and timbre), but the cognitive processes of categorizing the sounds make them similar when compared to other sound phenomena: both rely on "a set of discrete elements of little inherent meaning (such as tones or

---

[45] Ihde, *Listening and Voice*, 157.

[46] Lawrence M. Zbikowski, "Listening to Music," in *Speaking of Music: Addressing the Sonorous*, ed. Keith Chapin and Andrew H. Clark, 107 (New York: Fordham University Press, 2013).

[47] Zbikowski, "Listening to Music," 116.

[48] Zbikowski, 119.

phonemes) [which] are combined to form structures with a great diversity of meanings."[49] We are able to create a mental framework from both these learned sound categories, which we employ to make sense of what we hear. Within a particular culture, the sounds of both make sense because of our repeated exposure to, and thus familiarity with them.

Some Concluding Themes

A number of themes are common to all the intentional sound-types discussed here, and as a form of conclusion, it will be useful to consider the connections between listening and embodiment, listening and emotion, listening and social identity.

Listening in worship engages both the body and the mind, as the words, music, and ritual combine, and so it is natural that many commentators have considered the embodied aspect of listening. When we speak, chant, and sing, these sounds are heard as a bodily resonance, and we sense our breathing as well as the sound signals. Music which is sung, but particularly instrumental music, fills space in a way that the spoken voice alone does not, and the sound surrounds and penetrates us; it is not just experienced aurally. We hear physically, and I suggest that this physical experience, which requires our bodily presence, is an essential aspect of Christian worship. It would not have been necessary to say this in the era before digitally mediated worship, and it highlights the "de-incarnated" aspect of that worship. In general, we attend mentally to the sound of speech and chanted texts as the sounds require greater mental focus for their identification and interpretation, and consequently we become less aware of listening's physical effort.[50] Of course, certain speakers are able to project their voice to produce a physical effect in the listener; however, listeners will still be more alert to the words and search out semantic meaning.[51]

---

[49] Aniruddh D. Patel, *Music, Language, and the Brain* (Oxford: Oxford University Press, 2008), 10.

[50] Vanden Bosch der Nederlanden et al., "Music as a Scaffold."

[51] Andrew A. Cashner, *Hearing Faith: Music as Theology in the Spanish Empire* (Leiden: Brill, 2020), 79.

The body reacts physically to sonic stimuli in ways which are similar to emotions. Loud music with a heavy drum beat will raise the heart rate in the same way as if one were excited or aroused. Marcus Pearce and Geraint Wiggins showed that the emotional response to unexpected sounds, chords, and harmonies in music creates the same response as anxiety, having both an emotional and physical dimension described as "frisson." Frisson or chills are connected to physiological arousal, which has been identified by skin-conductance measurements. It is experienced as a pleasurable sensation, which brain studies have shown to be linked to reward and not to negativity.[52]

Emotions may or may not have a visible bodily aspect, although they should certainly be seen as a physical response to the situation. Augustine described his emotional and physical reaction to the singing in Ambrose's basilica in Milan: "During the days that followed [baptism] I could not get enough of the wonderful sweetness that filled me as I meditated upon your deep design for the salvation of the human race. How copiously I wept at your hymns and canticles, how intensely was I moved by the lovely harmonies of your singing Church! Those voices flooded my ears, and the truth was distilled into my heart until it overflowed in loving devotion; my tears ran down, and I was the better for them."[53] Compunction, leading to tears, was a highly valued emotion in both Western medieval as well as Byzantine worship, but it is not the only one.[54] Susan Karant-Nunn describes the new emotional culture that was brought about in the Reformation churches through sermons and, among Lutherans, through hymns. Singing about the passion and atonement should lead to rejoicing and love, which they were to demonstrate "not in obvious ecstasy or

---

[52] Marcus T. Pearce and Geraint A. Wiggins, "Auditory Expectation: The Information Dynamics of Music Perception and Cognition," *Topics in Cognitive Science* 4 (2012): 642.

[53] Augustine, *Confessions* IX.6, 14, in *The Confessions*, The Works of Saint Augustine, vol. 1, trans. Maria Boulding, ed. John E. Rotelle, 220–21 (Hyde Park, NY: New City Press, 2014).

[54] See Andrew Mellas, *Liturgy and the Emotions in Byzantium: Compunction and Hymnody* (Cambridge: Cambridge University Press, 2020); and Page, "To Chant in a Vale of Tears."

with tears but in the loving service of their neighbor."[55] The hymns, by their words and music, present and model an appropriate emotional response to God as well as generate it. In other Reformation churches, a godly preacher was also expected to arouse emotions in his listeners; as Hunt described for the seventeenth-century English preacher, "the tears of the people are the minister's praise."[56] In all these examples, emotions are generated by what the listener has heard, rather than as a result of an event which they have personally experienced.

It does seem though that music, chanting, and singing convey and generate emotions which speech finds it more difficult to do. In Patrik Juslin and John A. Sloboda's collection of essays *Music and Emotion*, they gather together a range of competing theories and perspectives about this, none of which touch upon the religious or liturgical context. The sources of emotion can be either intrinsic, being features of the sound itself (such as cheerful or melancholic), or extrinsic, arising independently of the sound.[57] Liturgical music operates intrinsically and extrinsically: the hymn tune or chant may reflect the emotional content of the text, which opens the possibility for that emotion to be generated or experienced by the listener, who may also be the performer. As liturgical texts convey authorized ideas about and attitudes to God, so too we should consider these emotional responses as scripted, anticipated, and authorized. But extrinsic factors may also play a part, notably the entire liturgical context within which the

---

[55] Susan C. Karant-Nunn, *The Reformation of Feeling: Shaping the Religious Emotions in Early Modern Germany* (New York: Oxford University Press, 2010), 82–83. Her example is Luther's hymn "Christ lag in Todesbanden," for which she provides this translation: "Christ lay in death's bonds / handed over for our sins; / he is risen again / and has brought us life. / For this we should be joyful, / praise God and be thankful to Him / and sing alleluia, / Alleluia."

[56] Arnold Hunt, *The Art of Hearing: English Preachers and Their Audiences, 1590–1640* (Cambridge: Cambridge University Press, 2010), 91.

[57] Patrik N. Juslin and John A. Sloboda, *Music and Emotion: Theory and Research* (Oxford: Oxford University Press, 2001). See also Patrik N. Juslin and Petri Laukka, "Expression, Perception, and Induction of Musical Emotions: A Review and a Questionnaire Study of Everyday Listening," *Journal of New Music Research* 33, no. 3 (2004): 217–38, for a survey of approaches and research results about how emotions are elicited in listeners as well as a table of intrinsic features of music and their relation to specific emotions.

music, hymn, or chant takes place: whether at a feast or fast, at a ritual prelude or climax, or in conjunction with powerful speech or ritual gesture. Liturgical composers and performers do not have the same freedom with regard to emotional expression as those in other musical contexts because of the need to model and generate only the desired and approved emotions. As new musical genres emerge, especially in popular music, their appropriateness is often discussed not in relation to the intrinsic aspects of a particular work, but by the overall emotional attitude of non-worship uses of the genre, evident in the suspicion of rock and roll, heavy metal, and punk, for example.[58]

Anticipation is a key emotional trigger for the auditory experience according to the research of Pearce and Wiggins, and anticipation involves memory. In an aural environment, the listener orientates herself with regard to other similar things which she has heard, and on that basis anticipates both the content of what is to come and her expected response. When the anticipated emotions are realized, the listener may respond with pleasure; when they are not, the listener experiences anxiety. The more experienced listener in the liturgical context is fully prepared for her role by anticipating what will come next, whereas the inexperienced is likely to be disorientated. By engaging memory, the listener compensates for when the perception or message is incomplete.[59] Memory can also function when some sounds trigger recall of memories with strong emotional content, either personal or cultural; the listener will be led away from the present sound event to past events which then contribute to the meaningfulness of the present event. The anamnetic character of Christian worship could also be usefully explored in relation to this.

In chapter 1, I showed how ecclesial communities have their own soundscape, which is informed by their religious and cultural musical traditions, their liturgical theologies, and, at a local level, by their resources. In moments of crisis these distinctive sounds take on

---

[58] See Anna Nekola, " 'More Than Just a Music': Conservative Christian Anti-Rock Discourse and the U.S. Culture Wars," *Popular Music* 32 (2013): 407–26; and Marcus Moberg, *Faster for the Master!: Exploring Issues of Religious Expression and Alternative Christian Identity within the Finnish Christian Metal Music Scene* (Åbo: Åbo Akademi University Press, 2009).

[59] Pearce and Wiggins, "Auditory Expectation."

increased importance as markers of identity, often leading to confrontation and violence. An early example of competitive hymn singing between Arians and Nicenes in Constantinople when John Chrysostom was archbishop of Constantinople (398–404) is an excellent illustration:

> The Arians . . . . congregated within the city gates about the public squares, and sang responsive verses adapted to the Arian heresy. This they did during the greater part of the night: and again in the morning, chanting the same songs which they called responsive, they paraded through the midst of the city, and so passed out of the gates to go to their places of assembly. But since they did not desist from making use of insulting expressions in relation to the Homoousians, often singing such words as these: "Where are they that say three things are but one power?"—John fearing lest any of the more simple should be drawn away from the church by such kind of hymns, opposed to them some of his own people, that they also employing themselves in chanting nocturnal hymns, might obscure the effort of the Arians, and confirm his own party in the profession of their faith. John's design indeed seemed to be good, but it issued in tumult and dangers. . . . on one of these nights, they engaged in a conflict; and Briso, one of the eunuchs of the empress, who was at that time leading the chanters of these hymns, was wounded by a stone in the forehead, and also some of the people on both sides were killed. Whereupon the emperor being angered, forbade the Arians to chant their hymns any more in public.[60]

Here the content of what was sung distinguished the two parties, but in Reformation Europe the sound itself—the use of hymns, the manner of singing the psalms, the presence or absence of the organ—acted as ecclesial boundary markers.[61]

As Chrysostom and the Arians knew only too well, and as recent research has confirmed, social bonding is facilitated more quickly by singing. In a 2015 study, Eiluned Pearce, Jacques Launay, and Robin I. M. Dunbar noted that, although humans do establish bonds through

---

[60] Socrates Scholasticus, *Ecclesiastical History* 6.8, trans. A. C. Zenos, Nicene and Post-Nicene Fathers 2nd series, vol. 2, ed. Philip Schaff and Henry Wallace, 144 (Edinburgh: T&T Clark, 1890).

[61] See Loetz, "Giving the Reformation a Voice."

one-to-one contact, this takes time and is not feasible when such bonding is required for large groups in a much shorter time frame.[62] Singing combines two particular effects: first, it produces ß-endorphins which are also produced in physical activity and which have been shown to be operative in relationships; and second, through synchronous activity, participants experience enhanced group cohesion. The study examined three adult groups engaged in seven-month singing and non-singing adult education classes. Their results showed that all participants reported increased closeness to their classmates over the time period, but those in the singing groups reported that social bonding occurred much more quickly because it bypassed the need to establish relationships with each individual member of the group. This also created the potential for developing deeper relationships in a shorter time period. In their final conclusions they remarked, "In this regard, it is interesting that religion, another potential mechanism for connecting large numbers of individuals, often incorporates singing or chanting in groups."[63] If we add to this music's ability to elicit appropriate emotions, we can see how powerful singing is as a means for performers and listeners to participate in communal emotions and attitudes.

---

[62] Eiluned Pearce, Jacques Launay, and Robin I. M. Dunbar, "The Ice-Breaker Effect: Singing Mediates Fast Social Bonding," *Royal Society Open Science* 2 (2015): 150221.
[63] Pearce et al., "Ice-Breaker Effect."

Chapter 5

Listening to Silence

"Silence may be kept" was a frequently occurring rubric in the Church of England liturgical book of my youth (*The Alternative Service Book*, 1980). This was an innovative addition to Anglican worship given that the BCP made no provision for silence in regular public worship.[1] This does not mean that silence was never a part of worship, only that it was not an intentional ritual sound. Contemporary worship seems to be much more attuned to silence, in all denominations, although what is less clear is the type, or value, or meaning of these silences, and therefore what it is that a worshipper is to *hear* during them. Unlike the other sounds in worship, silence needs to be performed by the listeners for them to hear and experience it.

There has been an astonishing lack of scholarship about silence in worship from liturgists. It is in inverse proportion to the number of times one has heard ministers complaining that the congregation do not know how to be quiet, by which they mean either to pray without making a noise, or to stop their chatter. Where there has been some attempt to discuss it, the results often demonstrate a lack of serious historical or theoretical perspective. Even the origins and practice of the silent recitation of the eucharistic prayer in the Catholic and Orthodox churches has been under-researched, despite the extensive research on the history of the Eucharist, as Jardine Grisbroke concluded about the silent Canon in an article on silent prayer: "this

---

[1] Silence is only mentioned once, at the ordination of priests, in the 1662 BCP.

category calls for little comment"![2] Often, the discussion fails to attend to the nuances of what silence is, what its function is, or who is silent. In a chapter on "Liturgical Silence," Charles Harris did not differentiate between the silence of the people while the priest or choir speak or sing, the (so-called) silent recitation of prayers in a low voice, or the quiet services such as a Low Mass.[3] Michael Downey, while acknowledging the "vital dimension" of silence to enable an "attentiveness to the word of God . . . and receptivity to the Spirit," described it in terms of occasions for barely audible presidential and popular prayers.[4] Clearly these do not attend to silence as a particularly sonic and auditory feature of worship.

There is some debate about the origins and spread of silent prayer in the early church. On the one hand, Pieter van der Horst suggested that the influence of Stoic and Platonic philosophers upon interpretations of the Hebrew scriptures first caused Philo to distinguish between physical spoken prayer and the silent prayer of the soul.[5] Subsequently, following Philo's impetus, writers such as Clement of Alexandria, Tertullian, and Cyprian promoted silent inner speech that only God hears, and it is this which eventually dominated monastic and ascetic practices, as evidenced by John Cassian and Ephrem.[6] Brouria Bitton-Ashkelony has cast doubt on this interpretation, insisting that silent prayer was not part of Christian practice until the fifth century through the influence of the neo-Platonic philosopher Proclus.[7] She notes that although Clement does say that the incorporeal God should be worshipped without the senses and that the true gnostic will not chatter to God, he does still affirm the conventional view that prayer is "a conversation (*homilia*) with God."[8]

---

[2] Jardine W. Grisbroke, "Silent Prayer," in *The New SCM Dictionary of Liturgy*, ed. Paul Bradshaw, 442–43 (London: SCM Press, 2002).

[3] Charles Harris, "Liturgical Silence," in *Liturgy and Worship*, ed. Lowther Clarke, 774–84 (London: SPCK, 1954).

[4] Michael Downey, "Silence, Liturgical Role of," in *The New Dictionary of Sacramental Worship*, ed. Peter E. Fink, 1189–90 (Collegeville, MN: Liturgical Press, 1990).

[5] Pieter W. van der Horst, "Silent Prayer in Antiquity," *Numen* 41, no. 1 (1994): 13.

[6] Horst, "Silent Prayer in Antiquity," 17–20.

[7] Brouria Bitton-Ashkelony, "'More Interior Than the Lips and the Tongue': John of Apamea and Silent Prayer in Late Antiquity," *Journal of Early Christian Studies* 20, no. 2 (2012): 308–9.

[8] Bitton-Ashkelony, "'More Interior Than the Lips,'" 312. Clement of Alexandria, *Miscellanies* (*Stromata*) 7.49.5-6.

Clement does suggest that the gnostic will engage in prayer without sound, but he will also participate in vocal prayer. Essentially, though, the topic is marginal in early Christian treatments of prayer by Tertullian, Cyprian, and Origen, and even Augustine has nothing to say on the subject. In the fourth century, monastic and ascetic practices promoted *hesychia* (stillness), within which silence functions as a disposition towards God, rather than prayer or liturgical practice. Only John Cassian explicitly refers to silent prayer as a way to avoid disturbing other monks at prayer, but this does not refer to communal vocal prayer.[9] Bitton-Ashkelony presents the writings of John of Apamea as a rare voice, and one whose influence is hard to determine. John devised a threefold model of stillness which corresponded to progression in the spiritual life: the cessation of speech; the stillness of the soul; and spiritual stillness. And he further defined levels of silence: "Thus there is a silence of the tongue, there is a silence of the whole body, there is the silence of the soul, there is the silence of the mind, and there is the silence of the spirit."[10] Only in the latter is there complete physical and intellectual silence before the silence of God; however, the journey starts with the cessation of speech. The impact of the monastic discipline of *hesychia* (stillness) upon the liturgical worship of the church is difficult to estimate; however, it is clear that this privileging of silence as the point of departure into true or pure prayer prioritized silence over other sounds in the worship of God.

The silent recitation of parts of the liturgy by the priest is evident in the Eastern church from the mid-sixth century when the emperor Justinian attempted, and failed, to stop the practice of reciting the anaphora inaudibly.[11] It was clearly widespread enough for the

---

[9] John Cassian, *Collations* (*Conlationes*) 9.35, in Boniface Ramsey, *John Cassian: The Conferences* (New York: Paulist Press, 1997), 353.

[10] John of Apamea, *On Prayer* 5, in "John the Solitary, On Prayer," trans. Sebastian Brock, *Journal of Theological Studies* 30, no. 1 (1979): 99. Cited in Bitton-Ashkelony, "'More Interior Than the Lips,'" 327–28.

[11] Justinian, *Novella* 137c6, dated 565, required that clergy recite the prayers at baptism and the Eucharist in a clear voice so that the faithful will be edified by the prayers; failure to do so would merit divine and secular punishment. See David Miller and Peter Sarris, *The Novels of Justinian: A Complete Annotated English Translation* (Cambridge: Cambridge University Press, 2018), 913–20. Anthony Gelston argued that Narsai (died c. 502) in *Homily* 17 provides the first explicit evidence of silent recitation of parts of the anaphora, but that it might also have been practiced by Theodore of Mopsuestia (c. 350–428; *Catechesis* 16.10). See Anthony Gelston, "The

emperor to consider that it merited a legal prohibition, but possibly not so established that he considered it impossible to reverse the practice. However, Maximus the Confessor (c. 580–662) omitted the anaphora in his *Mystagogia* on the eucharistic liturgy, and it has been suggested that he did so because of the custom of silent recitation.[12] A similar date for its appearance in the West was suggested by Gregory Dix, who credited the practice to Gregory the Great (c. 540–604) in order to prevent popular corruption of the words. G. G. Willis proposed that it was established practice only from the ninth century; after that, however, injunctions to preserve the Canon from misuse by the laity are common, and it seems there are no contrary voices until the Protestant Reformation.[13] Mary Hayes noted the prioritizing of divine speech as the priest ventriloquized Christ's words at the Last Supper; the cause of silent recitation was to avoid vulgarization of the words by the laity, and silence prevented the uttering of wicked speech or the accidental consecration of the bread by the laity. By the fourteenth century, congregations were so habituated to the silent Canon that a certain Johannes Andreas promoted it as a way of not impeding the people's private prayers during Mass.[14] What "silent" meant in this context is uncertain. Did the priest mouth the words but no sound came out? Or did he utter them in a low, barely audible voice (*tacita voce* or *submissa voce*)? Or was it that in the sanctuary the words could be heard, but not outside? That is, they were not silently recited but they might as well have been as far as the laity were concerned. In all these instances, "silent" means "inaudible," not the absence of sound.

Hayes has remarked that half of the medieval Mass was performed in silence,[15] but that does not mean that the laity were silent, only that they were not required to contribute to any intentional sounds

---

Meaning of Theodore of Mopsuestia's Sixteenth Catechetical Lecture and the Silent Recitation of the Eucharistic Prayer," *Journal of Theological Studies* 60, no. 1 (2009): 191–92.

[12] See Maximus the Confessor, *Mystagogia* 19, in *Maximus Confessor: Selected Writings*, trans. George C. Berthold (New York: Paulist Press, 1985), 202.

[13] See Mary Hayes, *Divine Ventriloquism in Medieval English Literature: Power, Anxiety, Subversion* (New York: Palgrave Macmillan, 2011), 8.

[14] Hayes, *Divine Ventriloquism*, 11.

[15] Hayes, 6.

of worship. Movement, muttered prayers, and conversations did not make for a quiet worshipping environment. The Reformation churches placed emphasis upon the people's comprehension of the liturgy, and especially upon the reading of Scripture and preaching, which required clear articulation by the minister and silent, attentive listening by the laity, who were also expected to participate vocally at the allotted moments. The scripting of silence is not in evidence, though. In the 1549 Book of Common Prayer, and in later versions, too, silence is only required during the ordination of priests: "After this, the congregacion shalbe desired, secretly in their praiers, to make humble supplicacions to God for the foresaied thinges; for the whiche praiers, there shalbe a certaine space kept in silence."

Some of the most fruitful scholarship about silence in religious communities has been undertaken in relation to those traditions in which silence is a fundamental aspect of their worship and religious practice, namely the Quakers and Buddhists.[16] Dana Fennell, in her ethnographic study of silence in Quaker and Buddhist worship practices, suggested that silence should be explored in relation to four continuums: speech–silence continuum, a body movement–body stillness continuum, a thinking–not thinking continuum, and an external sound/movement–external silence/stillness continuum. Her use of *continuum* is deliberate, as it rejects the notion of silence and noise as absolute categories in opposition to each other. It shows that silence may be experienced differently in relation to speech/noise, to bodily movement, to inner thought, and to external sounds depending on the context and the social interaction of the participants, and that groups may assign different meanings to silence as it is encountered in each of the continuums.[17] Thus, for example, she notes how in Quaker meetings the movement from silence, to speech, to silence is unpredictable and irregular, and that there is negligible concern about bodily movement (in contrast to the attention paid to

---

[16] On the Quakers, see Pink Dandelion, *A Sociological Analysis of the Theology of Quakers: The Silent Revolution* (Lewiston, NY: Edwin Mellen Press, 1996); Stanford J. Searl, *The Meanings of Silence in Quaker Worship* (Lewiston, NY: Edwin Mellen Press, 2005). For a comparative study of Quakers and Buddhists, see Dana Fennell, "Explorations of Silence in the Religious Rituals of Buddhists and Quakers," *Religion* 42, no. 4 (2012): 549–74.

[17] Fennell, "Explorations of Silence," 551.

it among Buddhist groups), nor about external sounds, but that variable inner thought occurs during the silence.[18] This is in contrast to the early monastic writers who emphasized bodily stillness and mental stillness, as well as abstention from speech.

Domenico Sartore proposed a typology of liturgical silence or, as he called it, "sacred silence," based upon a descriptive interpretation of contemporary Roman Catholic liturgical documents and practice, although his categories may well be applicable to other liturgical traditions too.[19] His approach to liturgical silence is functional: the type and quality is determined by where in the rite silence occurs. He proposed five types:

- "silenzio de raccoglimento" (silence of recollection), when the assembly collectively engages in private prayer as preparation for worship or at specific points in the liturgy; for example, at penitential sections or on Good Friday prostrations.

- "silenzio di appropriazione" (a silence of appropriation), when the laity, in spiritual union with the presider, is unified in silence while the priest prays the eucharistic prayer.

- "silenzio di meditazione" (a meditative silence), which many traditions employ in connection with the readings, psalms, and sermon.

- "silenzio di adorazione" (of adoration), such as that at the end of the eucharistic prayer and at other moments of adoration and attention on the sacrament.

- "silenzio orante" (a prayerful silence): Sartore seems to mean by this a devotional and wordless attentiveness before receiving communion, for example.

This typology takes account of the relationship between the communal and individual silences during the liturgy, but defines them more in relation to the texts and activities which they accompany and not to the experience and sonic quality of the silence itself.

---

[18] Fennell, 560.

[19] Domenico Sartore, "Silenzo," in *Liturgia*, ed. Domenico Sartore, Achille M. Triacca, and Carlo Cibien, 1864–73 (Milan: Edizioni San Paolo, 2001).

To my mind there are only three categories of intentional liturgical silence: an interval, a pause, and deep silence.[20] Interval and pause require there to be an ongoing stream of sound which the silence interrupts: an *interval* is what signals and allows a transition between ritual speech, music, or actions, and a *pause* is that which occurs within a liturgical unit. I suggest that it is the intervals of silence which actually provide the rhythm of worship rather than the sequence of sounds. They conclude one ritual activity and permit recollection before proceeding to the next. Relevant examples include the silences surrounding the reading of Scripture, before and after the sermon, before and after the eucharistic prayer, and after communion. Intervals provide the listeners with auditory space in which to re-tune their ears in preparation for the next ritual sound; essentially, this is an individualized listening experience. *Pauses* occur within liturgical or ritual units and therefore do not constitute the beginning or end of an auditory activity, but hold the listeners in an in-progress event or activity. The manner of praying the collect in the Mass provides a clear example: the priest "calls upon the people to pray," followed by a "brief silence," before he reads the collect (GIRM 54); many Anglican churches also follow this traditional practice. A pause may occur between petitions during intercessory prayer and during the words of institution in the eucharistic prayer. In the choral recitation of the psalms in the daily offices, a pause may punctuate the verses. For the listener, the silent pause causes a hiatus in the activity but does not interrupt it. The silent pause demands a heightened attentiveness to the activity in progress. It is often anticipatory and is marked by a communal listening.

Deep silence is connected to the great mysteries of Christ, represents the revealing and concealing of divine presence, and connects the temporal with the eternal. Deep silence participates in God's silence, because the Word has been silenced by death. Hans Urs von Balthasar wrote that "when the Son, the Word of God is dead, then no one can see God, or hear him, or attain him. And this day exists

---

[20] My categories do not correspond to those proposed by Bernard Dauenhauer, even though he also spoke of intervals and deep silence. See Bernard P. Dauenhauer, *Silence: The Phenomenon and Its Ontological Significance* (Bloomington: Indiana University Press, 1980).

when the Son is dead, and the Father, accordingly, inaccessible. . . . Then the silence closed around, as the sealed tomb will close likewise. At the end of the Passion, when the Word of God is dead, the Church has no words left to say."[21] Because this time is outside time, it can be considered neither as an interval nor pause; Balthasar refers to it as "non-time."[22] Ritually, it is performed by an absence of liturgical sounds. Such silence is not experienced in regular Sunday worship, but it is a feature of the Triduum in the Western Roman Catholic and some Anglican churches. The conclusion to the liturgies on Thursday and Friday is marked by a silent departure; the veneration of the Cross is conducted in a silence which is individual and communal. Holy Saturday is a day of complete liturgical silence in these churches (but not in the Orthodox church); the altar is bare and there are no liturgies.[23]

The silent intervals and pauses should not be confused as, even if they may be performed and heard in an undifferentiated way, they are intended and experienced differently. The rubrics may simply state that "Silence is/may be kept" or indicate a ritual action for which no sounds are required. At Catholic Low Mass or an Anglican Said Communion, the distinctive feature is that there is no music and minimal ritual to "fill in the gaps" between liturgical texts, and therefore silence becomes a by-product of decisions about ritual performance of a liturgy that could be validly celebrated without silence at others times in the week. The use of intervals and pauses differs between churches, and this is most evident with regard to the Eucharist. Thus, in the 1979 *Book of Common Prayer* of the U.S. Episcopal Church, silence (a pause) is mandated at the fraction of the bread, but there is no rubric for silence (an interval) after the Amen of the eucharistic prayer.[24] Robert Taft has indicated that liturgy hates a vacuum, and that words and music are added to silently performed, or wordless, rituals, but it is obvious even from a casual observation

---

[21] Hans Urs von Balthasar, *Mysterium Paschale: The Mystery of Easter*, trans. Aidan Nicols, OP (Edinburgh: T&T Clark, 1990), 49.

[22] Balthasar, *Mysterium Paschale*, 50.

[23] See Richard Bastable, "The Vigil of Pascha: Formation in Silence," *Anaphora* 3, no. 1 (1999): 57–66.

[24] U.S. Episcopal Church, *Book of Common Prayer* (New York: Seabury Press, 1979), 337.

that many of these extraneous elements are removed during processes of liturgical revision.[25] In modern liturgical texts, which have undergone considerable intentional revision, we should expect to find silences explicitly inserted into the liturgy through the rubrics when space has been created by the removal of other material.

It is interesting that in most traditions there is little explicit reference to the advisability of silence before and after the service in the liturgical books, even if that may be the firm practice in local congregations. Although I exclude these silences from my definition of intentional sound as they lie outside the ritual frame of the liturgy, they are frequently enjoined upon the laity. Romano Guardini (1885–1968), in his *Meditations before Mass*, strongly recommended bodily and mental composure and silence for the laity as a means of preparation for participation in the Mass: "Only in stillness can the congregation fundamental to the sacred ritual come into being. Only in stillness can the room in which the Holy Mass is celebrated be exalted into a church."[26] In contrast, the minister's edition of the 1978 *Lutheran Book of Worship* stated that the end of the liturgy is *not* a time for silence (or even an organ voluntary), but that this is the appropriate time for the people to greet each other![27]

The Length of a Liturgical Silence

What is the actual and desirable length of an interval and a pause?

Shortly after the introduction of the 1969 Roman Missal, one Roman Catholic commentator expressed concern that the laity no longer had the opportunity to "bring before the altar of God not a few intentions and in general speak with God in their own words in the intimacy of their hearts." We note that the writer, Benedict Heron, does not intend a listening silence. He urged the official and unofficial introduction of silence into the Mass, believing a parish could be

---

[25] Robert F. Taft, "How Liturgies Grow: The Evolution of the Byzantine 'Divine Liturgy,'" *Orientalia Christiana Periodica* 53 (1977): 8–30.

[26] Romano Guardini, *Meditations before Mass*, trans. Elinor Castendyk Briefs (Westminster, MD: Newman Press, 1957), 7. Originally published as *Besinnung vor der Feier der Heiligen Messe* (1939).

[27] Inter-Lutheran Commission on Worship, *Lutheran Book of Worship* (Minneapolis: Augsburg Fortress Press, 1978), 39.

"trained" to have up to ten minutes of silence; a few seconds after bidding prayers and half a minute after communion were considered inadequate.[28] The General Instruction on the Liturgy of the Hours (1971) recommended an "interval of silence" "as occasion offers and prudence suggests" after the antiphons and psalms; however, it warned, "Care must be taken to avoid the kind of silence that would disturb the structure of the office or annoy and weary those taking part" (202). A silence should be long but not too long!

If one looks at a number of U.S. Lutheran liturgical books and resources, we can see an increasing number of occasions for silence in worship, but less clarity about what the congregation will endure. Thus the 1978 *Lutheran Book of Worship* states that after the canticles in the Service of the Word, the silence "is integral to the service and should be more than a moment's pause if the people are to engage in reflection"; it is ended by the preacher approaching the reading desk.[29] In *Evangelical Lutheran Worship* (2006), there are references throughout to a "time of silence," a "brief silence," "an extended silence," and "sufficient silence."[30] These are distinguished by length, but again it presumably falls to the minister to determine quite how long each one should be. Only in the *Manual on the Liturgy* of 1979, produced for the Inter-Lutheran Commission on Worship, have I found a more precise discussion of the length of silences at different points in worship.[31] Thus it is suggested that at the confession "one or two minutes is not too long"; before the collect/prayer for the day "in accord with what appears to have been the ancient practice, silence of at least 5–10 seconds may be kept . . . to give the people time to collect their thoughts."[32] At morning and evening prayer the meditative use of psalmody is to be facilitated though silences of several minutes so that the laity are truly able to truly engage in

---

[28] Benedict M. Heron, "Silence during the Celebration of Mass and Other Rites," *Notitiae* 8 (1972): 180–81.

[29] *Lutheran Book of Worship*, 33, note 11.

[30] Evangelical Lutheran Church in America, *Evangelical Lutheran Worship* (Minneapolis: Augsburg Fortress Press, 2006).

[31] Philip H. Pfatteicher and Carlos R. Messerli, *Manual on the Liturgy* (Minneapolis: Augsburg Fortress Press, 1979).

[32] Pfatteicher and Messerli, *Manual on the Liturgy*, 21, 198.

meditation, proposing, also, that if time is short the length of the psalm should be cut and not the silence.[33]

Roy Rappaport distinguished calendrical ritual time by "periods" and "intervals," the latter being the "sacred time" that intervenes in the mundane. Although he was not at all discussing ritual or liturgical silence, I find his comment that intervals (his use) should be "long enough to experience being in them," to be highly pertinent to our investigation of the length of silence.[34] Each interval (my use) and pause does need to be long enough for the worshippers to perform, hear, and experience the silence, so that it constitutes ritual sound and is not a sign of ritual failure. But reports of people's experience of the length of silence can be misleading. Andrew Vogel Ettin commented: "Ask worshippers how long the 'moment of silence' has lasted at a religious ceremony and they will almost always overestimate it, often considerably."[35] A one-minute silence in memory of the departed may often last only thirty seconds even though one is sure it does indeed last the full minute. My own unscientific and surreptitious observations confirmed that intentional intervals and pauses in worship are often very short indeed, so that in traditions where the silence is intended for individual meditation or prayer, it has barely begun before being interrupted by speech or other intentional sound.

In his 1973 article on "Communicative Silences," Thomas Bruneau noted, in relation to dialogues, how silence distorts chronological time and that it can be experienced as fast or slow time.[36] Fast-time silence lasts about two seconds, occurs frequently, and is something like a verbal hesitation; slow-time silence is "closely associated with the semantic (and metaphorical) processes of decoding speech."[37] Slow-time silence enables the mind to explore memory and experience in relation to what has been heard. This is a willed and intentional act, and consequently causes highly individualized responses

---

[33] Pfatteicher and Messerli, 281.

[34] Roy A. Rappaport, "Ritual, Time, And Eternity," *Zygon* 27 (1992): 19.

[35] Andrew Vogel Ettin, *Speaking Silences: Stillness and Voice in Modern Jewish Thought* (Charlottesville: University of Virginia Press, 1994), 15–16.

[36] Thomas J. Bruneau, "Communicative Silences: Forms and Functions," *The Journal of Communication* 23 (1973): 21.

[37] Bruneau, "Communicative Silences," 26.

with regard to intensity and duration, and to the frequency of accepting the imposition of such silences. The decoder's (listener's or recipient's) ability and willingness to use this silence is related, he says, to their submission to the silence and its intended use, and their toleration of silence's ambiguity. Bruneau remarks that it is quite possible for the decoder to reject the silence.[38] He also connects this slow-time silence to mystical experiences.

The intentional silent intervals and pauses we have identified ideally operate as slow-time, but in performance they may be experienced as fast-time. These liturgical silences are not ritual hesitations, but the interval especially is a time for decoding speech or music. Bruneau explained the variability of the experience of time during silence: in moments of high intensity the experience will be of a slowing or cessation of time, even if in actual fact it is not. Our ability to perform, hear, and experience the silence depends upon an acceptance of the intention of the interval or pause, the extent to which we share the intensity, and our individual and communal memory of the significance of silence at that point in the liturgy. A useful example is the silence used in many traditions after the "Amen" of the eucharistic prayer. The priest can signal entry to the silence by physical stillness and the cessation of intentional sound, but the length of silence and how people experience it may differ from week to week despite the evident fact that the external performance of it may be unchanging.

Performing Liturgical Silence

A number of ethnographers and linguists have proposed typologies of silence based on the performative contexts and the perception of silence in conversational speech. Dennis Kurzon, for example, based his typology upon the circumstances in which silence may be meaningful, as opposed to its meanings.[39] His four types arise from the contexts in which they occur: conversational, thematic, textual, and situational. The thematic, textual, and situational types have

---

[38] Bruneau, 27.
[39] Dennis Kurzon, "Towards a Typology of Silence," *Journal of Pragmatics* 39 (2007): 1673–88.

more to say to our present study. He proposed that each type could be analyzed according to these criteria: the number of people involved; the identity of the (silent) "text"; and intentionality. Does silence indicate non-presence in the context? Does it originate with the one who is silent or is it externally imposed? *Thematic silence* is where the "text" is well known to all present but is intentionally avoided or ignored. As a case in point, he refers to the ignoring of women in much academic and social discourse, but he suggests that here silence should be understood metaphorically; there is no absence of noise or speech in the communication, but participants are silenced in and by the communication.[40] *Textual silence* occurs where the conventions of the event require that a shared text should be read silently by all present, and that this is a key part of the proceedings which do not originate with those keeping silent[41]; for example, where texts for private use are provided for use during the liturgical event. He distinguishes this from *situational silence*, which is an institutionalized form of silence, participated in by all present but for which no agenda or text is set or observable, and for which an authority figure or social convention establishes behavior. In this category he places Quaker worship and silent prayer within liturgical worship. By their silence, the participants do not signal their presence in overt ways, but by participation they are obviously present. Kurzon also mentions the silence of the audience at an artistic performance in which there is a "keeping silent" amidst sonic communication; although addressed rhetorically, the audience does not (normally) reply; their silence is intentional, much like during a sermon.[42]

Liturgical silence is a ritual performance like speech, music, or gesture, because it requires particular skills and techniques to perform, hear, and experience it. This is clearly the case in Quaker worship. Dana Fennell and Stanford J. Searl both indicate how worshippers employ techniques learned over time, and from those more experienced, about how to enter, keep, and use the silence in the meeting.[43] When to keep silent and when to speak, when to settle

---

[40] Kurzon, "Towards a Typology of Silence," 1677–79.
[41] Kurzon, 1679–81.
[42] Kurzon, 1681–84.
[43] Fennell, "Explorations of Silence," 549–51; Searl, *Meanings of Silence*.

into silence and when to emerge from it, were directed by the group in a relational way. Fennel found that the group settled into silence at the start of the meeting without any formal invitation, but within worship, participants examined themselves about when and whether to break the silence with speech. Individual techniques for achieving silence contributed to the performance of the communal silence: these included physical stillness, active attentiveness upon the gathered community and upon oneself, and the repetition of particular biblical verses such as "Be still and know that I am God"; knowing when and how to interrupt the silence was also a learned skill. Those interviewed in Searl's study of New England meetings did speak of the difficulties involved in learning to perform this ritual silence. Fennell reported that novices were given a pamphlet to explain how to behave, but that in fact the appropriate disposition was learned by watching and by informal explanation.[44] Participants preserved the external silence by abstention from speech and movement, while simultaneously trying to create silence/stillness in the mind and keeping their ears open for a possible spoken intervention.

Rachel Muers, though, distinguishes the performance of silence in a Quaker meeting from its scripted performance in a liturgical event. In the latter the meaning and use of silence is controlled by its having "a preparatory and auxiliary function to the acts of collective worship." Silence is bracketed from the other liturgical acts and functions to bring about other desired ends, and she proposes that silence itself could be "the organizing focus in relation to which words are weighted or judged."[45] It is silence which makes other sounds, speech, and music possible and therefore requires silence from the one who wishes to hear it. Muers also warns against considering the liturgical silence as a private and individualized moment within a communal ritual, but rather to consider the ethical imperative of hearing the sound and silence of others: "shared silence claims and enacts the reality of a given and non-verbalized common ground. To keep silence together is not merely for each to keep her own silence; *it is to keep one another's silence* [my emphasis], which in turn only makes

---

[44] Fennell, 570.
[45] Rachel Muers, *Keeping God's Silence: Towards a Theological Ethics of Communication* (Oxford: Blackwell, 2004), 150.

sense if it is also a keeping of God's silence, a sign and enactment of the silence in which God hears the whole of creation"[46]

Hearing Silence

Is it possible to hear silence, or is what one hears simply an absence of all sonic phenomenon? The latter is seemingly impossible: even if no sounds enter the ear from outside, the natural functioning of the body creates a resonance which is detected by the ears to be interpreted in the same way as external sound phenomenon. This is the experience of being in an anechoic chamber, which is not only isolated from external sounds, but also eliminates all reflected sound. Without a sound source in the chamber, one hears only oneself—the heartbeat, breathing, the twitch of nerves. Consequently, being removed from the sonic world makes one even more present to oneself. Normally, of course, one hears silence in the world, where the small and quiet sounds from outside combine with our inner sound to create a personal soundscape.[47] These tiny sounds require us to strain to listen to them; they clash with our expectations of ever-present identifiable and meaningful sounds. Silence, as Salomé Voegelin suggests, is not about the absence of noise, but it is, rather, the beginning of listening.[48] The strain to hear these barely-there sounds requires us to actively and self-consciously listen.

Silence is not the absence of noise but the ground out of which sound emerges. This should be especially the case in spoken communication, where my silence enables others to speak. I, as listener, have an ethical obligation to hear the other, and in authentic, attentive listening I will hear my own silence. Corradi Fiumara said that the ability to produce silence belongs to those who speak, and that it is therefore "the necessary condition of listening."[49] We become present to ourselves and to others in silence, and thus in hearing silence we

---

[46] Muers, *Keeping God's Silence*, 153.
[47] Salomé Voegelin, *Listening to Noise and Silence: Towards a Philosophy of Sound Art* (New York: Continuum, 2010), 83.
[48] Voegelin, *Listening to Noise and Silence*, 83.
[49] Gemma Corradi Fiumara, *The Other Side of Language: A Philosophy of Listening*, trans. Charles Lambert (London: Routledge, 1990), 95–99.

hear the potentiality of being. We are open to whatever will be revealed.

Hearing silence in worship is not to hear no sound at all, as that is not at all possible. As worshippers fall silent, they permit the speech of others and the proclamation of the Word of God. Liturgical silences are the ritual performance of an ethical and spiritual condition by which to listen to others and to God. In the silence, the potentiality of being is revealed in our awareness of the presence of God and of others. Ultimately, then, hearing liturgical silence is just another mode of ritual listening in which what is attended to is being and presence, rather than the intentional sounds of worship.

Experiencing Silence

How does the performer and hearer of silence experience it? That is, how do they make sense of the silence in which they find themselves? Unlike other intentional sounds for which there is a direct source and referent, silence is perceived as untethered to an identifiable source. Understanding this requires some attention to the origins, occurrence, and goal of silence. Thus we could ask, philosophically and theologically, whether silence is the source out of which speech and other sounds erupt; or whether silence is the necessary condition of dialogue, as "space between"; or whether silence is the consummation of speech and sound. Theologically, we could ask whether God's Word is sent forth from God's own silence, or does the Word and divine silence reflect the dynamics of the Trinity, or will, in the final consummation, when the Word has been fulfilled, all creation be gathered into God's silent presence? Of course, this assumes that God is silent, either in Godself or by choice. Rachel Muers has suggested that silence is part of God's fundamental communication: God "keeps silent" so that by exercise of our free will, humans are enabled to speak.[50] In contrast, Dauenhauer asserted that silence says nothing about God at all![51]

In Rojin Mazouji and Mohammad Raayat Jahromi's analysis of the function of silence in the thought of Søren Kierkegaard and Martin

---

[50] Muers, *Keeping God's Silence*, 13.
[51] Dauenhauer, *Silence*, 172.

Heidegger we find the paradox expressed more fully.[52] For both, silence occurs at the boundary of existence where the individual, her subjectivity and *Da-sein*, encounter God. Although they use speech as the opposite of silence, they are not concerned with silence as an acoustic phenomenon, but rather with its existential characteristics. Silence is a necessary condition for being authentically oneself, only possible when speech ceases and when one is before God. Authentic and intimate communication with God is possible only in silence, where the subject refuses to speak when confronted with the Incomprehensible and the Inexpressible. By being comfortable in this state of silence, by making the "house into a home," the individual is placed before God's Word and becomes continually receptive to it, and hence dialogue with God is possible. By cultivating silence the individual has a remedy for the forgetfulness of God's Word and for inattentiveness to it.[53] In Heidegger, silence is the ground of authentic speech (for him, poetry), which lets be what is: "By maintaining silence, *Da-sein* both abandons the quest for domination of everyday discourse and also a fall into idle-talk."[54] Silence is and makes possible hearing the call of conscience; it diminishes or restricts the "being-with-others" and reveals the authenticity of *Da-sein*, effecting also a return to the Holy who calls one into silence. According to Martin Heidegger in *The Phenomenology of Religion*, as interpreted by Sylvain Camilleri, the religious life organizes itself in concentric circles around silence at its very heart. It is no surprise that Heidegger privileged mystical prayer over liturgical prayer, an asceticism of speech in favor of revelation of God, without ever specifying a dominant mode by which God is revealed, or reveals Godself.[55]

---

[52] Rojin Mazouji and Mohammad Raayat Jahromi, "'Silence' as a Language of Faith and Being: A Comparative Study of Kierkegaard's and Heidegger's Uses of 'Silence,'" *Heythrop Journal* 62, no. 1 (2021): 39–52.

[53] Søren Kierkegaard, *For a Self-Examination*, trans. Howard V. Hong and Edna H. Hong (Princeton, NJ: Princeton University Press, 1876), 35. Cited in Mazouji and Jahromi, "'Silence' as a Language of Faith," 45.

[54] Mazouji and Jahromi, "'Silence' as a Language of Faith," 42.

[55] Sylvain Camilleri, *Phénoménologie de la religion et herméneutique théologique dans la pensée du jeune Heidegger: commentaire analytique des fondements philosophiques de la mystique médiévale (1916–1919)*, Phaenomenologica 184 (Dordrecht: Springer, 2008), 257ff.

The phenomenological reflections of Maurice Merleau-Ponty also place silence at the heart of experience, as that which precedes the conscious thought speech tries to articulate. Philip Walsh cites Merleau-Ponty from *The Prose of the World*, that essential to his idea is to "consider speech before it has been pronounced, against the ground of the silence which precedes it, which never ceases to accompany it, and without which it would say nothing. Moreover, we should be sensitive to the thread of silence from which the tissue of speech is woven."[56] This idea is developed by Bernard Dauenhauer, who notes that discourse receives its character from the specific sorts of silence with which it is conjoined.[57] Silence is the condition for speaking, and so too for listening. In Max Picard's *World of Silence*, he too remarks, "Thus the entire domain of human discourse is suspended between an originary silence whence discourse arises and a terminal silence, death, into which it departs."[58] Within this trajectory, silence may so overwhelm discourse that it is, itself, a form of death or the finitude of discourse. In prayer, though, there is a somewhat different dynamic according to Picard: "In prayer, the word comes again *of itself* into silence . . . it is taken up by God, taken away from man . . . Prayer can be never-ending, but the word of prayer always disappears into silence . . . Elsewhere, outside prayer, the silence of man is fulfilled and receives its meaning in speech. But in prayer it receives its meaning and fulfillment in the meeting with the silence of God."[59] In God the silence is not terminal, but eternal.

Silence is very often conceived spatially: statically as the center from which speech and other sounds emerge, or dynamically as movement out of or towards speech. The spatialization of sound functions metaphorically here, in contrast to the experiential spatialization of sound phenomenon. Rather than placing silence at the center, Don Ihde places it at the horizon, at the limit of speech beyond which

---

[56] Maurice Merleau-Ponty, *The Prose of the World*, trans. John O'Neill (Evanston, IL: Northwestern University Press, 1973), 46. Cited in Philip J. Walsh, "The Sound of Silence: Merleau-Ponty on Conscious Thought," *European Journal of Philosophy* 25, no. 2 (2017): 318.

[57] Dauenhauer, *Silence*, 89.

[58] Max Picard, *The World of Silence*, trans. Stanley Godman (London: Harvill, 1948). Cited in Dauenhauer, *Silence*, 136.

[59] Picard, *World of Silence*, 231–32, cited in Dauenhauer, *Silence*, 137.

there is the nothingness of the unsaid or the unsayable. This silence also functions as a frame surrounding the sounds I hear; it is what permits the sounds to come into being. Silence functions to bring the meaningful sound into relief, both as boundary marker and an unlimited field beyond it.[60] Conversely, a dynamic understanding of silence is evident in Dauenhauer: "the entire domain of human discourse is suspended between an originary silence whence discourse arises and a terminal silence, death, into which it departs."[61]

The dynamism is also evident in theological reflections which consider God's speaking and silence. God speaks the creation into being, but is that out of a ground of silence? For Oliver Davies this silence is "the primordial and generative ground, enabling God's own and subsequently all human speech." [62] If so, then we should consider silence to be prior to creation and to be part of God's own self. But the very speaking of creation and the incarnation of the Word also attest to a God who communicates with speech. But God is also silent. In the Old Testament, the Psalms and prophetic texts, especially, frequently ask why God is silent in light of the needs and requests of the people of Israel. In the New Testament, Jesus remains silent in front of Pilate, leading to the silence of the cross and the rupture of time. As Muers says, "Christ is not only made silent, but mute and passive. Christ's silence in one sense conceals nothing; but at the same time it apparently claims no power to communicate."[63] This silence is not one of absence but is a "listening silence" that enables human freedom and finitude, and it is this which characterizes God's relationship to creation. As Muers says, God hears God's own Word, which is silenced in the world but heard by God; the resurrection is God hearing God's Word, a hearing in love which is intrinsic to who God is.[64]

❖ ❖ ❖

---

[60] Don Ihde, *Listening and Voice: Phenomenologies of Sound* (Albany: State University of New York Press, 2007), 161.

[61] Dauenhauer, *Silence*, 136.

[62] Oliver Davies, "Reading the Burning Bush: Voice, World and Holiness," *Modern Theology* 22, no. 3 (2006): 203.

[63] Muers, *Keeping God's Silence*, 14.

[64] Muers, 15.

For creation to hear as God hears requires, then, a listening silence. It is this which is fundamental to strategies for creating stillness and silence in religious practice: ascetics remove themselves from the noise of the world; mystics hear God in the silence of ecstatic experience; all the faithful are invited to participate in a listening silence which enables them to attend to God and their neighbor. Liturgical silences are neither ascetic nor mystical, but they do participate in God's silence in as much as they create a space for God's communication to happen. As Rachel Muers put it, "To fall silent is, after all, to create a space in which anything can be heard, and to offer it a hearing that will not necessarily result in a verbalized solution. It can be understood as an effective sign of God's hearing, of God's own Word and of the world."[65]

---

[65] Muers, 149.

Chapter 6

Hearing Noise

In this book I have used *sound* in a neutral sense for any acoustical phenomenon, but now I shall introduce *noise* as sound which is perceived negatively. Noise is sound which does not fit our categories of coherent speech, ordered sound (i.e., music), silence, or even natural sounds. We could think of it as a subset of sound, in the same way as music or speech, but even these can be considered noise if they are not produced and heard in the appropriate context. In this chapter we shall consider why we designate some sounds as noise, what their effect on us is, and examine what criteria are applied to noise in worship.

How we define noise will influence the way in which we designate some sounds as noises. Etymologically, the origin of the word is confused. It has been suggested that it comes from the Latin *nausea*, "seasickness," which would imply that noise is a sound which produces an unpleasant physical reaction to an external stimulus. The editors of the *Oxford English Dictionary (OED)* suggest another plausible origin in a range of Old and Middle French words around the themes of din, disturbance, or quarrel, and it is this range of meanings which fits more closely to our experience of using the word. *OED*'s other definitions and uses are almost all negative: noise is disturbing, dissonant, or unpleasant sounds. They offer only a single example of noise as a "pleasant or melodious sound," followed by the observation "Obsolete"![1]

---

[1] *Oxford English Dictionary (OED)*, s.v. "noise" (n) (Oxford: Oxford University Press, 2023), https://www.oed.com/.

Considering noise as "din" alerts us to the volume, intensity, and pitch of the sound and what it is from these factors that will make it unpleasant regardless of the context in which it is heard. In this case, noise is defined by the quality of its sound. Such a notion lies behind noise-pollution campaigns and the use of acoustical measurements to determine safe and dangerous levels of exposure. National health and environmental protection agencies determine the legally permissible safe limits in decibels, and international guidelines can be found in the World Health Organization's *Guidelines for Community Noise* (1999). We have personal comfort levels about the level and type of noise we can tolerate, and these are often based on perceptions of loudness; however, we are also aware of how our tolerance changes as we age and by exposure to different levels and types of background noise.

Definitions around "disturbance" or "quarrel" alert us to the potentially violent nature of noise. It may indicate actual aggression, or simply be perceived by us as violent and hence as a danger warning. Unexpected shouts, loud bangs, warning shots, car horns, fire alarms, and the like are effective warnings based upon their ability to be heard above environmental noise and to intrude on other sounds we want to hear.[2] Noise in these circumstances intrudes, but we do not attend to the noise itself but instead to its source or the message it conveys.

Noise can also be understood as any sound which is out of place. Peter Bailey and Karen Bijsterveld invoked Mary Douglas's notion of dirt as "matter out of place" as a useful analogy which is worth exploring more fully.[3] For Douglas, the designation "dirt" is based upon the way in which individuals and societies classify matter into appropriate and inappropriate elements: dirt is what is left over, what is rejected. Douglas also explored our approach to those elements which do not precisely fit our self-made categories, to those which are

---

[2] R. Murray Schafer referred to these as "signals." *The Soundscape: Our Sonic Environment and the Tuning of the World* (Rochester, VT: Destiny Books, 1994), 10.

[3] Mary Douglas, *Purity and Danger: An Analysis of the Concept of Pollution and Taboo* (London: Routledge, 2003), 41. Peter Bailey, "Breaking the Sound Barrier: A Historian Listens to Noise," *Body & Society* 2, no. 2 (1996): 50. Karen Bijsterveld, *Mechanical Sound: Technology, Culture, and Public Problems of Noise in the Twentieth Century* (Cambridge, MA: MIT Press, 2008), 37.

ambiguous or ambivalent; these categories have the potential to be redefined and incorporated into the approved category.[4] Noise as dirt is most evident in discussions about noise pollution and the harmful effect of the noises in our environment. This noise has been likened to "aural litter or aural trash," with the implication that it offers no meaningful message.[5] In worship, some sounds which in previous generations would have definitely been viewed negatively—for example, electronic music—are now viewed very positively in some churches.

In communication theory, noise is that which disrupts the transmission of a message. A deliberate interruption may occur in political protests or by silencing the speaker when one meaningful message is displaced by another which is "out of place." Or disordered sounds may jumble the signal so as to make audition impossible. Such sounds may not necessarily be noise in themselves, as Jacques Attali wrote: "Noise . . . does not exist in itself, but only in relation to the system within which it is inscribed: emitter, transmitter, receiver."[6] Attali suggested that "noise is violence," "a simulacrum of murder," in contrast to music which channels and organizes noise into "a simulacrum of sacrifice." These powerful images build on the idea of noise as dirt and pollution, which can be used as a weapon. There can be a message, too, in the disruption—one of power and censorship. At times of carnival these power relationships are temporarily overthrown, and a sign of this is the deployment of sounds/noises which are not normally permitted.

Erwin Straus distinguished sound and noise on the basis of their ontology. Sound, for him, has an ontological separation from its source; it is pure and autonomous, but "noise retains the character of indicating and pointing to."[7] As we have just seen, this is clearly the case with warning noises. Noise which interrupts also points to

---

[4] Douglas, *Purity and Danger*, 37.

[5] Charles W. Schmidt, "Noise That Annoys: Regulating Unwanted Sound," *Environmental Health Perspectives* 113, no. 1 (2005): A42–44.

[6] Jacques Attali, *Noise: The Political Economy of Music*, trans. Brian Massumi (Minneapolis: University of Minnesota Press, 1985), 26–27. Originally published as *Bruits: essai sur l'économie politique de la musique*, 1977.

[7] Erwin Straus, "The Forms of Spatiality," in *Phenomenological Psychology*, trans. Erling Eng, 3–37, here at 8 (New York: Basic Books, 1966).

its source. It promotes the source over the content, whereas sound always communicates and has value regardless of whether its source is known or not. Barry Smith makes this interesting comparison between sounds which originate in a subject and noises which originate in an object. Thus, he redefines some human "noises," such as groans, laughs, or cries, as a subject communicating experience even if the sounds are non-semantic; they are not noises but nonlinguistic communication.[8] If, as Smith, we concentrate on the source of the sound rather than the sound itself, that will cause a reassessment of our category of noise. Now we should not see noise as simply a disruption of, or an interference in, communication, but as the product of a thing or event. Inquiring into the event can change noise into sound.

Noise is subversive. Simon Reynolds has written that once we start to speak about noise, we give it cultural value and consequently tame it so that it no longer shocks; instead, he suggests, we should allow it to remain subversive.[9] The subversive nature of noise leads us to consider its social and political implications. Hillel Schwartz encouraged us to turn our attention away from the quality of the sound/noise (intensity, pitch, etc.) to how it reflects social relations and attitudes.[10] It is powerfully used in protests, as we shall see later with the events at Lumb church in the 1930s. Schwartz indicates its power: "Yet noise is a specific historic phenomenon that can signify more than outrage. It is an expressive and communicative resource that registers collective and individual identities, including those of nation, race and ethnicity . . . it is a ready form of social energy with the power to appropriate, reconfigure or transgress boundaries; it converts space into territory, often against the social odds."[11] Noise may be appropriated by the powerless as their voice against perceived injustice or oppression, but the designation of a group or

---

[8] Barry C. Smith, "Speech Sounds and the Direct Meeting of Minds," in *Sounds and Perception: New Philosophical Essays,* ed. Matthew Nudds and Casey O'Callaghan (Oxford: Oxford Academic, 2009).

[9] Simon Reynolds, "Noise," in *Audio Culture: Readings in Modern Music,* ed. Christoph Cox and Daniel Warner, chap. 10 (New York: Continuum, 2006).

[10] Hillel Schwartz, *Making Noise: From Babel to the Big Bang & Beyond* (New York: MIT Press, 2011), 20.

[11] Bailey, "Breaking the Sound Barrier," 64.

community's sound as "noise" reveals social hierarchies. As Karen Bijsterveld remarked, "The right to make noise, as well as the right to decide which sounds are allowed or forbidden, has long been the privilege of the powerful, whereas those lower in rank (women, children, servants) were supposed to keep silent, or were under suspicion of intentionally disturbing societal order by making noise. Positively evaluated loud and rhythmic sounds have had connotations of strength, significance, and being in control, whereas noise as unwanted sound has often been associated with social disruption."[12] A specific example of this was explored by Odd Are Berkaak concerning English Heritage's desire to create an appropriate sonic environment at Stonehenge.[13] Berkaak examined the principles behind the attempt to restore tranquility and dignity to the monument. Citing Jacques Attali's notion of "noise as denial of difference" for the way it imposes supposedly normative values on sound, Berkaak showed that the source of intrusion was the gathering of pagans, neodruids, and other spiritual groups who claimed the stone circle for their own ritual uses at the solstices and equinoxes. Their presence was like noise, which needs to be restrained. Behind English Heritage's aim, Berkaak sees the imposition of historically constructed English middle-class values favoring tranquility, in which anything not tranquil is "noise." The implicit discourse in the construction of tranquility at Stonehenge, through changes to landscaping and access, "does not just reduce other voices to silence but also bars the way to outsiders. Tranquility's binary other does not appear to be noise in the sense of loud sounds but intrusion . . . This inherited tranquility and silence, in its peculiarly English manifestation, creates a space where otherness is effectively shut out—an ontologically pure space."[14] Such ideas and attitudes are also prevalent in relation to historic churches and cathedrals, both within and outside worship. Noise is a sound

---

[12] Bijsterveld, *Mechanical Sound*, 40.
[13] English Heritage is a charity charged with caring for historic monuments and places in England.
[14] Odd Are Berkaak, "Noise and Tranquility at Stonehenge: The Political Acoustics of Cultural Heritage," in *The Oxford Handbook of Sound and Imagination*, vol. 1, ed. Mark Grimshaw-Aagaard, Mads Walther-Hansen, and Martin Knakkergaard, 315, 327 (Oxford: Oxford University Press, 2019).

made by someone else; it is a judgement on the sounds produced by people of whom we disapprove or wish to exclude. Noise is rarely made by ourselves.

Challenges to conventional classifications of noise as negatively perceived sounds have been made in the modern era. Highly influential was Luigi Russolo (1885–1947) in *The Art of Noises* (*L'arte dei Rumori*, 1913), where he explored the implications of the sound of industrial machinery on music and how technology would enable the creation of many more new, non-orchestral sounds. Noise, he wrote, "differs from sound . . . only to the extent that the vibrations it produces are confused and irregular."[15] His futurist manifesto advocated noise as a musical form, and he is considered as one of the first noise musicians, followed by others. Experimental composer Edgard Varèse (1883–1965) used industrial and urban sounds in his compositions.[16] Pierre Schaeffer (1910–1995), composer and musical theorist, also pioneered electronic music and incorporated "concrete" sounds from the real world into his compositions. He considered that all sounds were equal as they are experienced in the same way, and that sounds should not be evaluated on aesthetic terms.[17] Lastly, we could mention John Cage (1912–1992), who demanded a more intense and participative listening which was attentive to *all* sounds: "Wherever we are, what we hear is mostly noise. When we ignore it, it disturbs us. When we listen to it, we find it fascinating. The sound of a truck at fifty miles per hour. Static between the stations. Rain."[18] What unites these composers and musical theorists is their challenge to social conventions about the undesirability of certain noises and the challenge to listeners to attend more closely to a fuller range of sound. They invite us to reconsider what we designate as noise, and with what criteria.

---

[15] Luigi Russolo, *The Art of Noises* (*L'arte dei Rumori*), in *Audio Culture: Readings in Modern Music*, ed. Christoph Cox and Daniel Warner, 12 (New York: Continuum, 2006).

[16] Paul Griffiths, "Varèse, Edgard [Edgar]," in *Grove Music Online* (New York: Oxford University Press, 2001), n.p.

[17] Francis Dhomont, "Schaeffer, Pierre," in *Grove Music Online*, n.p.

[18] John Cage, "The Future of Music: Credo," in *Silence: Lectures and Writings*, 3 (Middletown, CT: Wesleyan University Press, 2011 [1st ed. 1961]).

Reactions to Noise

Noise may result in indifference or provoke strong reactions; rarely does it create a positive emotional response. Some intensities of sound will be universally perceived negatively because the decibel level is above that which the ear finds comfortable (around 80 decibels) or which is safe (over 130 decibels); reactions to low-level noise are much more subjective. Subjective responses can be due to the characteristics of the sound, such as its loudness, frequency, and periodicity, which produce emotions in the range from annoyance to anger. Even physiological sound sensitivity is also subjective.[19]

When we perceive a negatively experienced sound, we designate it as noise, but it is possible not to perceive it at all. Some noises can be "listened through"; that is, they are heard as noise but do not interfere with the listening experience, or are tolerated. We have become habituated to certain sounds such that, although we might categorize them as noise, we are largely indifferent to them. Low-level background noise and environmental noises generally go unnoticed, but in places and events where silence is expected, any sound is noise. So, as I work in the library, the noise of the city outside goes unnoticed; mostly the noise of typing can be ignored, but speech, mobile phones, and music leaking from headphones are definitely noises which I do not willingly tolerate.

Concern about the detrimental effect of environmental noise lay behind the noise-abatement campaigns of the twentieth century and were the impetus behind R. Murray Schafer's categorization of sounds in *Soundscape*. Noise can be considered as a harmful type of pollution, and it is particularly insidious because we are unable to shut our ears to it. In 1999 the World Health Organization produced a lengthy report, *Guidelines for Community Noise*, as a response to excessive exposure to intrusive noise levels in developed and developing countries and the lack of clear advice on the health impact and safe levels. They concluded that environmental sound was particularly problematic because, although the levels may not always be extremely high, the length of exposure has a cumulative effect. Detrimental health impacts were summarized as follows: "noise induced

---

[19] Bijsterveld, *Mechanical Sound*, 10.

hearing impairment; interference with speech communication; disturbance of rest and sleep; psychophysiologcal, mental-health and performance effects; effects on residential behaviour and annoyance; and interference with intended activities."[20] Consistent exposure to loud noises may also result in physiological problems related to high levels of psychological stress, such as susceptibility to viruses, heart disease, and high blood pressure.

There have been many acoustical analyses of church spaces (see chapter 8), but few which have evaluated exposure to noise during worship. A rare example is the investigation by Tiffany Bellamo's research group of noise levels in twenty congregations with very different worship styles in Washtenaw County, Michigan.[21] Safe levels for employees (worship leaders) and attendees (congregation) were determined according to Environmental Protection Agency guidelines. They found that 35 percent of measurements at the podium/altar were above recommended limits and posed a risk for staff and attendees, and that 8 percent exceeded the levels for occupational noise. The highest measurements were in nondenominational churches, where the source of noise exposure was primarily from the sound-amplification systems. They found that, despite the recorded levels being likely to result in noise-induced hearing loss, no institution had any noise-reduction processes. This does seem to reveal different attitudes to noise during worship, and noisy worship.

Theologies of Noise

Theological understandings of noise also implicitly underpin the censure of noise during worship. For centuries a key tenet of Christian doctrine has been *creatio ex nihilo*, the belief based on Genesis 1 that God created the world out of nothing. In this nothing there was a silence, a formless void, which was broken by God's creative act, described as speech.[22] The doctrine was elaborated by Athanasius,

---

[20] World Health Organization Occupational and Environmental Health Team, *Guidelines for Community Noise* (1999), viii.

[21] Tiffany R. Bellomo et al., "Characterization of Noise Exposure in Places of Worship," *Applied Acoustics* 180 (2021): 108–14.

[22] See Gary A. Anderson and Markus Bockmuehl, eds., *Creation Ex Nihilo: Origins, Development, Contemporary Challenges* (South Bend, IN: University of Notre Dame Press, 2017). Contributors to this volume review the development of the doctrine, as

Augustine, and Aquinas, among others, theologians active at the most formative periods for Christian liturgical development. An alternative and somewhat contrasting notion was developed by some Old Testament scholars who, interpreting Genesis 1:2 in light of Near Eastern myths, identified the formless void as "chaos" upon which God imposed order. *Chaos* in Greek means "void" or "emptiness"; however, David Toshio Tsumura demonstrates the semantic shift: chaos—emptiness—undistinguishedness—disorder—confusion—uncreation—evil.[23] Many have questioned the association of the pre-created world as chaos (i.e., disordered) rather than empty; however, the negative connotation persists in popular imagination.

The created world is, therefore, one where God speaks clearly, and noise is associated with the Fall. Most obviously, the association of noise with sin is made explicit in the story of Babel (Gen 11:1-10). In English an association was made between the biblical *Babel* and the unrelated Old English word *babble*, such that both signified disordered, incoherent, or meaningless speech.[24] Hillel Schwartz referred to the Tower of Babel as a supersonic Fall, after which "humanity became noisy unto itself."[25] Gregory the Great perceived God's voice as a whisper requiring silence, audible only in the absence of the inner and outer clamor. G. R. Evans summarized Gregory's teaching in his *Moralia on Job*: "the wrong sort of noise may be disturbing to tranquility. Those who 'sleep' without disciplining their minds to silence find their idle heads full of clanging and obtrusive noises (*turba, tumultus, perstrepitus*). Those who fall asleep to the world under discipline not only 'sleep' but 'dream,' experiencing the presence of God in the inward silence of their minds. Adam was created in that state. The Fall brings into man's head the noise of unruly desires."[26]

---

well as challenges posed to it by contemporary biblical scholarship and scientific cosmology.

[23] David Toshio Tsumura, "Chaos and Chaoskampf in the Bible: Is 'Chaos' a Suitable Term to Describe Creation or Conflict in the Bible?," in *Conversations on Canaanite and Biblical Themes: Creation, Chaos and Monotheism*, ed. Rebecca S. Watson and Adrian H. W. Curtis, 253–82 (Berlin: De Gruyter, 2022). Richard J. Clifford, "Creatio ex nihilo in the Old Testament/Hebrew Bible," in *Creation Ex Nihilo*, 55–76.

[24] See *OED*, s.v. "Babel" (n) and "babble" (n).

[25] Schwartz, *Making Noise*, 48.

[26] G. R. Evans, *The Thought of Gregory the Great* (Cambridge: Cambridge University Press, 1986), 103.

So if the fallen world and fallen humanity are noisy, for the Christian there is a moral and spiritual imperative to reject the noise of the world for the silence in which God can be heard. The ascetic and monastic movement institutionalized this quest. Paul Gehl shows how Augustine also promoted this in *Confessions* when he recounts a conversation with his mother, Monica, at Ostia. Their conversation ranged over spiritual topics and then "We returned to the clamor of our usual kind of speech, in which words have both beginnings and endings." Augustine continues meditating on achieving an ultimate silence, "so that we heard his Word not by means of a tongue of flesh, nor by the voice of an angel nor by the thundering of a cloud nor by the mystery of a mental image; so that we heard the Word himself, the one we love in all these things, yet heard him without them, created as they are."[27] As Gehl concludes, Augustine's setting for this conversation "within but remote from the crowd (*turbis remotus*), is echoed in the description of the conversation itself which, as merely human language, is noise (*strepitus*). So, right and holy language is surrounded by a meaningless noise which extends into the only half-closed circle of this private human conversation."[28] The noise of the world and of human speech is contrasted with the Word, a matter which will become essential in the Reformation churches' much closer association of this Word with the Word of Scripture.

It is then a small step to contrast the peace, order, tranquility of the saved and of heaven with its opposite, the noise and disorder of the absence of God, and ultimately hell. Hell is noisy; it must be so to create a proper contrast with a tranquil heaven. Schwartz draws attention to Bede's account of Dryhthelm's miraculous rising from the dead in which he saw, smelled, and heard the din of hell:

> When I had stood there a long time in great terror, uncertain what to do or where to turn or what end awaited me, I suddenly heard behind my back the sound of wild and desperate lamentation, accompanied by harsh laughter as though a rude mob were insulting their captured foes. As the noise grew clearer and fi-

---

[27] Augustine, *Confessions* 9.10, 24–25, in *Augustine: Confessions*, trans. Carolyn J.-B. Hammond, Loeb Classical Library 27, 46–49 (Cambridge, MA: Harvard University Press, 2016).

[28] Paul F. Gehl, "*Competens silentium*: Varieties of Monastic Silence in the Medieval West," *Viator* 18 (1987): 132.

nally reached me, I beheld a crowd of evil spirits, amid jeers and laughter, dragging five human souls, wailing and shrieking, into the midst of the darkness. I could see that one was tonsured like a clerk, one a layman, and one a woman. The evil spirits dragged them down into the midst of the burning pit; and it came about that, as they descended deeper, I was unable to discern clearly between human lamentations and devilish laughter, but there was a confused noise in my ears.

Finally, he sees the "the abodes of the blessed spirits," where he "heard the sweetest sound of people singing."[29] The noises of hell are produced by the evil spirits as well as the damned. In John Bunyan's sermon on the parable of the rich man and Lazarus, the former's cries from hell, which repeat the noise of sin, are described as follows:

> . . . it is like he was laughing, jesting, jearing, drinking, mocking, swearing, cursing, prating, persecuting of the godly in his prosperity, among his filthy companions; but now the case is otherwise; now he is in another frame; now his proud, stout, currish carriage is come down, as is clearly signified by these words, And he cried. Therefore by these words you may secondy observe, that the laughter of the ungodly will not last alwayes, but will be sure to end in a cry.[30]

It is no surprise, then, that hell is frequently depicted in medieval art as an open mouth surrounded by chaotic scenes. Gary D. Schmidt placed the origins of this iconography in tenth-century monastic reform in France under Odo, and in England under Dunstan, the latter producing the first depictions in the *scriptorium* in Winchester. From thence the key features of the iconography became commonplace in religious and popular contexts up to the Renaissance.[31] As a literary or exegetical theme it had developed much earlier as a

---

[29] Bede, *The Ecclesiastical History of the English People*, book V.XII, trans. Bertram Colgrave and R. A. B. Mynors, 492–95 (Oxford: Oxford Medieval Texts, 2022).

[30] John Bunyan, *A FEW Sighs from Hell: OR The Groans of a damned Soul: OR, An Exposition of those words in the 19th. of Luke, ver. 19. &c*, in *The Miscellaneous Works of John Bunyan*, vol. 1, ed. Roger Sharrock and Ted L. Underwood, 278 (Oxford: Clarendon Press, 2014).

[31] Gary D. Schmidt, *The Iconography of the Mouth of Hell: Eighth-Century Britain to the Fifteenth Century* (London: Susquehanna University Press, 1995), 19–24.

conflation of four main themes: hell as an open pit which swallows up unbelievers, Satan as a roaring lion who devours, Satan as a dragon, and the Leviathan. What changed was that the mouth of hell became anthropomorphic.[32] It was depicted in psalters and liturgical and devotional books, in wall paintings and relief sculptures, on church furniture and even a bishop's crozier,[33] and was brought to life in popular plays.[34] It formed, then, a visual warning against noise and its consequences.

The Book of Revelation (13:5-6) describes the beast: "The beast was given a mouth uttering haughty and blasphemous words, and it was allowed to exercise authority for forty-two months. It opened its mouth to utter blasphemies against God, blaspheming his name and his dwelling, that is, those who dwell in heaven." Revelation is full of powerful sonic representations of evil, and of triumph over evil. Thus, it was only yet another short step to equate noise with evil and demonic possession; demoniacs shouted blasphemies like the beast. The exorcism of evil spirits was a noisy affair, and those who were possessed could be identified by their noise. In the gospel, the Gerasene demoniac cried out in the tombs and shouted "at the top of his voice" (Mark 5; Luke 8:26-38); the two thousand pigs must have been pretty noisy, too. In the early church, exorcism was performed regularly as part of preparation for baptism, but these baptizands were not considered to be personally inhabited by evil spirits nor exhibiting noisy behavior. Nevertheless, combat with Satan by the exorcist involved loud adjurations of Satan and his spirits to leave the baptizands in order that the latter would be ready to receive Christ. Demoniac possession, evidenced by noisy behaviors, was dealt with primarily by either a holy man exercising his charism or by the relics of the saints, but it was not until the fifteenth century that formal liturgical texts were provided for exorcism.[35] Nancy

---

[32] Schmidt, *Iconography of the Mouth of Hell*, 32–34. See also Pamela Sheingorn, "'Who Can Open the Doors of His Face?' The Iconography of Hell Mouth," in *The Iconography of Hell*, ed. Clifford Davidson and T. H. Seiler, 1–19 (Kalamazoo, MI: Medieval Institute, 1992).

[33] Crozier Head, 14th century. Walters Art Museum, Baltimore, Accession No. 71.484.

[34] On popular drama, see the essays in *Iconography of Hell*, ed. Davidson and Seiler.

[35] Nancy Mandeville Caciola, *Discerning Spirits: Divine and Demonic Possession in the Middle Ages* (Ithaca, NY: Cornell University Press, 2015), chap. 5.

Mandeville Caciolab describes these exorcistic scripts as "a species of clamor with similarities to other such liturgies, such as excommunications, humiliations, and maledictions."[36] A "clamor," from the Latin *clamor/clamare* ("to shout or call out"), is a rhetorical form in which the volume of what is said is what makes it effective.[37] Among the ritual actions and words in these manuals are invocations in the "demonic language," which are unintelligible nonsense but mimic normal Latin.[38] The demoniac is also expected to speak for the demon so that it can describe itself and its effect, and the exorcist can direct his speech of expulsion more accurately.

For centuries, the Old English version of the Psalms has been used in worship, in which we frequently find the exclamation "Make a joyful noise unto the Lord." However, this is not noise, as we have defined it hitherto, but a pleasant sound which it is hoped will be pleasing to God. In normal social and theological contexts, noise is a sound which is negatively perceived for a whole variety of reasons, many of which remain implicit.

Noise in Worship

The discussion so far has looked at definitions of noise, the impact of noise, and how noise has been interpreted theologically; all these factors lie behind the identification and condemnation of noise in worship. Here I shall explore two main themes: noise as disruption, and noise as a socially constructed category linked to otherness. Congregations causing noise in worship, which disrupts the preacher, priest, or fellow worshippers, is a constant theme from late antiquity onwards; however, with the prioritization of hearing the Word in the Protestant churches, condemnations of such distractions became more systematic and commonplace.

Paul's statement that women should be silent in church (1 Cor 14:35) resulted in any female sounds being designated as noise; this includes their participation in the intentional sounds of worship, as well as disruptive noise. John Chrysostom complained that "there is

---

[36] Caciola, *Discerning Spirits*, 242.
[37] *OED*, s.v. "clamour," "clamor" (n).
[38] Caciola, *Discerning Spirits*, 247.

apt to be great noise among them, much clamor and talking, and nowhere so much as in this place. They may all be seen here talking more than in the market, or at the bath. For, as if they came hither for recreation, they are all engaged in conversing upon unprofitable subjects. . . . To such a degree should women be silent, that they are not allowed to speak not only about worldly matters, but not even about spiritual things, in the church."[39] Many other patristic writers comment in similar tones about women's chatter (Origen, for example[40]), but even men were guilty of chattering. Caesarius of Arles (c. 470–542) rebuked his congregation, "When you stand in church do not busy yourself in idle gossip with your neighbor. What is worse, there are people, some men but especially women, who talk so much in church that they neither hear the word of God themselves nor allow others to do so."[41] The medieval Western and Byzantine worshipper participated differently in the liturgy than their Reformation counterparts. Private devotions among the laity did not disturb the liturgical functions of the clergy; indeed, they were encouraged to engage in them. It is only in monastic contexts where silence was prioritized and noisy behavior was actively discouraged both for men and women, but then conversation was restricted outside the liturgy too.[42] It is no surprise that, with the focus of worship shifting to the sermon, people needed educating into a behaving in a quiet and orderly fashion.

The frequency with which noise, from speech and movement, is explicitly or implicitly criticized in English church homilies, canons, and visitation questions from the sixteenth and seventeenth centuries indicates that either the attempts to control it were largely unsuccess-

---

[39] John Chrysostom, *Hom. on 1 Timothy* 9.1, in *The Homilies of S. John Chrysostom, Archbishop of Constantinople, on the Epistles of St. Paul the Apostle to Timothy, Titus, and Philemon*, trans. J. P. Tweed, 69–70 (England: Rivington, 1853).

[40] Origen, *Hom. on Exodus* 13.3: "And especially, how do you think women understand in heart, who chatter so much, who disturb with their stories so much that they do not allow any silence?" *Origen: Homilies on Genesis and Exodus*, trans. Ronald E. Heine, Fathers of the Church, vol. 71 (Washington, DC: Catholic University of America Press, 2002), 379.

[41] Caesarius of Arles, *Sermon* 50.3, in *Caesarius: Sermons, Volume 1 (1–80)*, trans. Mary Magdeleine Mueller, Fathers of the Church, vol. 31, 255 (Washington, DC: Catholic University of America Press, 1956).

[42] See Gehl, "*Competens Silentium*," 125–60.

ful or that condemnation of noise was just a convention. In the Church of England's *Second Book of Homilies* of 1563, part 2 of the first homily warns against both:

> Note, well-beloved, what quietness in gesture and behaviour, what silence in talk and words is required in the house of God, for so he calleth it. See whether they take heed to their feet (as they be here warned) which never cease from uncomely walking and jetting up and down and overthwart the church, showing an evident signification of notable contempt both of God and all good men there present; and what heed they take to their tongues and speech which do not only speak words swiftly and rashly before the Lord (which they be here forbidden) but also oftentimes speak filthily, covetously and ungodly, talking of matters scarce honest or fit for the alehouse or tavern in the house of the Lord, little considering that they speak before God, who dwelleth in heaven . . .[43]

Canon 4.9 of 1571 is critical of "young men, especially countrymen (whose nature is more prone to the contempt of godliness and disorder)" that they should "neither ring bells, neither walk in the churches, nor have idle talk together, nor by laughing or noise or unhonest jesting, either let the minister or offend the people."[44] This is repeated in the canons of 1603 and again in 1874.[45] The latter also repeated the provisions of the 1860 Ecclesiastical Courts Jurisdiction Act for England and Wales, which made it an offense to "molest, let, disturb, vex or trouble or by any other unlawful means disquiet or misuse" any preacher or clergyman during divine service. It became a criminal offense to make a noise which prevented the minister from performing the liturgy.[46]

---

[43] Church of England, "An Homily of the Right Use of the Church or Temple of God, and of the Reverence Due Unto the Same," *Second Book of Homilies* (1563), in *The Books of Homilies: A Critical Edition*, ed. Gerald Bray, 205–16, here at 213 (Cambridge, UK: Lutterworth Press, 2015).
[44] Church of England, Canon 4 (1571), in Gerald Bray, *The Anglican Canons, 1529–1947*, Church of England Record Society Series, vol. 6 (Woodbridge, UK: Boydell & Brewer, 1998), 189.
[45] Church of England, Canon 18 (1603); Canon 56 (1874), in Bray, *Anglican Canons*, 288, 605.
[46] Ecclesiastical Courts Jurisdiction Act, 1860, Section 2, https://www.legislation.gov.uk/ukpga/Vict/23-24/32/section/2.

Francesca Cioni, in discussing disorderly worship in early seventeenth-century England, noted how the provision of seating introduced a new noise-scape. Fixed seating was intended to ensure good order in worship, both a social order through the hierarchical arrangement of seats and separation of the sexes, and an aural order by focusing attention forwards to the pulpit and altar.[47] This did not always work. Disputes over the allocation of pews could result in noisy disorder, as in the case of Edward Fosse versus Thomas Penrose of Sithney, Cornwall, in 1605. Fosse complained that his wife had been ejected from her pew at the beginning of service by a gang that "most Riottouslye and prophanelye and irreligiouslye repayred into the said parishes church," they "vsinge many foule vnseemlye and revillinge speaches towards" her, did "in most violent fierye barbarous and cruell manner breake open and enter into [Fosse's wife's] seate." Having violently assaulted and ejected her from the seat, the group "departed from the said church, much reioycing and bragging and triumphinge of that they had done."[48] The ritual requirements of Elizabethan worship could also be a cause of noise as people shifted in their (uncomfortable) wooden pews. The *Admonition to Parliament*, 1572, complained that "When Jesus is named, then of goth the capp and downe goeth the knees, with suche a scraping of the ground, that they cannot heare a good while after so that the word is hindred."[49]

Accusations of noisy behavior go both ways. In *Fosse v. Penrose*, the latter countered that it was not his supporters who had behaved riotously but Fosse's. And in 1616, a supporter of reverent rituals complained that those who refused to perform them were "like Elephants . . . they have no joints in their knees, they talk, whisper, and gaze about, without any kind of bodily reverence, and, as it may be thought, without any inward devotion at all."[50] This highlights a point made earlier, that noise is the sound of others and that accusations of noisiness in worship are signs of more widespread opposition

---

[47] Francesca Cioni, "'Confuse Noises, and Clatterings': Fixed Seating and Disorderly Worship in England, 1604–1632," *The Seventeenth Century* 35 (2020): 557–77.

[48] Cioni, "'Confuse Noises,'" 564.

[49] Laura Feitzinger Brown, "Brawling in Church: Noise and the Rhetoric of Lay Behavior in Early Modern England," *The Sixteenth Century Journal* 34 (2003): 968.

[50] Cioni, "'Confuse Noises,'" 563; Brown, "Brawling in Church," 970.

to individuals, as well as to forms of worship and church practice. The Puritan Ralph Buckland condemned the prayers of the Church of England as animal noises: "You erre if you THINKE their PRAiERS to be PRAiERS, whatsoever they say, what soever they sing, it is in my eares the howling of Wolves, the bellowing of Bulles, the Screetching of Owles, the mutual answering of night Ravens in the deserts."[51] Anglicans responded, as shown by Helen Wilcox's short article about Puritan "nose-twang," an insulting and satirical term for the noise of a Puritan preacher from the early seventeenth century onwards. She cites a poem by John Polwhele from the 1630s which contrasted the good order of established worship with the "nose-twang spoyling harmonie" of the Puritans.[52] Catholic worship and anything thought to resemble it (e.g., some forms of Anglican ritualist worship) was likened to Babel or even to the pagan worship of Babylon.[53]

Condemning the sounds of worship of others as noise is clearly a way of denigrating them; however, a group may adopt noise as a sign of subversion when excluded from power structures. In chapter 1 we discussed the soundscape of early Pentecostal worship. Grant Wacker commented that contemporaries described this worship as "deafening," and journalists used a range of negative epithets to describe the sound of the early revival movement: "jabbering in a strange gibberish," "howlings of worshippers," "the rapid chattering of a frightened simian," "hideous noise," "moan, scream and speak unintelligible words," "chatter, scream, gnash their teeth," "laughing, high-trebled, piercing exclamations," "barking like dogs, hooting like owls," and "unearthly shrieks and groans."[54] Daniels commented that Pentecostal sound was subversive, and that Pentecostals were also the subject of noise-abatement campaigns which attempted to exert social control. Their noise identified them as different: "The syntax of early Pentecostal sound was challenged by the majority of

---

[51] Brown, "Brawling in Church," 955.

[52] Helen Wilcox, "Puritans, George Herbert and 'Nose-Twange,'" *Notes and Queries* 26 (1979): 152–53.

[53] See Brown, "Brawling in Church," 966–67.

[54] Grant Wacker, *Heaven Below: Early Pentecostals and American Culture* (Cambridge, MA: Harvard University Press, 2001), 100. This list is summarized in David D. Daniels III, "'Gotta Moan Sometime': A Sonic Exploration of Earwitnesses to Early Pentecostal Sound in North America," *Pneuma* 30 (2008): 12.

their Protestant counterparts on the larger American religious soundscape."[55] And it also was used by them as a marker of social identity: "Early Pentecostals employed noise, silence, music-making, musicality, and the sonic organization of humanity to construct their Christian identity, locate themselves in the society, engage in culture-crossing, and advance a nonracialism that countered the hierarchies of race advanced by the government and the majority society."[56] What was noise for those outside was considered a sweet and joyful sound to those within.

Intentionally noisy devotions, such as wailing, groaning, and loud tears, did in certain cultural contexts arouse criticism. Margery Kempe (c. 1373–1438), in her *Book*, records some particularly disruptive bouts of weeping, cries, and screaming during her private devotions in church and at Mass. During her pilgrimage to the holy sites in Jerusalem, at each location the *Book* records that she engaged in loud, boisterous, and unrestrained sobbing.[57] At Mass, she would weep and cry so loudly that she was given communion in a private chapel, but when this arrangement stopped and she returned to her parish church, her shouts could be heard in the street outside.[58] Although tears were approved of as a practice of piety by most clergy, clearly other parishioners considered it unusual to say the least. Santha Bhattacharji comments that Kempe seemed quite unaffected by disapproval of her noise, unlike the embarrassment of other medieval women with the gift of pious tears and screams, such as Marie d'Oignies and Angela of Foligno.[59] In the seventeenth century, opponents of formal liturgy promoted prayer in the Spirit, which did not necessarily require words. John Craig cites George Foxley's 1639 treatise, *The Groanes of the Spirit or the Triall of the Truth of Prayer*, in which the author argued that "Prayer . . . consisteth not in words, though they be ornat, or well set forth with seeming holynesse, but

---

[55] Daniels, "'Gotta Moan Sometime,'" 12–13.

[56] Daniels, 20.

[57] Margery Kempe, chap. 29 in *The Book of Margery Kempe*, ed. Anthony Bale (Oxford: Oxford University Press, 2016).

[58] Santha Bhattacharji, "Tears and Screaming: Weeping in the Spirituality of Margery Kempe," in *Holy Tears: Weeping in the Religious Imagination*, ed. John Stratton Hawley and Kimberley Christine Patton, 232–33 (Princeton, NJ: Princeton University Press, 2018).

[59] Bhattacharji, "Tears and Screaming," 236.

in powering out of the heart by sighes and groanes inexpressible."[60] For the godly Puritans, groaning for their sins was an acceptable noise in worship and a sign of prayer, but noise could intrude into the sermon when listeners might respond with sighs, exclamations, or murmurings. As Craig notes, this contradicted the injunctions for quiet and orderly participation enjoined in official church documents.[61]

A noise which would have been common in early modern England, and which would be considered highly inappropriate in contemporary worship, is that arising from the presence of dogs. Craig presented evidence from churchwardens' records for dog-whippers, employed to chase dogs out of church and to keep order among those in church. He cites Bishop Whitgift's injunctions at Worcester Cathedral of 1577, in which the beadsmen and sextons were to ensure "in the time of public service or of sermons there be no walking, talking, crying or playing of children, or fighting or brawling of dogs." The presence of dogs was not the issue, but the behavior of them was: fighting other dogs, disturbing worshippers with aggressive behavior, wandering around, and ringing bells attached to their collars. Statements were made against dogs attending church in subsequent centuries, but, Craig shows, these were largely ineffectual.[62]

A vexed issue in some worship environments is the noise of children, and most discussion of this rarely goes beyond the level of anecdotes of particularly disruptive episodes. Some churches adopt strategies which separate the children from normal worship: soundproofed rooms, separate worship, special seating areas in the church, or "family Masses." Others rarely make such provision, such as the Eastern Orthodox churches, and yet others employ children for a variety of liturgical ministries. Lydia Van Leersum-Bekebrede compared the experience in two contemporary Dutch congregations.[63]

---

[60] George Foxley, *The Groanes of the Spirit or the Triall of the Truth of Prayer* (Oxford, 1639), 7–8. Cited in John Craig, "Psalms, Groans and Dog-Whippers: The Soundscape of Sacred Space in the English Parish Church, 1547–1642," in *Sacred Space in Early Modern Europe*, ed. Will Coster and Andrew Spicer, 109 (Cambridge: Cambridge University Press, 2005).

[61] Craig, "Psalms, Groans and Dog-Whippers," 113.

[62] Craig, 113–21.

[63] Lydia Van Leersum-Bekebrede et al., "Sounds of Children in Worship: Materiality and Liturgical-Ritual Spaces," *Material Religion* 17, no. 5 (2021): 557–79.

In the first, a Surinamese Lutheran congregation, the children chatted, ran around, and shouted during the service, and these sounds were greeted with tolerance. Mirella Klomp had concluded that this was because the community was inclusive, participatory, and was not so concerned about the aesthetics of worship; however, the children did not contribute at all to the ritual performance.[64] In the second congregation, a Reformed church influenced by pietism, the younger children had Bible classes in soundproofed rooms while older ones were present but made quiet sounds; here, though, children's sound-making was channeled into the choir where it was highly respected. These two reports reveal attitudes to worship which are influenced by ecclesiology—who is the church; by social attitudes; and by the sonic traditions of congregations—but they reveal unspoken attitudes to the way in which sound is considered as noise. Adults can also be noisy in worship, even though it is assumed that, unlike children, they know the norms of participation, but their presence is never questioned. Many adult noises are those which break social conventions, e.g., the repertoire of bodily noises: breaking wind, belches, yawns. Then there are those which indicate a lack of attentiveness: sniggers, foot tapping or finger drumming, the chinking of loose change in pockets. And then there are those which are definitely "dirt" and sound out of place: mobile phones ringing, beeping, or audibly vibrating.

The purposeful intrusion of noise in worship has been used as a sign of protest, and in England and Wales it could be punished by fines under the 1860 Ecclesiastical Courts Jurisdiction Act. In the late 1920s and into the 1930s in the parish of Lumb-in-Rossendale, near Manchester, a long-running dispute between the vicar and parishioners made news headlines and ended up in the ecclesiastical and civil courts. The *Manchester Guardian* of December 23, 1929, records, "There was an unusually large congregation for Matins and the Vicar's words were completely inaudible during the greater part of the service owing to continuous coughing, shuffling of feet, and kicking and knocking on the woodwork of the pews. . . . As the noises

---

[64] Mirella Klomp, *The Sound of Worship: Liturgical Performance by Surinamese Lutherans and Ghanaian Methodists in Amsterdam*, Liturgia Condenda 26 (Leuven: Peeters, 2011).

continued the Vicar went to the door to call the police who were again on duty outside, into the porch . . . The congregation, with six exceptions, filed out of the church before the sermon."[65] A week later the police had to enter the church during morning service to restore order. The use of noise to express disapproval of the minister or the form of worship has a long history.

Also intruding into worship is noise from outside the church. Legislation about permitted activities on Sundays were not only to ensure proper regard for the Christian Sabbath, but also to reduce distracting noises in the surrounding environment. In the modern era, the amount of background noise in the environment has increased and humans have shown great ability to adapt to it, such that it is normally not noticed. These sounds are often machine made: traffic, pedestrian crossing signals, train whistles, airplanes, or air-conditioning and heating systems. They form the background to the daily life of worshippers, and our attention to them varies. Charles Hirschkind wrote that "sound and aurality are part of the material-sensory world that human life must accommodate and respond to,"[66] and, in theological terms, the presence of the worshipping Body of Christ in that sonic environment witnesses to the incarnation.

Conclusion

Our attitudes to noise in worship are formed implicitly, but we express our reactions to it in very clear terms. Generally, we designate a sound as noise according to subjective criteria and social conventions, and just as we judge the sound negatively, so also we judge the maker of noise negatively. When the source is an inanimate object, the consequences are not so bad, as the machine or similar can be removed or switched off. But when the noise-maker is a member of the congregation, then we need to consider afresh our presuppositions about acceptable sound-making and to reevaluate our attitudes to other people. The former goes to the heart of what we think worship

---

[65] "More Noise at Lumb Church: Police Called into Porch. Protestors' Open-Air Service," *Manchester Guardian*, December 23, 1929.

[66] Charles Hirschkind, "Religion," in *Keywords in Sound*, ed. David Novak and Matt Sakakeeny, 168 (Durham: Duke University Press, 2015).

is: the dominance of the sermon after the Reformation required a much more tranquil environment than the multisensory, multi-participative medieval parish Mass. Our theologies and practices of worship are formed in ever-changing ecclesial and social contexts, and these directly influence the way we hear noise. What is clear, though, is that noise is a sound which intrudes and which directs our attention away from the listening activity which is required from us at that moment. Worshippers are required to pay attention to the intentional sounds of worship, and how successfully they might do that is the subject of the next chapter.

Chapter 7

Paying Attention

Even of those who do come [to church], we find many behaving themselves in such a careless Manner, as if the Worship of God was either not their Business there, or not worth minding,- Some sit all the Time of the Prayers; or put themselves into such other lazy and irreverent Postures, as shew sufficiently that they have no Sense of what they should be doing, nor any Awe or Reverence of the glorious Being they come to address. Others lay themselves to sleep, or trifle away their Time thinking of their worldly Affairs. Others gaze and stare upon the Congregations, or keep talking and whispering with their Neighbours; and this is especially observable while the Lessons are reading; as if the Holy Scriptures, though given by Inspiration of God, were not always to be heard, marked, learned and inwardly digested, . . . Others there are, who do indeed shew some Inclination to mind the Prayers and all the rest of the Service; but they do it with so much Ignorance, Distraction, or Confusion, as discover that they do not rightly understand the Difference between one Part of the Service and another . . . We often find them repeating after the Minister what he alone should speak, and they should only hearken to. They are also apt, when they join the Prayers, to say them after him so loud, as must needs be troublesome, and disturb those that are near them. . . .[1]

---

[1] *Directions for a devout and decent behaviour in the public worship of God; more particularly in the use of the Common Prayer appointed by the Church of England* (London: F. and C. Rivington, 1799).

So wrote the anonymous author of the tract *Directions for a devout and decent behaviour in the public worship of God; more particularly in the use of the Common Prayer appointed by the Church of England*, first published in the early 1700s. It was so popular that by 1799 it had reached the thirtieth edition and had been translated into both Welsh (1752) and French (1751). Of course, such concerns were not only the preserve of those with set forms of liturgy; the 1645 *Directory of Public Worship*, prepared on Presbyterian principles, also required the following:

> The publick worship being begun, the people are wholly to attend upon it, forbearing to read any thing, except what the minister is then reading or citing; and abstaining much more from all private whisperings, conferences, salutations, or doing reverence to any person present, or coming in; as also from all gazing, sleeping, and other indecent behaviour, which may disturb the minister or people, or hinder themselves or others in the service of God.

In the *Directory*, signs of inattentiveness are exhibited in the sort of behaviors which, we have seen, result in noise, but in the *Directions for a devout and decent behaviour in the public worship of God* the writer is much more concerned with the interior disposition of the worshippers which results in these behaviors. Aural attentiveness is certainly a mental activity which can be demonstrated by physical behaviors, but in religious terms it is often presented as a sign of spiritual maturity. Paying attention in worship is certainly a desirable thing, but deciding what it is and how it is achieved is complicated by the different ways it manifests itself.

What Is Aural Attentiveness?

As we have already indicated, we do not have "ear flaps" which allow us to physically switch off the sound signals entering our ears. We are, though, capable of separating sound signals so that we hear one but exclude the others. This is called "selective auditory attention." How we do this has been the subject of some interesting research from the 1950s onwards, primarily among psychologists and more recently by cognitive scientists. Their focus has been on hearing speech, but the findings seem to be applicable to chant as well.

In 1953, Colin Cherry identified the "cocktail party effect" where, in an environment with multiple conversations, we are able to focus upon the one in which we are involved and exclude those around us—until, that is, some external stimulus, such as hearing our own name, causes us to switch our attention.[2] In these contexts, we are fully aware of the other sounds, but we have chosen to ignore them, and as Donald E. Broadbent, writing in 1958, showed, we are able to filter out some sounds.[3] It seems, therefore, that there is an intermediate stage, between the sound entering the ear and the brain making sense of it, before the sounds are processed. This is necessary because we only have a limited capacity for processing among the other simultaneous cognitive tasks. However, the processing-out of unwanted sounds is not total, because clearly some sounds are able to break through our focus and impinge upon our awareness, and we have some limited ability to recall them. Thus it was proposed that there is a "bottleneck" in processing auditory signals; some receive full processing, whereas others get stuck in the bottleneck and do not make it through. Barbara Shinn-Cunningham referred to it as a competition between sound objects which occurs in the brain, but what wins out will be determined by our own goals and inner disposition just as much as the external stimuli; this was confirmed by Alexandra Bendixen and Iring Koch.[4] It is also possible to be so focused on one sound source that we completely fail to hear another one; this is called "inattentional deafness." In this situation, we can recall very little about the rejected source.

---

[2] Donald Cherry's original research was published here: "Some Experiments on the Recognition of Speech, with One and with Two Ears," *Journal of the Acoustical Society of America* 25 (1953): 975–79. The subsequent research is so vast that I will rely on the surveys provided by these authors: Elizabeth Styles, *The Psychology of Attention* (New York: Psychologists Press, 2006); Alfred W. Bronkhorst, "The Cocktail-Party Problem Revisited: Early Processing and Selection of Multi-Talker Speech," *Attention, Perception & Psychophysics* 77, no. 5 (2015): 1465–87; Barbara Shinn-Cunningham, "Auditory Selective Attention," in *The Handbook of Attention*, ed. Jonathan Fawcett et al., 99–117 (Cambridge, MA: MIT Press, 2015).

[3] Donald E. Broadbent, *Perception and Communication* (New York: Pergamon Press, 1958).

[4] Shinn-Cunningham, "Auditory Selective Attention," 101; Alexandra Bendixen and Iring Koch, "Editorial for Special Issue: 'Auditory Attention: Merging Paradigms and Perspectives,'" *Psychological Research* 78 (2014): 301–3.

A number of factors seem to influence what is attended to, which relate to the sound itself, the speech message, and the recipient. The quality of the sound—loudness, pitch, and timbre—are obviously important, but research has shown that memory of previous speech by the same person also makes it more likely that it will be attended to.[5] An abrupt sound will trigger an immediate shift in attention and often a visual response, too; "hearing is an important early warning system and as such must be constantly sensitive to new sounds arriving from different locations, even when we are engaged in another task."[6] So our ears need to be open to receive these warning signals, but as we are unable to process all sounds at once, we select the sound source which fits our needs and desires at each moment. Our auditory attention is a balance between "voluntary prioritisation of currently relevant stimuli and . . . a more involuntary capture of attention," which means that, despite our best efforts to control our capacity to be attentive, there is always the potential for distraction.[7] We can shift our total attention from one source to another and continue with the same level of attentiveness as before, or, as sometimes happens, we find ourselves surrounded by sounds whose signals are jumbled; this we call "noise."

All listening environments have multiple sound sources, and to focus on one requires two tasks: "One is to separate, at any time, target elements from other speech (*segregation*). The other is to connect elements across time (*streaming*)." Segregation happens at a pre-attentive phase, where the sounds are ordered for future processing on the basis of voice characteristics and the "spatial separation of the target and interfering sources."[8] Once the sounds are separated, then the signals from the one to which we wish to attend can be coherently ordered into a meaningful message. Streaming is the selection and grouping of sounds based upon already known patterns, and for this we need to tune in so that we attend to a single one and exclude the rest. Learned and practiced patterns mean our ability to

---

[5] Scott Bressler et al., "Bottom-Up Influences of Voice Continuity in Focusing Selective Auditory Attention," *Psychological Research* 78, no. 3 (2014): 349–60.

[6] Styles, *Psychology of Attention*, 138.

[7] Polly Dalton and Robert W. Hughes, "Auditory Attentional Capture: Implicit and Explicit Approaches," *Psychological Research* 78 (2014): 313–20, here at 313.

[8] Bronkhorst, "Cocktail-Party Problem Revisited," 1471.

do this becomes refined over time.[9] It will be interesting to see later in this chapter how early modern writers emphasized both the elimination of nonrelevant sounds, as well as the training of the ear to enable proper attentiveness to the sermon.

The pertinence, or salience, of the sound signal's content is clearly important: sound signals with low informational content, often ambient sounds, will be filtered out, so that we can process what we deem to be significant. Shinn-Cunningham notes that when in a state of high auditory focus, the chosen sound source takes on an overriding priority in our processing system. This can result in inattentional deafness to other sound sources present in the environment; the unwanted information is filtered out and never processed, regardless of the actual importance of the content. Similarly, inattentional deafness can occur when there are high demands on the auditory and processing system.[10] These demands can be such that other sensory stimuli, such as touch, are also ignored.

Investigations into how we process sounds, especially speech, have highlighted the role of memory. In normal speech situations, listeners are rarely focused on every individual word but upon the meaning conveyed by the whole discourse. Attentiveness does not mean, therefore, a complete focus upon every syllable or word, but upon the meaning conveyed through sentences and in the back-and-forth of a conversation. Only when the whole utterance has been transmitted will the listener know whether it was worth attending to or not. It has been suggested that we have a brief high-capacity memory in which sounds are stored for several seconds before processing. Even the unimportant sounds are stored temporarily, which was demonstrated by Ulrich Neisser and identified as echoic memory. He showed, as we probably know from our own experience, that when we ask a speaker to repeat what she has just said, we are able to respond or complete the sentence before they have uttered it again.[11] This temporary memory is also important when listening to longer discourses, when we need to construct meaning from an argument

---

[9] Important research on this was undertaken by Albert S. Bregman, *Auditory Scene Analysis: The Perceptual Organization of Sound* (Cambridge, MA: MIT Press, 1990).
[10] Shinn-Cunningham, "Auditory Selective Attention," 107.
[11] Styles, *Psychology of Attention*, 128.

set out over a period of time; our memory capacity enables us to combine what we heard earlier with what we hear now to construct coherent meaning.

Speech to which we have been attentive will be retained in the long-term memory and is available for recall after the event. Our long-term memory also operates when we are only partially attentive to a speech in the present which is the same or close to that which we have heard before, and in these cases we are able to use our memory to fill in the blanks. In liturgical worship, frequently repeated texts are retained in our memories, and when we perform them it is often unclear whether we recite from memory or participate in the present performance of the text. It appears that, as Kristina Backer and Claude Alain suggested, "attention is a balancing act between focusing on events from our external and internal worlds."[12] The early modern treatises are helpful here, because they also encourage memory strategies to enhance attention on the sermon; above all, the regular private meditation on Scripture provides a foundation for recall of familiar texts during the sermon and thus enables the listener to tune in more effectively.

Sound arrives in both ears, and the imperceptible "interaural time difference" enables us to locate the sources without turning our ears, as we need to do with our eyes. It seems we are able to prioritize one ear, choosing to attend to one spatially located sound over another, either intuitively or as an act of will. However, there can be a failure to select or focus on one because of competing sounds at nearby locations, or the sound is muddled and its source cannot be identified; consequently, the listener is distracted and not properly inattentive to any of the sounds.[13] Certain strategies can compensate or improve our ability to select: the speaker might give cues to the listener about the priority of his speech, or we might consciously decide to orientate ourselves to one sound by moving our head. In chapter 3 we presented the gospel procession as an example of ritualized listening, and here we can see how it operates to direct the attentiveness of listeners to the priority of the speech event through auditory and

---

[12] Kristina C. Backer and Claude Alain, "Attention to Memory: Orienting Attention to Sound Object Representations," *Psychological Research* 78 (2014): 440.

[13] Shinn-Cunningham, "Auditory Selective Attention," 103.

visual clues. Styles explained that auditory cues can attract both auditory and visual attention, but that visual cues on their own have no effect on auditory attention. The senses clearly combine in our perception of the world, but for aural attentiveness there is a limit to this because of the need to actively select one signal over another. Thus Styles noted that it is not possible to combine two auditory and two visual tasks at the same time, but we are able to combine taste, touch, and smell without interference.[14] Dana Raveh and Nilli Lavie showed that a high visual-perceptual load will result in decreased hearing sensitivity even as we are expecting an auditory stimulus. They called this "load-induced deafness" and concluded that it demonstrated that our capacity for attentiveness is shared between vision and hearing.[15] Nevertheless, attentiveness does seem to be related to the position of the sound object in space and is improved if we are able to visually focus on it; however, inattentional deafness will occur if the demands for visual attentiveness are too dominant.

These reflections on the role of space and the senses in attentiveness lead us to further consider the embodied experience of worship. Thomas Csordas reiterates that embodiment is not the same as the body; embodiment combines perceptual experience, the mode of presence, and engagement with the world, and is thus more than our material physicality. Combining Maurice Merleau-Ponty's notion that perception is always embedded in the cultural world with Pierre Bourdieu's notions of the socially informed body and *habitus*, Csordas proposed "somatic modes of attention," which he defined as "culturally elaborated ways of attending to and with one's body in surroundings that include the embodied presence of others." It requires sensory engagement with an object which is attended to with the body through the physical operation of the senses rather than simply at a cognitive level. This sensing of the world, and the way we employ our senses to do so, is culturally constituted and not just a physical process.[16] Our worship traditions reveal, usually implicitly, a particular mode

---

[14] Styles, *Psychology of Attention*, 6.

[15] Dana Raveh and Nilli Lavie, "Load-Induced Inattentional Deafness," *Attention, Perception, & Psychophysics* 77, no. 2 (2015): 483–92.

[16] Thomas Csordas, "Somatic Modes of Attention," *Cultural Anthropology* 8, no. 2 (1993): 135–56.

of bodily, sensorial attentiveness through the dynamic of active and passive participation through rituals and sacraments, all of which are culturally determined, that is developed from historical, theological, and social contexts. Hitherto we have been concerned with individual listeners and their cognitive processes to be attentive or not, but Csordas asks us to consider attentiveness as a cultural phenomenon, that is, something developed and practiced in congregational or ecclesial contexts. Varied worship styles across denominations clearly make different demands upon what or who is to be attended to, how the senses are combined or prioritized, and how that is manifested bodily, even though all would say that, ultimately, the congregation is to be attentive to God.

Attentiveness as a Dimension of Ethics and Spirituality

Attentiveness as an ethical and spiritual practice reveals theological and philosophical ideas of the relationship between ourselves, the world, and God.

Nicholas Davey proposed a hermeneutic of attentiveness drawn in part from Iris Murdoch's essays on moral philosophy in *The Sovereignty of Good* (1970). For Murdoch, attentiveness changes the quality of an experience by transforming our everyday consciousness through the surrendering of ourselves to the world. It works in two directions which join the external world to our interior perception: "Attentiveness is centripetal in that it is a heightened mode of being aware and centrifugal in that it entails a sharpened consciousness of what it is aware of."[17] Attentiveness denotes a focus beyond oneself through which comes the realization of something more, and by which one acquires knowledge of the reality of the other. As Davey continues, "The disposition of attentiveness to the voice of another, albeit a text, artifact, or person, is essentially a *dialogical* disposition in that it is willing to listen, its spirit of questioning springs from both an honest recognition of its own limitations of understanding and its desire to understand more, and it is open to the risk of having its initial presuppositions about a subject-matter substantially trans-

---

[17] Nicholas Davey, "On the Polity of Experience: Towards a Hermeneutics of Attentiveness," *Renascence* LVI.4 (2004): 220.

formed."[18] The transformation is not just about some*thing*, but also of ourselves; attentiveness requires us to overcome our subjectivism, but in doing so we "become more fully aware of who we are by moving both beyond and yet towards ourselves."[19]

Murdoch's ideas were developed from an ethical approach to attention which is found in Simone Weil, who also started from the idea that attention is the subjugation of the self. As Eric O. Springsted summarizes, "Attention has the flavor of altruism to it, or, better put, a sense of self-sacrifice, of kenosis, the self-emptying that allows another sufficient room in which to exist."[20] Attention is based on love, faith, desire, and consent and is contrasted with will, language, and the intellect. It is, thus, an ethical turning to the other so that they are seen (and heard), and a contemplation without words which happens in the heart of the inner person and not in the intellect. It is, then, for Weil as for many others, like prayer: "Absolutely unmixed attention is prayer"[21]: a turning to an object which lies beyond oneself, is as yet unknown or inconceivable. "Attention alone—that attention which is so full that the 'I' disappears—is required of me. I have to deprive all that I call 'I' of the light of my attention and turn it on to that which cannot be conceived."[22] In French, *attention* is derived from *attendre*—"to wait" or "to expect." This multi-valency brings a new dimension to our anglophone discussion. Attentiveness is not simply about the way in which audition functions but is about contemplation, and this is what the monastic and ascetic movement in the early church sought to achieve.

Inbar Gravier has examined the centrality of attentiveness in monastic spiritual discipline in late antiquity; the monks aimed to "develop a constant sense of divine presence and devote themselves single-mindedly to the contemplation of God."[23] This was to be

---

[18] Davey, "On the Polity of Experience," 229.
[19] Davey, 233.
[20] Eric O. Springsted, *Simone Weil for the Twenty-First Century* (South Bend, IN: University of Notre Dame Press, 2021), 56.
[21] Simone Weil, "Attention and Will," in *Gravity and Grace* (New York: Putnam, 1952), 169–76.
[22] Weil, "Attention and Will," 169–76.
[23] Inbar Gravier, "The Paradoxical Effects of Attentiveness," *Journal of Early Christian Studies* 24, no. 2 (2016): 199.

achieved by prayer, and by the ascetic practices which diminished distractions or temptation and required attention to oneself. Psalmody and repetitive prayer, along with bodily practices, controlled and stilled the mind so that the monk could achieve the continual contemplation of God. Attentiveness begins by taming the thoughts in one's mind. Mark the Monk explained, "The cause of everything that happens to a person is something that person has thought (αἰτία ἐστιν ὁ λογισμός). I ought to have said that this includes both words and deeds, but since these do not precede thought, I attribute everything to thoughts. With thought leading the way, words and deeds follow."[24] For the monks, training the sensory dispositions is related to the discipline of their inner inclinations. It is within this program that we should place the exemplary physical attentiveness so obvious in the reports of monastic liturgy, where they both practiced and exhibited the total contemplation developed through individual spiritual activity. The monk is to be attentive to and for the signs of God's presence in his own and others' lives which are conveyed from Scripture, worship, daily life, and ascetic practice. Although all these require the operation of the senses, this attentiveness is not primarily auditory, but arises in the heart and mind.

Direct speech from God is rarely attested in the monastic literature; instead, we often find monks trying *not* to hear speech from the devil and his proxies. The relationship between temptation and attention was interestingly explored by Günter Bader in light of Martin Luther and Immanuel Kant. For Kant, attention has a twofold characteristic, positive and negative, each of which arises from a decision to turn towards something or someone, or to turn away. In negative attention, the subject never loses control of his cognitive processes, whereas positive attention is ruled by the senses. Temptation was, for Kant, a perversion of positive attention.[25] On Luther, Bader starts with his 1541 German translation of Isaiah 28:19, *"Anfechtung lehrt auf das Wort merken,"* which can be rendered, "Temptation leads to attention to

---

[24] Mark the Monk, *A Monastic Superior's Disputation with an Attorney* 18, in *Counsels on the Spiritual Life: Mark the Monk*, trans. Tim Vivian and Augustine Casiday, 229 (Crestwood, NY: St. Vladimir's Seminary Press, 2009). Cited by Gravier, "Paradoxical Effects of Attentiveness," 207.

[25] See Günter Bader, "La tentation comme attention— l'attention comme tentation," *Revue de théologie et de philosophie* 146, no. 2 (2014): 139–41.

the Word," although one would not find that in any modern translation of the Old Testament. This, Bader finds, corresponds to both the monastic and Kantian view: temptation can only be countered by a yes/no decision to be attentive to the Word.[26]

(In)attentiveness in Worship

In every generation it seems that those who have bothered to turn up to church have not also been bothered to pay attention once they got there. Although inattentiveness can manifest itself physically (by fidgeting) or visually (by looking around), it is auditory attention which is particularly enjoined upon congregations, with these other activities being manifestations of an auditory inattentiveness. The historical sources provide clues as to what was considered inattentive behavior and strategies to alleviate it.

Robert Taft gave a typically colorful summary of the problem in the early church:

> One should not imagine the congregation primly seated like Methodists at a wedding in Indianapolis. . . . Late Antique congregations in East and West were an unruly lot, wandering around and chattering even during the Scripture readings and homily. Chrysostom in Constantinople (398–404) accuses his congregation of roaming around; of either ignoring the preacher or pushing and shoving to hear him, when not bored or downright exasperated with him; of talking, especially during the homily and Scripture lessons; of leaving before the services are over . . . and, in general, of causing an uproar and acting—the words are Chrysostom's—as if they were in the forum or the barbershop—or worse still, in a tavern or whorehouse.[27]

The *Didascalia Apsotolorum*, a third-century Syrian text, indicates the allocation of personnel to deal with unruly behavior: "And the deacon should also observe that nobody is whispering or going to sleep or laughing or gesticulating, for it is fitting that they should be watching in the church respectfully and attentively, with ears alert to the word

---

[26] Bader, "La tentation comme attention," 145.
[27] Robert F. Taft, *Through Their Own Eyes: Liturgy as the Byzantines Saw It* (Berkeley, CA: Interorthodox Press, 2006), 77.

of the Lord."[28] Later on, the doorkeeper would become responsible for this when the deacon's role became more concerned with liturgical duties.[29] But complaints in sermons are our best evidence for congregational behavior. In addition to producing inappropriate noise (see chapter 6), Chrysostom's congregations would engage in other distracting behavior; for example, entering the church ostentatiously with a retinue, pickpocketing, and sealing business deals. Unlike the noise we discussed in the last chapter, which can be a response to preaching and readings, these activities have no connection to the ritual at all.[30]

It is notable that the early Christian writers who are most concerned with behavior indicative of inattentiveness are those who were heavily influenced by the emergent monastic and ascetic movement: Athanasius, Jerome, Ambrose, Augustine, Chrysostom, Cassian, Caesarius, and others.[31] Here, as in other aspects of Christian life in this period, the model proposed for all, including the laity, was the silent attentiveness of the cenobitic monks during worship. Jerome tells Eustochium that after the prayers when the "father" (abbot) starts to preach on the reading, "While he is speaking the silence is profound; no man ventures to look at his neighbor or to clear his throat."[32] Augustine described certain approved noises as signs of their attentiveness: "They listen with incredible zeal and perfect silence, however, making known the dispositions of their own souls, insofar as the words of the speaker moves them, either with groans or with tears or even with a modest joy free from every out-

---

[28] *Didascalia Apostolorum* 12.10-11, in *The Didascalia Apostolorum: An English Version*, trans. Alistair C. Stewart, Studia Traditionis Theologiae 1, 176 (Turnhout: Brepols, 2009).

[29] Juliette Day, "The Status and Role of Doorkeepers in the Early Medieval West," *Studies in Late Antiquity* 6, no. 1 (2022): 148–73.

[30] See Wendy Mayer, "John Chrysostom: Extraordinary Preacher, Ordinary Audience," in *Preacher and Audience: Studies in Early Christian and Byzantine Homiletics*, ed. Mary Cunningham and Pauline Allen, 105–37 (Leiden: Brill, 1998).

[31] See Neil A. Adkin, "A Problem in the Early Church: Noise during the Sermon and Lesson," *Mnemosyne* 38 (1985): 161–63.

[32] Jerome, *ep*. 22.35, in *Letters*, trans. W. H. Freemantle and G. Lewis, Nicene and Post-Nicene Fathers 2nd series, vol. 6, 38 (New York, Oxford: Parker & Co., 1893).

burst."[33] Isidore of Seville and John Cassian also describe the monks' behavior in similar ways. Quite clearly they equate spiritual attentiveness, an interior disposition, with physical and auditory attentiveness in worship. Behaviors which display inattentiveness are a sign of spiritual and moral weakness, of succumbing to temptation.

In the medieval West and Byzantine East, the liturgy develops in such a way as to distinguish the participation of the clergy from laity; the former concern themselves with the words and rituals, while the latter mostly engaged in privatized ritual practices. Corporate congregational attentiveness is only required at particular high points when the clergy engage with the laity in the performance of shared texts (the Creed or *Sanctus*) or at the readings; apart from that, the laity are encouraged to occupy themselves by closely following the Mass, but with their own devotional strategies. Although many of these would have been learned from observation and participation, by the later medieval period we find their codification in manuals such as the *Lay Folks Mass Book*, or in manuals to help priests teach the congregation such as John Myrc's *Instructions for Parish Priests*, and occasionally as additions to the Book of Hours. The *Lay Folks Mass Book* indicates what the reader might pray at particular points in the Mass. These are given in the vernacular and in rhyming couplets. Thus, at the gospel, the layman is to pray:

> Ihesu, my Lord, grant me thy grace,
> And of amendment might and space,
> Thy word to keep and do thy will.
> The good to choose and leave the ill:
> And that it may be so,
> Good Ihesu, grant it me. Amen[34]

---

[33] Augustine, *The Catholic Way of Life and the Manichean Way of Life (De moribus ecclesiae Catholicae et De moribus Manichaeorum)* 1.31,67, in *The Works of Saint Augustine*, part 1, vol. 19, *The Manichean Debate*, trans. Roland Teske and Boniface Ramsey, 62 (Charlottesville, VA: Past Masters, 2014).

[34] Modern English translation by Thomas F. Simmons in *The Lay Folks Mass Book; Or, The Manner of Hearing Mass: With Rubrics and Devotions for the People, in Four Texts, and Office in English According to the Use of York, from Manuscripts of the Xth to the XVth Century* (England: Early English Text Society, 1879), xxviii.

Such manuals were found all over Europe. In Italy the most popular was *Il soccorso dei poveri (Help for the Poor)* by Girolamo da Siena, but there were numerous others which focus on behavior in church and not faith or spirituality.[35] Sometimes the layman is to join with the priest in the *Confiteor* and the Creed, or to listen to the gospel; at others he is to recite his own prayers to accompany the ritual act or words. Thus,

> [w]hen you see the priest bow before the consecrated host, you shall first say this verse: "Thou hast loosed my bonds. I will offer to thee the sacrifice of thanksgiving and call on the name of the Lord" [Ps. 116:16–17]. Then say: "I offer infinite thanks to you, most holy Savior, because you have deigned to make manifest your most holy son Jesus Christ, in pure and true flesh." And call upon his mercy and say: "I am guilty, my Lord, of that which I have done to offend you in the days of my life." And pray to him for all Christian souls, and especially for those who are in mortal sin and those who are in the pains of Purgatory.[36]

Similar prayers are suggested to accompany the veneration of the chalice.

It is no surprise that both these examples begin with a warning about inattentive behavior in church. The *Lay Folks Mass Book* opens by emphasizing the "the virtue of Mass singing / And the profit of the Mass hearing" and warns "that thou at the Mass no jangling make."[37] Similarly, in *Del modo che si die tenire in chiexia* we find, "And thus you shall remain in your usual place in silence and dread, without looking here and there or making any uproar the way some people do, beating their breast and sighing disgracefully."[38] The worshipper was to be alert to the transition from private prayers to communal participation, which might be signaled acoustically by the sacring bell or a diaconal address, or ritually by movement out of the

---

[35] Daniel Bornstein, "How to Behave in Church and How to Become a Priest," in Miri Rubin, *Medieval Christianity in Practice*, 112 (Princeton, NJ: Princeton University Press, 2009).

[36] English translation of *Del modo che si die tenire in chiexia*, in Bornstein, "How to Behave," 110–11.

[37] *Lay Folks Mass Book*, 3–4 (my translation).

[38] Bornstein, "How to Behave," 109.

sanctuary. Attentiveness does not mean absolute unwavering focus on the priest, but the ability to negotiate the interior and exterior forms of participation, and it does not necessarily mean silence either, as the private devotions are likely to have been muttered rather than recited in the head alone.

The Protestant Reformation brought with it new modes of lay and clerical liturgical participation that also required new attentiveness strategies. The prominence of the Scripture readings and of the sermon demanded enhanced physical and auditory attentiveness, while at the same time an emphasis on individual moral responsibility required the inner attentiveness of the mind. In late sixteenth- and seventeenth-century sources, we see how public displays of attentiveness in worship were to mirror an interior, spiritual attentiveness on God which, to some extent, reflect what we have seen in early monastic practices. The laity needed training for the new attentiveness, and the many tracts about listening in church promote normative behaviors and advise attentiveness strategies.

In London in 1650, Joseph Caryl published this tract, closely typed on a single broadsheet:

> *Some plain Directions for the more profitable hearing of the Word Preached, together with the Lets and hinderances which usually keep people from profiting by Hearing; and also many Characters and clear Symptoms of good and profitable Hearers; with several Arguments persuadung a Christian to take heed how he hears, containing the heads of some Sermons lately Preached by the most unworthy of Christs Servants in the Ministry and now Printed for the further benefit of his Flock.*

The tract is a list of points grouped together by theme and almost all illustrated with a biblical quotation. For Caryl, attentiveness in church is about training the ear, which should not be "indisposed" or "itching," and about creating the right inner disposition. In section 2, "Things to be observed in time of hearing, or the qualifications of hearing the Word Preached," he advises prior preparation: "As you are going to the Congregation, remember, 1. to keep your hearts from the world, minding no earthly business. 2. To think how that you are going to meet with the great God of heaven, to deal about the eternall estate of your souls. 3. Think on some fit portion of Scripture as

Psal. 41.1,3." During the sermon, the reader is to apply the content to self-examination, and to "be courteous and hospitable to the faithfull preachers of the Gospel." It is after church that true attentiveness becomes evident. On the way home, the sermon should be discussed with others: at home, "sit down a little and chew the cud (as it were) on your spirituall meat," and later on "call on your relations, help them, putting them in mind of some most seasonable truth delivered." In the later seventeenth century, people were encouraged to take sermon notes, and this was especially seen as a way of keeping schoolboys occupied.

Inattentiveness in church can be exhibited by physical behavior during worship, but just as important is what is going on in the mind. In Henry Mason's 1656 treatise, *Hearing and Doing the Ready Way to Blessednesse: With an Appendix Containing Rules of Right Hearing Gods Word*, he provides a definition of attention which is more than simply hearing, which he dismisses as mere "ear-labour": "Attention is that which doth enlive our hearing and maketh it effectual and profitable. For if we heare, and attend not, we do not learn by the instructions . . . we are not moved by the exhortations . . . nor are we feared by the threatenings . . . But Attention in hearing is like the plough that goeth before the Sower. For as the plough openeth the ground that the seed may enter in, and take root under the furrows: so attention setteth open the heart that it may receive the word."[39] The problem of inattentiveness is described as follows: "For, how ever attention bee so necessary for right hearing . . . yet such is our frailty and folly, that usually our thoughts wander all the world over . . . For sometimes we do willingly busie our selves with earthly thoughts about our Trades, and our Lands, and our household affairs . . . And sometimes, the devill . . . standeth at our elbow, and casteth worldly thoughts in to our mindes or heavinesse of sleep, into our heads, to disesteeme of the word spoken, into our hearts."[40] For this he suggests a number of remedies. First, training oneself to meditate on Scripture outside worship so that our mind has more to think about than "baggs, and bonds and accounts" or the "works of fleshly de-

---

[39] Henry Mason, *Hearing and Doing the Ready Way to Blessednesse: With an Appendix Containing Rules of Right Hearing Gods Word* (London: John Clark, 1656), 605.
[40] Mason, *Hearing and Doing*, 615–16.

lights" or ambition. Secondly, "it will be an helpe also, if we use such posture of body as may be apt to keep our senses waking and to drive away heaviness and sleep." He recommends keeping the eyes fixed on the speaker, and also, surprisingly, standing up if "we find that by long sitting at ease, wee grow heavie and dull of hearing," and even using gestures if they are helpful. Thirdly, they should remove any impediments prior to worship, such as wine or strong drink, a heavy meal which "calleth the spirits to the stomach for concoction, and in their absence, the braine is disabled from contemplation and religious thoughts"; he also recommends refraining from "carnal sports." Finally, one should identify the distractions through a process of examining one's own thoughts.[41]

For these mostly Puritan writers, such as Henry Mason, Robert Wilkinson, and Cotton Mather[42], what enters via the ear has a direct route to the heart and then to the soul, and so aural attentiveness is not just about removing impediments to listening, but it will be demonstrated in a spiritual outcome. Obviously, one's bodily deportment in worship is important, but so too that which precedes and follows the service. It is surprising that Mason does not object to all physical movement, indicating clearly that for him attentiveness is an inner disposition and not about distraction. Failure to attend has some pretty serious consequences that go beyond missing vital messages in the sermon. Caryl closes his treatise with a list of biblical warnings: "A negligent hearing will, to the terror of a poor fool, plainly manifest five things: 1. That he is but a fool, *Matt.* 7.26. 2. That he is under the judgements of God, *Deut.* 29.4. 3. That he is in a lost condition, 2 *Cor.* 4.3. 4. That the Lord has a purpose to destroy him, 2 *Chron.* 25.16. 5. That he is nigh to cursing, *Heb.* 4.12. The word will make quick work."

Despite all the good advice in these many manuals with such evocative names as *A Jewell for the Eare* (Robert Wilkinson, 1593), *The Boring of the Eare* (Stephen Egerton, 1623), and the more prosaic *The Art Or Skil, Well and Fruitfullie to Heare the Holy Sermons of the Church Written First in Latin, by a Godly Minister Named Gulielmus Zepperus; and Now Truly Translated into English by T.W.* (1599), it is not evident

---

[41] Mason, 625–28.
[42] See Arnold Hunt, *The Art of Hearing: English Preachers and Their Audiences, 1590–1640* (Cambridge: Cambridge University Press, 2010), chap. 2.

that there was a general increase in attentiveness. In William Hogarth's *The Sleeping Congregation* (1736), which parodies the experience of worship in the Church of England in the eighteenth century, the preacher addresses a packed church, but below him, in the foreground, the clerk and a woman parishioner are evidently snoozing (fig. 1). Further sorts of inattentiveness were described in the anonymous tract with which I opened this chapter. For most of these centuries, the preacher had considerable responsibility for creating sermons that the people were able to attend to, and, of course, the quality varied considerably. Some, such as Charles Spurgeon, could keep huge crowds transfixed, but the experience in most parishes must have been quite different. We could consider the increase in congregational hymn-singing as a strategy for attentiveness, and the nineteenth-century Anglican Ritualists considered that seemly and aesthetic ritual worship would help. In the Roman Catholic Church, there was the revival of Gregorian chant and encouragements to increased sacramental participation, even though the laity were still expected to follow the Mass with their private devotions, such as the rosary. But as we move into the twentieth century, aural attentiveness was clearly replaced by more varied participation of the laity, including speech and ritual movement as well.

Conclusion

Theologians and philosophers promote aural attentiveness as an inner disposition, a moral act, and a sensorial practice, and to some extent attentiveness in worship is presented as an ideal of the human way of being in the world and before God. However, the difficulties of attending to the sonic signals seem to mitigate against full and complete attentiveness. The ears receive many sounds simultaneously, even in the quietest of environments, and the brain must work to filter out and prioritize which ones will be retained and rendered meaningful, which will be partially processed, and which ignored. We are able to exercise our will to listen to one person rather than another, but even then peripheral sounds can distract us, as indeed they must be able to. In worship, the situation is more complicated than a conversation. We receive different types of sound signals whose informational content is presented sometimes in speech, sometimes in chant or hymns, but also in ritual and by the physical environment. It can help when, with experience, the listener/worshipper either knows beforehand what is to be heard (e.g., a set prayer in the Mass) or has some prior idea of the topic of a sermon based upon passages of Scripture recently heard. But that is still no guarantee that the mind will not wander onto other thoughts, or the ears pick up unwanted noises, despite our best efforts to pay attention. When the goal of our attentiveness is God and his Word, then any disruption can be viewed as a sign of sin and spiritual weakness. The early modern writers' attention to the scriptural and theological foundations of aural attentiveness attempted to address just this fundamental problem: how can we listen attentively to God despite humanity's fallen nature? They, like the early monks and ascetics before them, suggest the training and disciplining of the ears in conjunction with a disciplining of the body and the mind. Modern Western liturgies are lean; that is, repetitions have been mostly removed and there is a very clear movement from start to finish. This produces a clean text on the page, but it may not help us to be attentive if repetition can help us hear and process words. Styles comments that "Redundancy in language is . . . useful when we try to listen to something in a noisy situation because even if we hear only part of the input there is enough redundancy for us to understand the message."[43] If attentiveness is not just about receiving the sounds but about also processing them into meaningful communication, then rather than considering that we only partially heard the sound the first time, we could consider that it necessarily requires repetition to achieve understanding and therefore complete the task of attentiveness.

---

[43] Styles, *Psychology of Attention*, 19.

Chapter 8

Aural Architecture

Aural architecture refers to more than the acoustic properties of a building or space. Instead, the expression, invented by Barry Blesser, denotes a listener's *experience* of the acoustic environment of a space. The space through which a sound signal travels modifies it in particular ways before it reaches the listener, but the listener's experience will be more than just the resulting sound alone. The listener will experience the aural architecture when they locate themselves by sound in the geophysical space, or when a sound reflected off a wall will be experienced as the sounding of the wall itself, and when they respond to the aural personality of the space through emotions and associations and in combination with its visual and aesthetic aspects.[1] Church buildings are usually studied in relation to the latter, and changes in the construction and interior discussed in terms of building technology, architectural style, and, sometimes, in relation to changes in worship. Church buildings have been subject to acoustical analyses, but these do not always attend to the auditory experience of intended and actual worshippers in that space; in this chapter, I will draw upon the work of some of the studies which have attempted this. Aural architecture is a useful corrective to the separate fields of enquiry, as it asks us to consider how and what the listener hears during worship in the place where it occurs.

As the sound signal leaves its source en route to the ears of the listener, it is modified by the space through which it travels by a

---

[1] Barry Blesser and Linda-Ruth Salter, *Spaces Speak, Are You Listening? Experiencing Aural Architecture* (Cambridge, MA: MIT Press, 2007), chap. 1.

whole range of factors: the shape and volume of the space; the material of the walls, ceiling, and floor; room-dividing features such as screens or pillars; the position of the main sound sources (speakers, singers, musicians) in relation to the congregation; and the presence or absence of sound-enhancement or -absorption features. Environmental factors are also important, such as the ambient temperature, humidity levels, and, of course, background noise from outside the church.[2] Blesser and Salter proposed that each space has its own sonic personality, the distinctive way in which sounds are heard in that space, so that even if two congregations use the same words, music, and ritual, what worshippers hear will not be the same. Worshippers implicitly recognize the sonic personality of their own places of worship, and each congregation forms an "acoustical community" whose boundaries are determined by the audible range of the sound in their space rather than any visible, or even ecclesial, boundary. Blesser and Salter refer to listeners being "immersed in the space's aural response," and this will combine the way they hear themselves at prayer, with the intentional and ritual sounds of their worship, as well as the distinctiveness of the space in which those prayers take place.[3]

Although ideally, theologically, and ritually, we might want to consider that all worshippers form a single acoustical community, the reality is that the location of worshippers and ministers in different places in the space creates different listening experiences. Gary Sieben suggested that there could be up to five communities in any one contemporary worship event and space: the leader, congregation, music director, choir, and technical staff.[4] Historically, there could have been many more: doorkeepers at the back; men and women occupying separate sides; penitents outside the door; cantors; deacons and sub-deacons forming new communities as they moved between sanctuary and nave. Additionally, because of the way that sound surrounds us and comes from all directions, each listener perceives

---

[2] Victor Desarnaulds, António P. O. Carvalho, and Gilbert Monay, "Church Acoustics and the Influence of Occupancy," *Building Acoustics* 9, no. 1 (2002): 29–47.

[3] Blesser and Salter, *Spaces Speak*, 16.

[4] Gary Sieben, "The Soundscape of Worship," in *Worship Space Acoustics: 3 Decades of Design*, ed. David T. Bradley, Lauren Ronsse, and Erica Ryherd, 7–9 (New York: Springer, 2016).

themselves to be at the center of what they personally hear. Each person inhabits their own sonic world, just as much as they share the acoustical arena and participate in the "acoustical community."[5]

This chapter will first survey the distinctive sonic properties of the principal styles of church architecture which contemporary worshippers have inherited, and then investigate the effect of architectural design on the listener's perception of reverberation and speech intelligibility.

Acoustical Features of Architectural Styles

It is interesting to note that, although in the Greco-Roman world the most effective acoustical environment was the amphitheatre, early Christians chose the basilica as the most appropriate architectural model for their public worship. A basilica church is typically long and narrow, with high wooden ceilings. The space may be divided longitudinally by rows of columns, and at one end there is a raised semicircular apse, often with a semi-dome above, as the focal point from which the sound usually emanates. These spaces enabled a large congregation to gather, but acoustically were not optimal for speech intelligibility due to excessive reverberation, although the raised apse (or *bema*) and ambo may have helped carry the voice further.[6] The basilica shape with modifications, such as the additions of side chapels and transepts, remained the basic model for centuries, although developments in building techniques did bring about changes in the acoustics. Thus, the introduction of stone vaults into Romanesque churches caused the lowering of the ceiling, enabling a more effective diffusion of the sound. The pointed vaults of the gothic period caused sound to be reflected sideways as well as down, which was particularly good for chant, but as the ceiling height increased so speech intelligibility decreased.[7] The cult of relics, the requirements for multiple daily Masses, the monastic movement, as well as philosophical notions of spatial harmony resulted in the space being divided into

---

[5] Blesser and Salter, *Spaces Speak*, 12, 22.

[6] Victor Desarnaulds, "De l'acoustique des églises en Suisse—une approche pluridisciplinaire" (PhD diss., École Polytechnique Fédérale de Lausanne, 2002), 20.

[7] Rafael Suárez, Juan J. Sendra, and Alicia Alonso, "Acoustics, Liturgy and Architecture in the Early Christian Church: From the *Domus Ecclesiae* to the Basilica," *Acta Acustica united with Acustica* 99 (2013): 296–99.

separate "rooms." Each room had its own sonic personality, and the dividing barriers between them obviously affected the way in which sound traveled through the major and minor spaces of the church. The mendicant orders, with their emphasis on preaching, did concern themselves with the audibility of the sermon, but without any radical change to the basic shape and organization of the space; what they did do, however, was to place the pulpit in an acoustically more advantageous place.[8] The Byzantine tradition developed in a different direction from the basic basilica shape, and its most distinctive acoustical and architectural feature was the dome; in some churches there could be multiple domes. The domes gather, redirect, and scatter the sound such that it seems to emanate from above rather than from the clergy or singers. Hagia Sophia produced multiple reverberations of different lengths such that the sound was perceived as fluid and moving; Bissera Pentcheva described it as stirring "the sensation of multiple waterfalls staggered at different times and places as the sounds reach the listener."[9]

The spatial and acoustical requirements for Protestant worship caused some significant changes to the aural architecture experienced by worshippers. With speech intelligibility as a priority, it was important to reduce the distance between minister and people, and to reduce the reverberation. Modifications to existing medieval churches resulted in the removal of barriers or screens between rooms, the placing of the minister in closer proximity to the congregation, and concern about the position of the pulpit in relation to the altar.[10] This often resulted in two focal points and created distinctive acoustic environments for the sacrament of the Word and the sacrament of the Eucharist (see fig. 7, Sauvo church). Churches designed especially for certain Protestant communities were not bound to the traditional architectural styles, and there are many examples of churches and temples in which the congregation is arranged in closely packed seats around a centrally placed pulpit[11] (fig. 3). For Roman Catholics, the

---

[8] Desarnaulds, "De l'acoustique des églises en Suisse," 24.

[9] Bissera Pentcheva, *Hagia Sophia: Sound, Space, and Spirit in Byzantium* (University Park, PA: Penn State University Press, 2017), 12.

[10] A useful survey of the changes at the time of the Protestant Reformation can be found here: Jack C. Whytock, "The Reformation of Space for Public Worship: Past and Present—Continuing the Discussion," *Die Skriflig/In Luce* 52, no. 3 (2018): a2307.

[11] Desarnaulds, "De l'acoustique des églises en Suisse," 26–28.

Figure 3

Jean Perrissin, *Le Temple de Paradis* (Lyon, France, 1569–1570). Oil on canvas. Bibliothèque de Genève, now in the Musée internationale de la Réforme, Geneva. This painting depicts the newly built temple for Calvinist worship in Lyon, France. Speech intelligibility would have been enhanced by the densely packed congregation seated around the centrally placed and raised pulpit.
Wikipedia Commons License CC-BY-SA 4.0.

Council of Trent mandated the removal of stone choir screens, which improved sight as well as sound of the altar. Although the spaces themselves remained highly reverberative and thus not optimal for speech, the additional, even excessive, ornamentation in baroque churches did have a modifying effect.[12]

[12] Desarnaulds, 33–34.

Despite the importance of acoustics in worship spaces, it is strange that the application of acoustical research to church design does not really happen until the twentieth century, and not always even then. In 1627, Francis Bacon's treatise *Sylva Sylvarum* was posthumously published, and despite his observations on room acoustics, it clearly had little influence in the design of the churches such as those seen in the Hogarth engravings in chapter 1. In the nineteenth century, acoustical observations were applied to the new cultural forms of the opera house and theatre, which were designed with a lower sound source and raked seats arranged around the stage. Churches did not have raked seats except in galleries. Revivalist preachers often shunned traditional church spaces in order to reach those who did not attend them, and thus we find John Wesley and the early Methodists preaching outdoors, and, in the United States, Charles Grandison Finney taking over the Chatham Theatre in Manhattan in 1832. Here, the slope of the floor was increased so that everyone could see the preacher who was placed centrally on the stage; reportedly, he could be heard from every seat in the house. Shortly afterwards, Finney oversaw the construction of the Broadway Tabernacle, which was designed like a classical amphitheatre and used the latest acoustical science[13] (fig. 4). Jeanne Halgren Kilde presents numerous examples of experiments with auditorium-type churches among Protestant congregations in North America during the later nineteenth century, but these were not considered appropriate for Catholic or Episcopalian congregations.

Many liturgical reforms of the twentieth century resulted in increased participation by the laity, which has multiplied the sound sources and types which worshippers experience. New architectural technologies, especially the use of concrete, and changed aesthetics have created innovative spaces that cannot be so easily distinguished according to denomination or worship style.[14] Acoustical science

---

[13] Jeanne Halgren Kilde, *When Church Became Theatre: The Transformation of Evangelical Architecture and Worship in Nineteenth-Century America* (New York: Oxford University Press, 2002), chap. 2.

[14] Edwin Heath and Laura Moffat gathered together two hundred examples in their book *Contemporary Church Architecture* (London: Wiley, 2007). These indicate varied architectural styles, and sometimes new ways of arranging the people and ministers in the space. It is not obvious, though, whether any were designed with acoustical principles in mind.

Figure 4
The Broadway Tabernacle, New York, 1850. The steeply raked seats were set in a semi-circle around the stage, from which Finney could preach. The congregation enjoyed unimpeded visibility and enhanced speech intelligibility for the sermon. (Image: The Miriam and Ira D. Wallach Division of Art, Prints and Photographs: Print Collection, The New York Public Library. New York Public Library Digital Collections.)

enables the measurement and planning of spaces to achieve a particular quality of sound, or to modify the acoustical infelicities of a space by electronic means.[15] Increasing background noise in (post-)industrial societies also creates its own problems. Modern worshippers are likely, therefore, to find themselves in a much more diverse aural environment, even if they worship with similar historic texts and music.

The term "earcon" was coined by Blesser and Salter as a sonic analogy to the icon. It describes the symbolic meaning of the sound,

---

[15] See the essays in David T. Bradley, Lauren Ronsse, and Erica Ryherd, eds., *Worship Space Acoustics: 3 Decades of Design* (New York: Springer, 2016).

independently of the meaning of the content it conveys.[16] The acoustic properties of a building are usually accidents of architectural design, but when that design becomes associated with religious ritual and its sounds, the visual, material, and sonic combine to create a normative (that is, traditional) way of worship. Consequently, new spaces are constructed along the same lines as the previous ones, even if it is impossible to recreate the liturgical and aural experience of earlier worshippers. Nevertheless, this explains why new church buildings still have high reverberation, even when it is known that this hinders the much-desired characteristic of intelligibility. Blesser and Salter explain that "for those who repeatedly attended services in these religious spaces, aural and visual symbolism became tightly linked. In this context, long reverberation indirectly acquired its meaning from the religion, with its liturgy, icons and visual designs. And this link was further strengthened by religious music written for this highly reverberant space."[17] All these aspects combine to create the idea that "this is the way our community worships," which is indistinguishable from the notion that "this is the way our community sounds when it worships"; conformity with tradition and thus orthodoxy ("right worship") is demonstrated by these acoustical means.

The acoustics of worship spaces have also been interpreted in spiritual and theological ways, in addition to the more pragmatic issues. Mendel Kleiner, David Klepper, and Rendell Torres emphasized that "a worship space must be designed to assist the communication sought by worship"[18] and thus enable intelligibility. However, if in worship there is a divine-human encounter, then how human participants hear God through the sounds of worship is not just a matter of acoustics. In a study of Catholic churches in Goa, the acoustical environment, especially that produced by the reverberation, was reportedly intended to engender a reverential awe, to produce religious comfort and solace, and to provide a background of silence out of which these could emerge.[19] Alaa Algargoosh's research

---

[16] Blesser and Salter, *Spaces Speak*, 88.

[17] Blesser and Salter, 93.

[18] Mendel Kleiner, David Lloyd Klepper, and Rendell R. Torres, *Worship Space Acoustics* (Fort Lauderdale, FL: Ross Publishing, 2010), 2.

[19] Menino A. S. M. P. Tavares et al., "Prediction of Acoustic Comfort and Acoustic Silence in Goan Catholic Churches," *Inter-Noise* (2009): n.p.

group took a slightly different approach and explored the impact of acoustical features of a space on the emotional experience of worshippers.[20] They observed that multiple sound reflections from the architectural surfaces "makes identifying the sound source difficult—the sound source may appear to be invisible, which influences listeners' emotions," and that "the resonance effect of some historic buildings influences both the state of mind and the emotions; this can appear as a physiological effect (e.g. change in heart rate, breathing rhythm)."[21] Their research compared artificially produced "dry" and "wet" acoustics, "dry" being without resonance produced in an anechoic chamber, and "wet" being highly resonant, such as Hagia Sophia. For the latter, participants reported more intense spiritual feelings accompanied by a physiological reaction in terms of increased heart rate. They used words such as "calming, uplifting, awe-inspiring, and, mostly, spiritual."[22] What was also interesting in this research was the role of memory and expectation and how the visual appearance of the space affected their expectations of what such a space should sound like, and hence what sort of emotional response would be appropriate in such an environment.

Liturgical Acoustics

A sound initially travels in all directions as an ever-expanding spherical wave until it strikes an object. Some objects (wood, fabric, people) will absorb the sound energy, but others (marble and other stone, metal) will reflect the sound. As these reflections hit yet more objects, they in turn produce fresh but weaker reflections until the energy dissipates and the sound fades away. When these are heard as two distinct sounds from separate sources, they are an echo; but when there are multiple reflections which arrive in the ear at different times such that the message and the source is indistinct, this is a reverberation. The listener initially hears the original, direct sound and then the reflections in staggered waves, first from those reflecting

---

[20] Alaa Algargoosh et al., "The Impact of the Acoustic Environment on Human Emotion and Experience: A Case Study of Worship Spaces," *Building Acoustics* 29, no. 1 (2022): 85–106, here at 86.

[21] Algargoosh et al., "Impact of the Acoustic Environment," 87.

[22] Algargoosh et al., 101.

surfaces close to the source, and then those progressively further away.[23] The listener perceives the early reflections as being more intense and clearer, but the later the reflection, the more intrusive it can be.

Reverberation in church buildings was an accident of architectural design which was compensated for by cantillation and chant and then exploited in polyphonic, melismatic chant and other musical developments. Ettore Cirillo and Francesco Martellotta suggested these optimal reverberation times for different liturgical sounds: the organ—over three seconds; chant—arounds two seconds; instrumental music—around one and half seconds; and speech—less than one second.[24] Speech intelligibility is a desirable feature in worship which prioritizes the clear articulation of the biblical texts and preaching. The intentional sounds of any worship event, the verbal and musical components, require quite different acoustic environments to be present simultaneously in the same space, so the study of the aural architecture of worship needs to attend to the benefits, difficulties, and compromises required to enable the worshippers to listen attentively.

Reverberation

The design, material, and decoration of a worship space all have a direct effect upon the quality of the sound and the amount of reverberation. Churches built of stone with walls of polished plaster or marble revetment have the longest reverberation, but this can be modified to some extent if the vaults are of unplastered brick and if there are lots of wooden pews; large stained-glass windows can also diminish reflections from stone walls. The most sound-absorbing spaces will have wooden ceilings, close-packed wooden pews, carpets, and curtains.[25] The narrow and high space of an early Christian basilica with marble revetment on the walls produces strong lateral reflections, which hinders sound traveling along the length of the nave, although it produces good speech intelligibility for those near

---

[23] Dorothea Baumann and Christina Niederstätter, "Acoustics in Sacred Buildings," in *Sacred Buildings: A Design Manual*, ed. Rudolf Stegers, 54–59 (Basel: Birkhäuser, 2008).

[24] Ettore Cirillo and Francesco Martellotta, *Worship, Acoustics, and Architecture* (Brentwood, UK: Multi-Science Pub. Co., 2006), 48.

[25] Cirillo and Martellotta, *Worship, Acoustics, and Architecture*, 202–3.

the source. Stone vaults and domes diffuse the sound, producing mixed reflections which are helpful for polyphonic chant. The ceiling produces late reflections, and thus the effect of this will be related to the height of the chancel and nave, and will be particularly complicated when they are of different heights. Desarnaulds's acoustic measurement of Swiss churches revealed that Reformed churches had a much lower ceiling height than Catholic ones, which resulted in improved speech intelligibility.[26] Also important will be the floor surface, and again the material will determine the reverberation time: almost eliminating it when carpeted, reducing it when covered with sound-absorbing wood or, as in the medieval church, with straw, but exacerbating it when of stone.

Cirillo and Martellotta suggest that the surface material will be more influential on sound quality than the volume of the space, but volume is certainly a factor. Dorothea Baumann and Christina Niederstätter proposed that to achieve a compromise acoustics for both speech and music, the maximum amount of seating should not exceed 1,800 to 2,000 seats.[27] Desaunaulds's research revealed that a competent speaker should be heard without amplification in a church of less than 3,000 square meters with a seating capacity of less than 1,000 people.[28] The seating capacity of a church is directly related to its volume, and in historic church buildings reverberation will inevitably increase as size increases. In modern, purpose-built auditoria churches, though, reverberation can be almost completely eliminated or kept within the desired limits.

Acoustical measurement of historic churches reveal them to be highly reverberant. Hagia Sophia (completed 537) has a reverberation time of ten seconds and St. Paul's Cathedral, London (completed in 1711), has eleven seconds, even though they were built centuries apart and for quite different worship styles.[29] In Hagia Sophia the highly

---

[26] Desarnaulds, "De l'acoustique des églises en Suisse," 71–72.
[27] Dorothea Baumann and Christina Niederstätter, "Acoustics in Sacred Buildings," in *Sacred Buildings: A Design Manual*, ed. Rudolf Stegers, 57 (Boston: Walter De Gruyter, 2008).
[28] Desarnaulds, "De l'acoustique des églises en Suisse," 88.
[29] For Hagia Sophia, see Pentcheva, *Hagia Sophia*, 12. For St. Paul's Cathedral, see Sara Girón, Lidia Álvarez-Morales, and Teófilo Zamarreño, "Church Acoustics: A State-of-the-Art Review after Several Decades of Research," *Journal of Sound and Vibration* 411 (2017): 378–408, here at 381.

elaborate polyphonic chant exploited the acoustics to produce a fluid and enveloping sound; Pentcheva argued that this aural "obfuscation," which went together with the visual obfuscation produced by the tesserae of the mosaics, was enhanced by placing the singers under the dome. The effect was to "disintegrate the linear composition of meaning in order to produce a sound that functions outside the register of human speech" and thereby produce a sense of transcendence.[30] St. Paul's Cathedral, designed for Anglican worship which prioritized speech intelligibility and the sermon, is singularly unsuited for its task. The vast volume of the church, and especially the dome, means that speech travels neither very far nor very clearly; Frances Knight has described the exhaustion of Henry Parry Liddon after preaching there for over an hour in the 1870s.[31] The Episcopalian church of St. Thomas on Fifth Avenue in New York City, completed in 1913 in the High Gothic style, employed interior cladding to reduce the reverberation to 2.5 seconds, making it ideal for speech but not for the organ or singing.[32] Significant comparative acoustical measurements were undertaken by Desarnaulds for Catholic and Protestant churches in Switzerland; by Cirillo and Martellotta for Catholic churches in southern Italy; by António Carvalho on Portuguese Catholic churches; and by Menino and others on Catholic churches in Goa.[33] These all do seem to testify to unhelpful acoustics for the typical sonic activities of liturgical worship, but as Antonio Pedrero commented, "it is implausible that an architectural model that has endured for centuries should fail to respond correctly to the functional needs of its own activities. . . . It would hardly have survived for centuries as an architectural model without properly fulfilling its duties, and its acoustic conditions were essential elements of that function."[34] As I said earlier, the reverberant nature of the sound in

---

[30] Pentcheva, *Hagia Sophia*, 70.

[31] T. H. Lewers and J. S. Anderson, "Some Acoustical Properties of St. Paul's Cathedral, London," *Journal of Sound and Vibration* 92, no. 2 (1984): 285–97. Frances Knight, "Preaching in Britain's 'Parish Church': Sermons at London's St. Paul's Cathedral in the Eighteenth and Nineteenth Centuries," *Sermon Studies* 3, no. 2 (2019): n.p.

[32] Pentcheva, *Hagia Sophia*, 109.

[33] A review of the most important of these studies can be found in Girón, Álvarez-Morales, and Zamarreño, "Church Acoustics," 378–408.

[34] Antonio Pedrero et al., "Acoustical Study of Toledo Cathedral according to its Liturgical Uses," *Applied Acoustics* 85 (2014): 23–33, here at 23.

worship spaces is expected by most listeners and does not necessarily detract from their experience, except when they actually want to listen attentively to the sermon.

Worship spaces are rarely a single space with regular angles, but are divided into 'rooms' and may also have apses as well as irregular niches or alcoves. Concave surfaces, as a barrel vault, apse, or dome concentrate sound to a focal point, and acute angles and niches can lead to localized sound accumulation.[35] Pedrero's study of Toledo Cathedral (constructed between the thirteenth and eighteenth centuries) emphasized that the building is composed of many different spaces—apse, sanctuary, choir, radiating chapels, presbytery, transepts, nave, and aisles—which are demarcated by boundaries, such as the six-meter-high wall separating the choir from the nave and the pillars between the nave and aisles. Each space was devoted to a different liturgical activity and intended for different types of participants who were distinguished by hierarchy, social status, and gender: clergy were in the sanctuary; high status laymen could be in the presbytery; but women remained in the crossing. The space was so reverberant that Pedrero and others concluded, "The results of a global analysis of the measurements obtained would lead to the conclusion that the cathedral is a highly reverberant space, with low speech intelligibility, and unsuited to listening to spoken or musical sound signals."[36] The choir had the best results, but even there it was not optimal; for those in the presbytery the reflections from the side walls gave them as good a listening experience as the officiants, but in the women's area the measurements revealed very poor acoustics.[37] Cirillo and Martellotta considered the speech intelligibility so bad in these large medieval churches that only the priests and those very close would have been able to hear at all.[38]

Although the apse originates in Greco-Roman buildings as a niche for a statue, in Christian basilicas it was the place for the altar, and often behind it stood the bishop's chair surrounded by the *synthronon*, amphitheatre-style benches for the presbyters. Apses may be roofed

---

[35] Baumann and Niederstätter, "Acoustics in Sacred Buildings," 55.
[36] Pedrero et al., "Acoustical Study of Toledo Cathedral," 32.
[37] Pedrero et al., 27–32.
[38] Cirillo and Martellotta, *Worship, Acoustics, and Architecture*, 15.

with one or more semi-domes, or later on with a vault, but the effect is pretty much the same. Iegor Reznikoff remarked that, "The reason for the complex curved shape of the apse is obviously acoustic: it focuses the sound of the singing voice facing the apse where the altar is located . . . From there the voice can be heard very distinctly up to 100m away."[39] But the effectiveness of the acoustical properties of the apse is dependent on the position and orientation of the speaker. If the speaker faces the wall, there is some benefit; but if, for example, the bishop speaks from his *cathedra*, then it is of very little use. Lidia Alvarez-Morales and Francesco Martellotta specifically examined the effect of varying the position of the altar and priest in celebrations of the Latin Mass in different historic Roman Catholic churches, that is with the priest facing away from the people. They concluded that, "As expected, when the priest turned his back to the congregation the intelligibility dropped in all the churches, but those having the altar in the apse showed a less dramatic variation than those having a free-standing altar and consequently distant reflecting surfaces."[40] Church of England priests in the sixteenth and seventeenth centuries celebrated the Eucharist from the north side of the altar. This was hardly practical, as the large congregational paten and chalice needed to be placed on the narrow part of the altar, but it would have made some improvement in intelligibility.

The use of cantillation has been seen as a practical response to the acoustic properties of church spaces. It aids intelligibility by breaking down the text into smaller units with clear pauses and modulating the frequency. As Rafael Suarez with others concluded from their survey of St. John's Lateran and other basilicas, "The slow, syllabic monotones of chant with louder passages increasing sound levels reduced the interference of reverberation and helped improve intelligibility. Gregorian chant was not a musical arrangement for the liturgy, but rather the liturgy in sung form, supported and enhanced

---

[39] Iegor Reznikoff, "The Evidence of the Use of Sound Resonance from Paleolithic to Medieval Times," in *Archaeoacoustics*, ed. Christopher Scarre and Graeme Lawson, 77–84, here at 82 (Cambridge, UK: McDonald Institute for Archaeology, 2006).

[40] Lidia Alvarez-Morales and Francesco Martellotta, "A Geometrical Acoustic Simulation of the Effect of Occupancy and Source Position in Historical Churches," *Applied Acoustics* 91 (2015): 47–58.

by the great reverberation of the basilica."[41] Polyphony and the melismatic chants of the Byzantine liturgy indicate a sophisticated exploitation of the acoustic properties of the reverberant spaces, because lengthening the notes created the impression of hearing a fuller sound composed of harmonies which were not at all present in the melody; these effects were entirely due to the acoustics. Nevertheless, many of these reverberant spaces were, and remain, completely unsuited to worship focused on preaching and congregational hymnody.

Speech Intelligibility

In 1880, E. C. Gardner published *Common Sense in Church Building*, an imagined epistolary dialogue between churchgoers and an architect about the ideal space for Protestant worship. The correspondent remarks, "The preaching—oh! I never mind that—not in these beautiful churches. I am always sorry when the sermon comes—the speaker seems so small and feeble and far away. Half the time I can't hear him if I try. I don't think anybody cares much about the sermons." To which the architect replies, "the chief object in building your church is to afford convenient opportunity for a large number of people to listen to the voice of one man. To this fundamental idea everything else must be subservient. . . ."[42] The famous nineteenth-century Baptist minister Charles Spurgeon, who was personally instrumental in the design of the Metropolitan Tabernacle in London, was acutely aware of the acoustical requirements for preaching. He explained his ideas in his address at the opening meeting of the Tabernacle on August 21, 1860: "Concerning this vast chapel, I believe it is the most perfect triumph of acoustics that has ever been achieved. If it had been a failure at present, I should not have been at all disappointed, because the walls have yet to be covered with matched boarding, so that not a particle of brickwork is to be exposed, — it being my theory that soft substances are very much the best for hearing, having proved in a great number of buildings that stone walls are the main creators of an echo, and having seen hangings put up

---

[41] Suárez, Sendra, and Alonso, "Acoustics, Liturgy and Architecture," 299.

[42] E. C. Gardner, *Common Sense in Church Building* (New York: Bicknell & Comstock, 1880), 39, 41.

Figure 5
Interior View of the Metropolitan Tabernacle, depicting Charles H. Spurgeon preaching from pulpit. (Image from Henry Davenport Northrop, *Life and Works of Rev. Charles H. Spurgeon* [Ontario: Bradley, Garretson, 1890], 200, plate.)

to break the reverberation, and to give the speaker a hope of being heard"[43] (fig. 5).

Technologies of sound absorption have been used to adjust the acoustics, and in particular to reduce reverberation. Some of this would have been the accidental result of changed worship styles, such as the insertion of wooden pews and galleries; in fact, the presence of a congregation makes one of the most significant improvements in acoustic quality. Alvarez-Morales and Martellotta's acoustical study of Italian and Spanish churches showed that the pews themselves had a negligible effect compared to when they were filled with a densely packed, and well dressed, congregation.[44]

How much sound absorption is necessary is rather subjective. Baumann and Niederstätter were of the opinion that "The excessive

---

[43] Charles Spurgeon, *C. H. Spurgeon's Autobiography: Compiled from His Diary, Letters, and Records*, vol. 2 (Cincinnati: Curts and Jennings, 1899), 355.

[44] Alvarez-Morales and Martellotta, "Geometrical Acoustic Simulation," 51.

use of sound insulation causes sacred spaces to lose one of their most essential qualities: the sense of otherworldliness, the atmosphere that creates the conditions for transcendental experience."[45] Algargoosh suggested that too much reduction in reverberation resulted in an acoustic environment which does not match what is expected from the architectural design, and that has a potential impact on the worshipper's experience and emotions.[46] In modern acoustical design for churches, sound absorption can be added as panels to ceilings and walls; the most effective have a "soft fuzzy finish," but thickness and position are also key. *Worship Space Acoustics* by Bradley, Ronsse, and Ryherd contains numerous case studies of acoustical projects in a range of American places of worship and these describe the different types of site-specific sound-absorption solutions.[47] It is interesting to note those churches that chose not to install the recommended sound absorption solutions; mainly these were Roman Catholic churches.

Although it is not obvious now, many early Christian basilicas used curtains between the pillars and in doorways: visual representations of these are incidental in mosaics and on portable items.[48] During her visit to the Holy Land in the 380s, Egeria described that at Epiphany in the Church of the Holy Sepulchre in Jerusalem and at the Church of the Nativity in Bethlehem, there were wall hangings and curtains of silk with gold stripes, presumably placed between the pillars and covering the marble walls.[49] This would have created a markedly different acoustic environment than at other times of the year. Medieval churches had textiles on the altar, and sometimes tapestries on the wall.[50] Alicia Alonsi and Francesco Martellotta add

---

[45] Baumann and Niederstätter, "Acoustics in Sacred Buildings," 58.
[46] Algargoosh et al., "Impact of the Acoustic Environment," 86.
[47] Bradley, Ronsse, and Ryherd, *Worship Space Acoustics*. See especially the discussion in appendix A, 325–32.
[48] On curtains in churches, see Sible de Blaauw and Klára Doležalová, "Constructing Liminal Space? Curtains in Late Antique and Early Medieval Churches," *Convivium Supplementum* (2019): 46–67.
[49] Egeria, *Itinerarium* 25.8, in Paul F. Bradshaw and Anne McGowan, *The Pilgrimage of Egeria* (Collegeville, MN: Liturgical Press, 2018).
[50] See, for example, the tapestry now in the Metropolitan Museum of Art, New York (accession number 38.28). It was commissioned for a sixteenth-century bishop of Burgos and presumably displayed with others in the series on the redemption

that there would also have been textile coverings for shrines, veils for crucifixes and altarpieces, and other draperies, which are recorded in inventories: Seville Cathedral, for example, had velvet draperies for use on the walls and columns. The area immediately in front of the altar might also have had some sort of carpet. Such textiles fell out of favor in the plainer style of Protestant churches and with the architectural decoration of the Catholic baroque. In modern times, textiles have returned to some church spaces in the form of upholstered seating and carpets, which are essential given the widespread use of (highly reverberative) concrete.[51] Textiles are particularly effective at reducing reverberation because they are "essentially porous absorbers which dissipate acoustic energy due to friction inside the pores." They are more effective when there is a gap between the material and the wall, rather than being placed directly against it, and even more so if they have folds and are not lying flat.[52] Although the research of Alonso and Martellotta was based upon simulated acoustic effects, the results do correspond with our experience. They concluded that "From the listener's perspective, the addition of textiles brought about a notable reduction in reverberation time (probably not so dramatic under fully occupied conditions) and a slight increase in clarity," and said that clarity increased when textiles were closer to the listener.[53]

A less visible technology was acoustic pots inserted high into walls and especially vaults. The first mention of them is by Vitruvius (c. 80 BC–c. 20 BC), who described earthenware or bronze pots being placed in niches around the seating in theatres to amplify the voice, although none have been found in these locations. Nevertheless, many ceramic

---

of man in the vast space of Burgos Cathedral: https://www.metmuseum.org/art/collection/search/467650. See also Laura Weigert, *Weaving Sacred Stories: French Choir Tapestries and the Performance of Clerical Identity* (Ithaca, NY: Cornell University Press, 2004).

[51] See Young-Ji Choi and John S. Bradley, "Effects of Varied Row Spacing and Adding Cushions, Carpet and Occupants on Pew Sound Absorption," *Applied Acoustics* 99 (2015): 110–17.

[52] Alicia Alonso and Francesco Martellotta, "Room Acoustic Modelling of Textile Materials Hung Freely in Space: From the Reverberation Chamber to Ancient Churches," *Journal of Building Performance Simulation* 9, no. 5 (2016): 469–86, here 471–73.

[53] Alonso and Martellotta, "Room Acoustic Modelling," 483–84.

pots have been found in churches from the eleventh century onwards, in both East and West. They seem to have been used to improve clarity rather than loudness by absorbing some of the (unwanted) reflections and amplifying the desired frequencies. Jean-Christophe Valière suggested that they were tuned to enhance specific voices, and that they particularly improved chant. In the small monastery church at Aber-Wrach in Brittany, founded in 1507, 110 unglazed pots had been placed in the walls of the choir: "Seven kinds of pots have been found with frequencies uniformly distributed between 150 and 300 Hz. . . . This frequency range corresponds to male signing voices (Baritone-Tenor)."[54] At Dalby church in Sweden, the pots were placed behind holes in the ceiling, although normally they would have been fully enclosed in the vault or walls.[55]

Contemporary churches frequently make use of electronic amplification systems to compensate for the acoustic deficiencies of the space. These do not eliminate the reverberation, but, by positioning speakers nearer to the worshippers, they reduce the distance of the direct sound.

The Pulpit

The position of the speaker in relation to the listeners quite obviously affects audibility: if attentive listening can be enhanced by sight, as I discussed in chapter 7, having a clear view of the speaker by raising them above the congregation is beneficial. Listeners with a clear view of the speaker also receive a more direct sound, and this reduces the risk of too many unhelpful reverberations.

The solution for when the congregation were to be addressed directly in the readings and the sermon was to install a raised platform such as the ambo or *pulpitum*, or the *bema* was raised by a number of steps. Differences in floor level provide visual focus and reflect the

---

[54] Jean-Christophe Valière, Benedicte Bertholon-Palazzo, and Nadia Barone, "An Example of the Restoration of a Monastic Church with Acoustic Pots: L'Abbaye des Anges of L'Aber-Wrach (Brittany)," *The Journal of the Acoustical Society of America* 141, no. 5 (2017): 3774.

[55] Delphine Bard, "Acoustics in Dalby Church in Middle Ages and Today," *The Journal of the Acoustical Society of America* 141, no. 5 (2017): 3773. Desarnaulds, "De l'acoustique des églises en Suisse," 110ff.

Figure 6
The choir of San Clemente, Rome, with its double ambos. (Photo: Dnalor 01, Wikipedia Commons License CC-BY-SA 3.0.)

hierarchy in the community. Pedredo's survey of Toledo Cathedral noted very great differences in the floor levels with the sanctuary and high altar 1.7 meters above the presbytery and 2.4 meters above the nave and transepts.[56] Placing the minister on a raised platform aids visibility and demonstrates status, but also enhances audibility; however, determining which of these reasons takes precedence is not always straightforward.

The significance of the ambo can be shown by the excessively long description which Paul the Silentiary gave it in his ekphrasis of Hagia Sophia, as well as by the surviving examples of imposing monumental structures from early Byzantine and medieval churches. The ambo or *pulpitum* could be an extension of the *bema* which protruded into the nave, or it could be set up in the congregational space, connected to the *bema* by a raised walkway, the *solea*. With the latter, the

---

[56] Pedrero et al., "Acoustical Study of Toledo Cathedral," 25.

speaker was able to address the congregation from the midst of the nave.[57] In the West, pulpits appear in the naves of churches from the twelfth century exclusively for preaching, and they are clearly separated from the ambo or lectern used for readings, but this double arrangement was preceded by a phase of having two equal ambos to the left and right such as we see in San Clemente, Rome. Later medieval pulpits, especially in the churches of the mendicant orders, were not freestanding but were a balcony protruding from one of the walls. This position was for acoustic reasons, as Nirit Ben-Aryeh Debby pointed out: placing it in the nave meant the preacher avoided reverberations from the transepts, and the wall behind reflected the sound into the nave.[58] Acoustical considerations also determined whether the pulpit was placed on the north or south side.

The pulpit was obviously essential for Protestant worship. It remained raised but was often moved to a more central position, especially when the altar was no longer the main architectural focus. In Calvin's church in Geneva, the pulpit was placed on the north wall of the nave; the chancel, screen, and altar were removed and galleries introduced. The result was that the people surrounded the pulpit and were much closer to the preacher.[59] Fixed seating was also an aid to effective hearing of the Word, given that sermons were apt to be rather lengthy (see fig. 3, *Le Temple de Paradis*). Francis Bacon, in his *Sylva Sylvarum, Or, A Naturall History*, "Century III," explored the nature of sound. He stated that sound "moves round. That is to say On all sides, Upwards, Downwards, Forwards and Backwards. . . . They move strongest in a Right Line, Which nevertheless is not caused by the Rightness of the Line, but by the Shortness of the distance." Because of this, "you shall heare the Preachers voice, better, before the Pulpit than behind it or on the Sides"; he adds: "Sounds doe move better Downwards, than Upwards. Pulpits are placed high above the people . . . But this may be impouted to the Stops and Obstacles, which the voice meeteth with, when one Speaketh on the

---

[57] See Liudmila G. Khrushkova, "What Is a Solea? The Solea in Rome, Constantinople and Other Places," *Hortus Artium Medievalium* 25, no. 2 (2019): 263–82.

[58] Nirit Ben-Aryeh Debby, *The Renaissance Pulpit: Art and Preaching in Tuscany, 1400–1550*, Late Medieval and Early Modern Studies 6 (Turnhout: Brepols, 2007), 55.

[59] See Jeanne Halgren Kilde, *Sacred Power, Sacred Space* (New York: Oxford University Press, 2008), chap. 4.

levell. But there seemeth to be more in it. For it may be, that Spirituall Species, both of Things Visible and Sounds, doe move better Downwards than Upwards."[60]

Contemporary with this was the reordering of Sauvo parish church in southern Finland. A pulpit was installed in the center of this medieval church, with pews on all sides and a raked gallery immediately opposite. The pews on the east side have benches which can be flipped depending on whether the liturgical focus was the pulpit or the altar. Although the pulpit is visible from all parts of the nave, the best view of the preacher is from the gallery, which suggests that worshippers there may also have heard him better (fig. 7). The architect of St. Paul's Cathedral, Christopher Wren, had a "rule of thumb" about church acoustics: "A moderate voice may be heard 50 feet distant before the preacher, 30 feet on each side and 20 feet behind the pulpit, and not this unless the pronunciation be distinct."[61] In the nineteenth century, acoustical science showed that an auditorium in which the audience was placed in concentric circles around a lower stage was acoustically more effective, but for most traditional churches such a design was not considered appropriate. We note that Finney was using a theatre at the same time as the Gothic Revival in church architecture led to the construction of very reverberant spaces. Spurgeon's pulpit was, though, at a mid-height between the floor and the galleries.

Although raised pulpits minimize the obstruction to sound caused by other people, they can result in early resonance from the ceiling, which is exacerbated by vaults. Consequently, sounding boards, or testers, were placed above the pulpit to direct the sound downwards; the French term *abat-voix*, "beat down the voice," clearly indicates its purpose. Their use was ubiquitous, but as many were flat, which simply directs sound to the nearest listeners, or shaped like the inside

---

[60] Francis Bacon, *Sylva Sylvarum, Or, A Naturall History in Ten Centuries: Whereunto is Newly Added the History Naturall and Experimentall of Life and Death, Or of the Prolongation of Life* (London: William Ravvley, 1651), 49–50. *Sylva Sylvarum* was first published in 1627, one year after Bacon's death.

[61] Christopher Wren, *Parentalia* (London, 1750), quoted in T. Roger Smith, *A Rudimentary Treatise on the Acoustics of Public Buildings; Or, The Principles of the Science of Sound Applied to the Purposes of the Architect and Builder* (England: J. Weale, 1861), 34.

Figure 7

Sauvo parish church, southern Finland, was consecrated in 1472 and the interior substantially altered in the 1600s for Lutheran worship. In 1651 the pulpit with sounding board and altar painting were installed. In this period, the priest was obliged to start the liturgy from the pulpit and remain there until after the sermon, only moving to the altar to celebrate the Eucharist. (Photo: Juliette Day.)

of a top hat, which focuses the sound for the speaker alone, their usefulness was limited for most of the congregation.

Desarnaulds produced a theoretical analysis of the effectiveness of pulpits and sounding boards in Swiss churches. He concluded that a horizontal sounding board is only really effective for a radius of between two and five meters, but that its effectiveness increases in proportion to its size and angle; even with a 10 percent inclination, sound will be projected to over ten meters.[62] But the effect is very limited in churches where the listeners are spread throughout the building and was only ever useful when they were grouped around the pulpit. Desarnaulds's results correspond with the practical attempts to resolve the acoustical problems of Attercliffe church in 1829 by the Reverend John Blackburn. These were reported in one of the earliest treatises on room acoustics by Roger Smith in 1861. Blackburn found that the reverberations were so bad that speech was entirely unintelligible. First, Blackburn tried different positions of the pulpit, which was three meters high, with no discernable effect, and then he introduced a sounding board. Initially, this was a flat board, which enhanced the sound for those immediately in front but made it worse for everyone else. Then he tried a parabolic reflector which was fixed with an incline of ten to fifteen degrees. Although it was unsightly, Blackburn reported that those in the galleries were now able to hear even better than those in proximity to the pulpit.[63]

Conclusion

This is clearly not an exhaustive treatment of worship acoustics, but even this brief foray into an increasingly complex science enables us to consider how the listener's perception of a sound is highly influenced by the space in which it is heard. Traditional church designs, which have endured for centuries, have provided a distinctive and recognizable acoustical environment for liturgical worship, the principal characteristic being the long reverberation times which are

---

[62] Desarnaulds, "De l'acoustique des églises en Suisse," 183.
[63] Smith, *Rudimentary Treatise*, 62–63. Christ Church, Attercliffe (Sheffield, UK), was consecrated as the Anglican parish church in 1826, but was badly damaged in bombing during the Second World War and subsequently pulled down.

unhelpful for the spoken voice. However, these properties do not always seem to bother worshippers who associate the acoustical features with the authentic sound of their congregation's worship. When they hear themselves before God, they hear what the acoustics enable them to hear, not the intentional sounds alone. Some commentators have noticed that high reverberation produces an emotional and/or spiritual effect on listeners as the sound is seemingly displaced from its source; that is, it arrives as if from an unseen source. This does not suit all worship traditions, and we have seen how in those which have prioritized the "right hearing" of the Word that all attempts to improve speech intelligibility need to be tried, even if this means altering the traditional internal arrangement of the church. It is a moot point whether contemporary congregations should modify the intentional sounds of their worship to better suit the acoustics of their spaces—for example, increasing the use of chant—or modify their spaces to achieve the desired acoustical outcome for their style of worship. Whatever is decided, it is as well to realize that any solution will always involve a compromise.

Conclusion:
Listening and Liturgical Listening

Listening

Listening is not the same as hearing. Our ears are always open to receive sounds regardless of whether we wish or intend to hear them, and thus hearing denotes a more passive engagement with the auditory situation we find ourselves in. Although it appears to us that hearing sounds requires no very great effort on our behalf, the research which investigates why we hear some sounds but not others shows that, however passive we think we might be, our brains are actively processing the sounds into those we wish to attend to and those we wish to reject, and assessing the value of the ones we become aware of but might choose to ignore. Added to our aural filtering, the sounds we hear are affected by other more practical matters before we even reach the meaningfulness of the sound: for example, our proximity to the source, the volume of the sound signal, and our level of attentiveness to it; that is, our mental and emotional attitude. So, having said that, it is probably not at all accurate to say that hearing is entirely passive, but simply that we are mostly unaware of the effort which enables us to hear.

I have, though, distinguished hearing from listening, but I no longer wish to distinguish them by passive and active modes of audition, but rather to consider listening to be an *intentional act of audition*, whereas hearing does not have to be. Listening involves no change in the reception and processing systems of sound signals, but it does involve a more active cognitive processing by which we seek out the meaning of what we hear. There is an anticipation that the sound contains information which we want to or should want to know and therefore an openness to what it might reveal. And this is the case even if we have heard it before. The information and meaning is not entirely revealed in the sound, and we are required to make sense of it by connecting it to prior knowledge and experiences lodged in our memory. Listening is an active seeking out of these connections, such that what is newly heard is recognized as belonging to particular types of knowledge and experience, as well as attaching value to it. The criterion of novelty is not normally why we listen; indeed, we are often very pleased to hear a personally significant piece of music many times. As we do, we may identify the elements which make it familiar, but also compare with other times we have heard it. Possibly we may be able to identify what is different, but in any case, even with recorded music and speech our own disposition and the listening environment affect each new hearing of it.

Once tuned into a sound signal, listening does still require some effort, particularly in extracting one sound stream from others which compete for our attention. Attentive listening does sometimes seem effortless if we are completely focused, but at other times it is a great effort when distracted by competing claims on our attention, or if we are tired or bored. To listen means that we are open to what might be revealed, to the possibility that it will add to our understanding of ourselves and the world, that it has the potential to change us and our situation. Listening also requires a turning of the ear towards the source of the sound, and this takes on an ethical dimension when the source is another person, or a spiritual dimension if God is the presumed source. We listen to those whom we consider have something to add to our sense of self or our understanding of others and of the world. Already there has been a prior judgement about the value of the sound before it has begun, and by implication also a value judgement about its source. Part of our ethical responsibility as listeners is to reflect on what criteria we apply when deciding what sounds are worth listening to: are they social, political, aesthetic, emotional, or intellectual?

Liturgical Listening

The elements from which a model of liturgical listening can be constructed have been put forward throughout this book. In chapter 1, I suggested that the methodological considerations of the *sound-*

scape are a useful starting point for two reasons. First, they force us to acknowledge the totality of sounds which are available to be heard in the worship event and not just those to which we actively attend. The presence of many sounds competing for our attention presents a more complex listening environment than simply attending to the sounds produced from our liturgical books and hymnals. It is useful to remember Ari Kelman's assertion that "background sounds are not background at all," and to realize that it is these sounds which enable us to situate ourselves in the world. Second, soundscape theories invite us to consider the ways in which certain sounds are privileged in the communities where they are heard; authority and social convention prioritize some sounds over others. Communities create and inhabit their own soundscape, which they compare, usually negatively, with the soundscape of others. In the church, the "others" are invariably congregations whose theological and ecclesial as well as social differences are negatively compared with our own.

Listing the distinctive elements of the soundscape of one worshipping community will not account for all the possible sounds that are present, and it creates unhelpful, value-laden comparisons between communities for the presence or absence of sounds which one personally considers important. Consequently, I have suggested that a more useful way to consider the liturgical soundscape is to use the categories of *intentional sounds*, *non-intentional sounds*, and *noise*. What sounds fall into each category will be determined by each denomination, by each congregation, and will be further determined by social and contextual factors. *Intentional sounds* are intended to be meaningful: they have been authorized by those in authority and/or by tradition, and are anticipated by worshippers. Principally, this category includes prayers, Scripture readings, hymns and songs, and the sermon, as well as instrumental music and ritual sound; even the community notices can be considered as intentional sounds. It is important to remember that intentional sounds do not necessarily need to be semantically intelligible to the worshippers. *Non-intentional sounds* are those which are heard and tolerated but do not form the intentional content of the liturgical event. These are ambient noises from the church building or the locality that do not intrude or overwhelm the attention of worshippers. Additionally, I have placed in this category the sounds which accompany rituals, those sounds which are a by-product of ritual actions and to which they add little additional significance. The final category is *noise*: any sound which does not belong, which is not tolerated, and which disturbs auditory attention to the intentional sounds. These categories can be used to investigate the auditory environment of worship of both contemporary and historical churches, and to produce descriptions of the soundscape of specific congregations that include the totality of the sound to be heard. Only once we know what the liturgical soundscape is can we consider the auditory task facing worshippers.

The words we use for "audition" reflect our relationship to what is heard. This is true for mundane auditory environments just as much as in the liturgy. *Hear* refers to any act of audition, whether it is willed or not, but *listen* always means an intentional and active hearing; the archaic English *hearken* also carries the sense of intensive listening. It is through the senses that we perceive and understand the world: the phenomenological philosophers referred to in chapter 2 emphasize the openness of our ears to the world, an alertness to what is there to be received and a responsibility to strain to hear and thus to understand. Audition also places us in relationship with others, because, as Gemma Corradi Fiumara has said, "there can be no saying without hearing, no speaking which is not an integral part of listening, no speech which is not somehow received."[1] Biblical models of audition present God's hearing as a model for human hearing, which, in the New Testament, is linked to faith in Christ. This hearing, or perhaps hearkening, is connected to Christian responsibility to listen properly in worship; that is, to be attentive to the preacher as well as to have faith. This raises an interesting question about how we can use our senses to perceive the immaterial God and, particularly, how we hear God when his speaking does not activate our auditory system. The notion of spiritual senses was originally conceived as a separate, and higher, sensorium by which God communicated directly, bypassing the physical sensorium, but modern theologians prefer to consider that we hear God with the physical sensorium through the proclamation of the Word and the sacraments in the church's worship. Hence, in worship, we are to have our ears attuned for the continuing revelation of Christ in the world.

---

[1] Gemma Corradi Fiumara, *The Other Side of Language: A Philosophy of Listening*, trans. Charles Lambert (London: Routledge 1990), 1.

Listening is not a single undifferentiated activity in worship, as in life, and listeners adopt different roles depending on their relationship to the producer of the sound. Listeners are also speakers: in the liturgy, we hear ourselves address God and each other; we are not simply overhearers or eavesdroppers of the speech of others. Listeners are also active in the creation of the sonic event and in its meaning, as audience studies have revealed. But liturgical listening also asks us to be attentive to sounds which appear not to have a physical origin, either because of ritual play which conceals the source, or because it is God who addresses the congregation through the words of others, speaking, as it were, to the heart. Liturgical listening places a responsibility upon worshippers to be open to the transformative Word of God, which is set before them to be gathered and taken into themselves; it is anything but passive.

I have also argued in this book that listening is not just the means by which the liturgical sounds are received—that is, a necessary corollary to the performance of the intentional sounds—but it is a ritual activity in its own right. Thus, liturgical listening is not the same as ordinary listening because it is framed by the ritual, and because within the liturgy the listeners are attuned to the immanence of God and not solely to the informational content which the verbal content might convey, and which participants usually know already. Indeed, the meaning of the ritual is never conveyed by the verbal content alone, but always in conjunction with ritual gesture, other sonic and sensory phenomenon, and the context.

Liturgical listening is also paradigmatic of authentic listening when worshippers participate in acts of what I have called *ritualized listening*. A simple and often repeated injunction like "Let us pray" requires and is fulfilled by an act of ritual listening when worshippers are invited to be attentive to God and to the prayers addressed to him. Scripted and unscripted dialogues between ministers and people put them into a relationship that is constituted by attentiveness to each other. The most powerful acts of *ritualized listening* occur when it is God or Christ who are presumed to be the speaker, as is the case in the reading of the gospel and in the sermon. Ritualized listening demands heightened auditory attentiveness and may be accompanied by other focusing rituals. Although the entire act of worship requires attentive listening, it is in these moments of ritualized listening that worshippers model the ideal of attentive listening to God by their auditory and physical behaviors.

The intentional sounds of worship are primarily verbal, the liturgical texts performed by speech or by singing, but also involve music and silence. Setting aside liturgical silence for now, the other intentional sounds of worship should be placed on a spectrum according to the mode of performance, which does not place speech and music in opposition to each other, but shows how choices about the performance of the liturgical texts affect how they are heard. Such choices are commonly made for pragmatic reasons related to the skills and resources of the congregation, but given that the spoken word, the chanted word, and the sung word require very different listening strategies, it really does matter how one chooses to perform them. Many factors affect the listener's ability to latch onto the words and hence be able to make sense of what they convey. For spoken words, speed and intonation are key elements which affect comprehension. The listener must be particularly attentive to the start and end of semantic units, as these may not be clear from the rapid sequence of syllables. Choral recitation emphasizes that the roles of speaker and listener are mutual and interchangeable, and it facilitates the creation of communal interpretations of the texts. Cantillated readings of Scripture and chant are much easier to follow, because the delivery is slower and the melody provides clues to the listener about when a semantic unit comes to an end; it also improves intelligibility in the very resonant acoustics of traditional church buildings. Communal singing has been shown to be very important in creating social cohesion, and hymns in particular model communally authorized emotional and theological responses to God, which the listener appropriates for herself as she sings. Questions over the suitability of instrumental music in worship arise, first, because of the emphasis on clearly hearing the word/Word and faith; and, second, because without verbal content there is no guide to how it is to be interpreted. Music, more than other sounds, surrounds the listener and produces physical and emotional responses which speech is rarely able to do.

The combination of these intentional sounds are the most significant elements in the liturgical soundscape of the congregation and are often the primary way of distinguishing between different communities, even within the same denomination. It is by them that congregations hear themselves before God, and with them that they hear God in their midst. When making sense of liturgical and scriptural texts and sermons, listeners do more than attend to the propositional content of each one individually; in worship, each auditory experience is interpreted in light of the whole ritual event, of which the performance of the texts is part.

Silence is an integral part of the liturgical soundscape, and it is not an absence of sound or a ritual hiatus. Christian tradition has valued silence as a way of listening to God, and when used appropriately in worship it can act as another mode of ritualized listening. It is important not to confuse *hesychia*, which is an ascetical act of physical and mental stillness, with silence, which is a sonic phenomenon; in much writing on prayer and spirituality, these are conflated. It is the case, though, that one can lead to the other; without physical stillness it is not possible to create the conditions for silence, and without silence it is impossible to create stillness in the mind. The observation that silence can only be heard by those who perform it is very apt.

The liturgical event consists of a series of spoken and sung texts, and ritual gestures which are interspersed with moments of silence, but these silences do not have the same value or purpose. I have suggested that instead of thinking about silence in terms of what worshippers should be doing during it (usually forms of silent, yet verbal, prayer), it is more useful to consider how it functions to structure the ritual—that is, by *intervals* that indicate a transition between ritual units and enable the listener to recollect themselves to complete one listening activity and prepare for the next, and by *pauses* during which the congregation hears itself in a communal silence within a ritual unit. The latter are particularly powerful in holding the listeners in a state of heightened attentiveness to the ritual and/or to the presence of God. Attempts to legislate for the length of a liturgical silence ignore the ritual dynamic implied by the intervals and pauses; essentially, a silence need only be long enough for one to experience being in it, because at each occurrence one's experience will depend on the context. Silence creates the space from which speech and other intentional sounds of worship can emerge and be heard, rather than being a sign that a sound has been completed. In silence we can anticipate revelation.

The liturgical soundscape includes *all* the sounds present to be heard during worship, and that includes *noise*. Any sound can be noise if it is heard in the wrong place or is deemed to be distracting, offensive, inappropriate, or valueless by the listener or community. Noise does not normally refer to the quality of the sound itself, despite the fact that listening to very loud sounds and sound signals with very jumbled frequencies will usually cause aural discomfort. The designation of a sound as noise is the result of personal or social perceptions, to which may be added theological ideas that connect noise with the Fall, sin, the world, and hell. These notions are implicit when worshippers and ministers complain about noise during worship. Superficially, there may be a judgement about a sound which does not belong, but subliminally are fears of an intrusion of sin/the world into sacred time; only this can explain why there are such frequent complaints about noise in worship throughout Christian history.

Liturgical noise is accompanied by disruptive behaviors, and there is a pretty consistent catalog of chattering, moving around, coughing, and shifting in the pews in the literature; in the modern era, the mobile phone comes at the top of the list. It is only a short jump from condemnation of the noise to condemnation of the source of the noise, and this raises complicated social and ecclesial issues. In many churches, how to "deal with" the noise of children during worship is a delicate topic; no solutions are offered here, except to invite congregations to reflect on what personal, social, cultural, and theological factors lie behind the designation of some sounds as noise. Challenging our presuppositions may well be a better place to start the conversation than with the removal of a member of the church from worship. It is useful to reflect, too, that although noise has been understood as a sound without communicative significance by those who perceive and designate it, it can be used as a powerful signal to a community; in these cases it is intended to be noticed and is not the result of inattentive behavior. Noise is most powerfully used as a sign of protest, and in churches it has been used to protest against the minister or preacher, as well as against forms of worship. Invariably, civil and canon law can be brought to bear against the noise-makers. Interestingly, noise has also been used as an approved sign of spiritual gifts or spiritual maturity in certain contexts, when the noise-maker's style of prayer challenges the mainstream. Social, cultural, and ecclesial conventions determine whether such noises intrude or are another intentional sound.

Noise is particularly bothersome because it distracts the worshipper from the aural attentiveness required for liturgical listening. Complaints against noise in church may mask a wider complaint about a lack of attentiveness and an improper hearing. This became a particular problem in the post-Reformation era when whole communities and nations needed to learn new ways of worshipping which were physically passive and required much greater auditory attention. The many tracts produced in the seventeenth century mix biblical and theological ideas of audition, faith, and behavior to bring about a disciplining of the ears so that people might hear aright the word/Word of God, that is, the Scriptures and the preaching. Inattentiveness in church was not invented in the sixteenth century, but it certainly became more of a congregational problem.

Contemporary psychological and cognitive research reveals how very difficult it is for us to pay attention aurally, despite our best efforts. Certain things may help, such as frequent exposure to a context in which attentive listening is required, and memories of the content or of the sound source enable the listener to more easily make sense of what they hear. Spiritual and ethical dimensions of attentiveness ask us to be physically, sensorially, and emotionally present to God and/or to the other. Attentiveness is potentially more than directing our auditory capacities exclusively to a single sound source, but is more of an inner disposition or attitude. Worshippers are asked or expected to be attentive when a failure to attend is perceived, and, in these instances, it is worth considering what sort of inattentiveness is meant. It is all too easy to see signs of physical inattentiveness as a sign of auditory inattentiveness, and one or both as signs of interpersonal and spiritual inattentiveness, when in fact an individual may experience their own inattentiveness as only one of these.

As this book has made clear, the auditory experience of worship is much more than simply hearing the intentional sounds alone. There are two competing acoustical requirements for most Christian liturgy: reverberation, which is essential for chant and music, and speech intelligibility, which is essential for the sermon and usually also the Scripture readings. Modifications to a building are often made to reduce the former and enhance the latter. What are usually considered decorative features, such as curtains, wall hangings or tapestries, carpets, and altar textiles, have the potential to considerably reduce reverberation and render speech more intelligible: the use of more textiles at certain times can combine with the visual impact of the liturgical color, to aurally signal the importance of a feast. Modern electronic sound amplification has done much to improve speech intelligibility, and in many instances made the pulpit redundant. However, the history of the pulpit reveals much about the intentional acoustic design of worship: its position and height, the sounding board, as well as the visual focus provided by a large and often highly decorated location for the sound source, the preacher.

The study of aural architecture draws our attention to the context in which liturgical listening takes place, and the effect of the building and our position in it upon the transmission and reception of the sound signals. From the perspective of contemporary acoustical design, Christian worship spaces appear eminently unsuited to the aural activities they facilitate. The intentional sounds of worship—speech, chant, communal singing, instrumental music, and silence—each require such different acoustical environments that it would be impossible to create the optimum environment for a single liturgy in which all are combined. Interestingly, though, worshippers seem mostly untroubled by the acoustic infelicities and compromises because they identify their own community's worship with the particular way it sounds in their worship space. The sonic personality of their church building provides the way that a congregation hears itself, and hears itself before God. The way a congregation sounds has significance for its spiritual, ecclesial, and social identity, which is more than the sum of meanings conveyed by the intentional sounds.

❖   ❖   ❖

Liturgical listening

- attends to a limited range of intentional sound signals within the fixed temporal and spatial boundaries of the worship event and the space designated for it;
- is never an individual and private aural experience, but takes place in and is influenced by a communal listening;

- is not primarily engaged in a situation of information exchange, but displays spiritual, social, and ecclesial identity and values;
- is not a passive mode of liturgical participation but a ritual performance of "right hearing" of the Word of God; and
- is not just the physical operation of the human auditory system, but participates in and makes present God's hearing of his people and the world.

Bibliography

Adkin, Neil A. "A Problem in the Early Church: Noise during the Sermon and Lesson." *Mnemosyne* 38 (1985): 161–63.

Ælfric, *Letter to the Monks of Eynsham*. In Christopher A. Jones, *Ælfric's Letter to the Monks of Eynsham*. Cambridge: Cambridge University Press, 1999.

Albrecht, Daniel E. *Rites in the Spirit: A Ritual Approach to Pentecostal/Charismatic Spirituality*. Sheffield, UK: Sheffield Academic Press, 1999.

Algargoosh, Alaa, Babak Soleimani, Sile O'Modhrain, and Mojtaba Navvab. "The Impact of the Acoustic Environment on Human Emotion and Experience: A Case Study of Worship Spaces." *Building Acoustics* 29, no. 1 (2022): 85–106.

Alonso, Alicia, and Francesco Martellotta. "Room Acoustic Modelling of Textile Materials Hung Freely in Space: From the Reverberation Chamber to Ancient Churches." *Journal of Building Performance Simulation* 9, no. 5 (2016): 469–86.

Alvarez-Morales, Lidia, and Francesco Martellotta, "A Geometrical Acoustic Simulation of the Effect of Occupancy and Source Position in Historical Churches." *Applied Acoustics* 91 (2015): 47–58.

Amidon, Philip R., trans. *Philostorgius: Church History*. Atlanta: Society of Biblical Literature, 2007.

Anderson, Gary A., and Markus Bockmuehl, eds. *Creation Ex Nihilo: Origins, Development, Contemporary Challenges*. South Bend, IN: University of Notre Dame Press, 2017.

Anderson, James, trans. *John Calvin: Commentary on the Book of Psalms*. Edinburgh: Calvin Translation Society, 1845–49.

Anderson, Michael Alan. *Music and Performance in the Book of Hours*. New York: Routledge, 2022.

Attali, Jacques. *Noise: The Political Economy of Music* (*Bruits: essai sur l'économie politique de la musique*, 1977). Translated by Brian Massumi. Minneapolis: University of Minnesota Press, 1985.

Augustine. *The Catholic Way of Life and the Manichean Way of Life (De moribus ecclesiae Catholicae et De moribus Manichaeorum)*. In *The Manichean Debate*, translated by Roland Teske and Boniface Ramsey. Vol. 1/19 of *The Works of Saint Augustine*. Charlottesville, VA: InteLex Corporation, 2014.

Augustine. *Augustine: Confessions*. Translated by Carolyn J.-B. Hammond. Vol. 27 of the Loeb Classical Library. Cambridge, MA: Harvard University Press, 2016.

Augustine. *The Confessions*. Translated by Maria Boulding and edited by John E. Rotelle. The Works of Saint Augustine. Vol. 1. Hyde Park, NY: New City Press, 2014.

Augustine. *De doctrina Christiana*. Translated by Edmund Hill and John E. Rotelle. Vol. 1/11 of *The Works of Saint Augustine*. Charlottesville, VA: InteLex Corporation, 2014.

Augustine. *Sermon 57*. In *The Works of Saint Augustine*, edited by John E. Rotelle. Vol. III/3 of *Sermons (51–94) on the Old Testament*. Translated by Edmund Hill. Hyde Park, NY: New City Press, 1991.

Austin, John L. *How to Do Things with Words: The William James Lectures Delivered at Harvard University in 1955*. Oxford: Clarendon Press, 1962.

Backer, Kristina C., and Claude Alain. "Attention to Memory: Orienting Attention to Sound Object Representations." *Psychological Research* 78 (2014): 439–52.

Bacon, Francis. *Sylva Sylvarum, Or, A Naturall History in Ten Centuries: Whereunto is Newly Added the History Naturall and Experimentall of Life and Death, Or of the Prolongation of Life*. London: William Ravvley, 1651.

Bader, Günter. "La tentation comme attention—l'attention comme tentation." *Revue de théologie et de philosophie* 146, no. 2 (2014): 137–53.

Bailey, Peter. "Breaking the Sound Barrier: A Historian Listens to Noise." *Body & Society* 2, no. 2 (1996): 49–66.

Bale, Anthony, trans. *The Book of Margery Kempe*. Oxford: Oxford University Press, 2016.

Balthasar, Hans Urs von. "Seeing, Hearing, and Reading within the Church." In *Spouse of the Word*, translated by A. V. Littledale and Alexander Dru, 473–490. Vol 2. of *Explorations in Theology*. San Francisco: Ignatius Press, 1991.

Balthasar, Hans Urs von. *Mysterium Paschale: The Mystery of Easter*. Translated by Aidan Nicols, OP. Edinburgh: T&T Clark, 1990.

Bard, Delphine. "Acoustics in Dalby Church in Middle Ages and Today." *The Journal of the Acoustical Society of America* 141, no. 5 (2017): 3773.

Barney, Stephen A., W. J. Lewis, J. A. Beach, and Oliver Berghof, trans. *The Etymologies of Isidore of Seville*. Cambridge: Cambridge University Press, 2006.

Bastable, Richard. "The Vigil of Pascha: Formation in Silence." *Anaphora* 3.1 (1999): 57–66.

Baumann, Dorothea, and Christina Niederstätter. "Acoustics in Sacred Buildings." In *Sacred Buildings: A Design Manual*, edited by Rudolf Stegers, 54–59. Basel: Birkhäuser, 2008.

Bede. *The Ecclesiastical History of the English People*. Translated by Bertram Colgrave and R. A. B. Mynors. Oxford: Oxford Medieval Texts, 2022.

Bellomo, Tiffany R., Sanjana Prasad, Jacob Abou-Hanna, Sai Talluru, Yanjun Xie, Linyan Wang, Glenn E. Green, and Richard L. Neitzel. "Characterization of Noise Exposure in Places of Worship." *Applied Acoustics* 180 (2021): 108–14.

Bendixen, Alexandra, and Iring Koch. "Editorial for Special Issue: 'Auditory Attention: Merging Paradigms and Perspectives.'" *Psychological Research* 78 (2014): 301–3.

Berkaak, Odd Are. "Noise and Tranquility at Stonehenge: The Political Acoustics of Cultural Heritage." In *The Oxford Handbook of Sound and Imagination*. Vol. 1. Edited by Mark Grimshaw-Aagaard, Mads Walther-Hansen, and Martin Knakkergaard, 311–31. Oxford: Oxford University Press, 2019.

Bhattachaiji, Santha. "Tears and Screaming: Weeping in the Spirituality of Margery Kempe." In *Holy Tears: Weeping in the Religious Imagination*, edited by John Stratton Hawley and Kimberley Christine Patton, 229–41. Princeton, NJ: Princeton University Press, 2018.

Bijsterveld, Karen. *Mechanical Sound: Technology, Culture, and Public Problems of Noise in the Twentieth Century*. Cambridge, MA: MIT Press, 2008.

Bitton-Ashkelony, Brouria. "'More Interior Than the Lips and the Tongue': John of Apamea and Silent Prayer in Late Antiquity." *Journal of Early Christian Studies* 20, no. 2 (2012): 303–31.

Blesser, Barry, and Linda-Ruth Salter. *Spaces Speak, Are You Listening? Experiencing Aural Architecture*. Cambridge, MA: MIT Press, 2007.

Bornstein, Daniel. "How to Behave in Church and How to Become a Priest." In *Medieval Christianity in Practice*, edited by Miri Rubin, 109–14. Princeton, NJ: Princeton University Press, 2009.

Boulding, Maria, trans. *The Confessions*. Edited by John E. Rotelle. The Works of Saint Augustine. Vol. 1. Hyde Park, NY: New City Press, 2014.

Bouras, Laskarina, and Robert F. Taft. "Ambo." In *The Oxford Dictionary of Byzantium*, edited by Alexander P. Kazhdan. Oxford: Oxford University Press, 1991.

Bownde, Nicholas. *The Doctrine of the Sabbath*. London: Widdow Orwin, 1595.

Bradley, David T., Lauren Ronsse, and Erica Ryherd, eds. *Worship Space Acoustics: 3 Decades of Design*. New York: Springer, 2016.

Bradshaw, Paul F., and Anne McGowan. *The Pilgrimage of Egeria*. Collegeville, MN: Liturgical Press, 2018.

Braun, Lucinde. "The *Syntagma musicum* in Lutheran Organ Sermons of the Seventeenth and the Eighteenth Centuries." *De musica disserenda* 15, nos. 1–2 (2019): 179–200.

Bray, Gerald. *The Anglican Canons, 1529–1947*. Church of England Record Society Series. Vol. 6. Woodbridge, UK: Boydell & Brewer, 1998.

Bray, Gerald, ed. *The Books of Homilies: A Critical Edition*. Cambridge, UK: Lutterworth Press, 2015.

Bregman, Albert S. *Auditory Scene Analysis: The Perceptual Organization of Sound*. Cambridge, MA: MIT Press, 1990.

Bressler, Scott, Salwa Masud, Hari Bharadwaj, and Barbara Shinn-Cunningham. "Bottom-Up Influences of Voice Continuity in Focusing Selective Auditory Attention." *Psychological Research* 78, no. 3 (2014): 349–60.

Broadbent, Donald E. *Perception and Communication*. New York: Pergamon Press, 1958.

Brock, Sebastian. "John the Solitary, On Prayer. " *Journal of Theological Studies* 30.1 (1979): 84-96.

Bronkhorst, Alfred W. "The Cocktail-Party Problem Revisited: Early Processing and Selection of Multi-Talker Speech." *Attention, Perception & Psychophysics* 77, no. 5 (2015): 1465–87.

Brown, Laura Feitzinger. "Brawling in Church: Noise and the Rhetoric of Lay Behavior in Early Modern England." *The Sixteenth Century Journal* 34 (2003): 955–72.

Brownrig, Ralph. *Twenty-Five Sermons by the Right Reverend Father in God, Ralph Brownrig, Late Lord Bishop of Exeter*. Cambridge, UK: W. Martyn, 1664.

Bruneau, Thomas J. "Communicative Silences: Forms and Functions." *The Journal of Communication* 23 (1973): 17–46.

Bunyan, John. *A FEW Sighs from Hell: OR The Groans of a damned Soul: OR, An Exposition of those words in the 19th. of Luke, ver. 19. &c*. In *The Miscellaneous Works of John Bunyan*. Vol. 1. Edited by Roger Sharrock and Ted L. Underwood, 221–49. Oxford: Clarendon Press, 2014.

Caesarius of Arles. *Caesarius: Sermons, Volume 1 (1–80)*. Translated by Mary Magdeleine Mueller. Vol. 31 of Fathers of the Church. Washington, DC: Catholic University of America Press, 1956.

Cage, John. "The Future of Music: Credo." Chap. 1 in *Silence: Lectures and Writings*. Middletown, CT: Wesleyan University Press, 2011.

Calvin, John. *John Calvin: Commentary on the Book of Psalms*. Translated by James Anderson. Edinburgh: Calvin Translation Society, 1845–49.

Camilleri, Sylvain. *Phénoménologie de la religion et herméneutique théologique dans la pensée du jeune Heidegger: commentaire analytique des fondements philosophiques de la mystique médiévale (1916–1919)*. Dordrecht: Springer, 2008.

Carside, Charles. "Calvin's Preface to the Psalter: A Re-Appraisal." *The Music Quarterly* 37 (1951): 566–77.

Carter, Tim. "Word-Painting." In *Grove Music Online*. New York: Oxford University Press, 2001.

Cartledge, Mark. *Testimony in the Spirit: Rescripting Ordinary Pentecostal Theology*. Farnham, UK: Ashgate, 2010.

Cashner, Andrew A. *Hearing Faith: Music as Theology in the Spanish Empire*. Leiden: Brill, 2020.

Chase, Nathan P. "The Ascent into Heaven: An Answer to the Problem of Time in Liturgical Anamnesis." *Studia Liturgica* (2022).

Cherry, Donald. "Some Experiments on the Recognition of Speech, with One and with Two Ears." *Journal of the Acoustical Society of America* 25 (1953): 975–79.

Choi, Young-Ji, and John S. Bradley. "Effects of Varied Row Spacing and Adding Cushions, Carpet and Occupants on Pew Sound Absorption." *Applied Acoustics* 99 (2015): 110–17.

Chupungco, Anscar. *Cultural Adaptation of the Liturgy*. New York: Paulist Press, 1982.

Chupungco, Anscar. *Liturgies of the Future: The Process and Methods of Inculturation*. New York: Paulist Press, 1989.

Church of England. Canons of 1571. In *The Anglican Canons, 1529–1947*, edited by Gerald Bray. Church of England Record Society Series. Vol. 6. Woodbridge, UK: Boydell & Brewer, 1998.

Church of England. *Common Worship: Services and Prayers for the Church of England*. London: Church House Publishing, 2000.

Church of England. "An Homily of the Right Use of the Church or Temple of God, and of the Reverence Due Unto the Same." In *The Second Book of Homilies* (1563). In *The Books of Homilies: A Critical Edition*, edited by Gerald Bray. Cambridge: Lutterworth Press, 2015.

Cioni, Francesca. " 'Confuse Noises, and Clatterings': Fixed Seating and Disorderly Worship in England, 1604–1632." *The Seventeenth Century* 35 (2020): 557–77.

Cirillo, Ettore, and Francesco Martellotta. *Worship, Acoustics, and Architecture*. Brentwood, UK: Multi-Science Pub. Co., 2006.

Clement of Alexandria. *Clement of Alexandria: Christ the Educator [Paedagogus]*. Translated by Simon P. Wood. Vol. 23 of Fathers of the Church. Washington, DC: Catholic University of America Press, 1954.

Clifford, Richard J. "*Creatio ex nihilo* in the Old Testament/Hebrew Bible." In *Creation Ex Nihilo: Origins, Development, Contemporary Challenges*, edited by Gary A. Anderson and Markus Bockmuehl, 55–76. South Bend, IN: University of Notre Dame Press, 2017.

Colgrave, Bertram, and R. A. B. Mynors, trans. *Bede: The Ecclesiastical History of the English People*. Oxford: Oxford Medieval Texts, 2022.

Coolman, Boyd Taylor. "Alexander of Hales." In *The Spiritual Senses: Perceiving God in Western Christianity*, edited by Paul L. Gavrilyuk and Sarah Coakley, 121–39. Cambridge: Cambridge University Press, 2011.

Corbin, Alain. *Village Bells: Sound and Meaning in the 19th-Century French Countryside*. New York: Columbia University Press, 1998.

Corradi Fiumara, Gemma. *The Other Side of Language: A Philosophy of Listening*. Translated by Charles Lambert. London: Routledge 1990.

Coster, Will, and Andrew Spicer, eds. *Sacred Space in Early Modern Europe*. Cambridge: Cambridge University Press, 2005.

Craig, John. "Psalms, Groans and Dog-Whippers: The Soundscape of Sacred Space in the English Parish Church, 1547–1642." In *Sacred Space in Early Modern Europe*, edited by Will Coster and Andrew Spicer, 104–23. Cambridge: Cambridge University Press, 2005.

Csordas, Thomas J. *Language, Charisma, and Creativity: The Ritual Life of a Religious Movement*. Berkeley and Los Angeles: University of California Press, 1997.

Csordas, Thomas J. "Somatic Modes of Attention." *Cultural Anthropology* 8, no. 2 (1993): 135–56.

Cunningham, Mary. "Dramatic Device or Didactic Tool? The Function of Dialogue in Byzantine Preaching." In *Rhetoric in Byzantium*, edited by Elizabeth Jeffreys, 101–13. Aldershot, UK: Ashgate, 2003.

Cunningham, Mary, and Pauline Allen. *Preacher and Audience: Studies in Early Christian and Byzantine Homiletics*. Leiden: Brill, 2017.

Cyril of Jerusalem. *Procatechesis*. Translated by E. J. Yarnold, SJ. In *Cyril of Jerusalem*. London: Taylor and Francis, 2002.

Daley, Brian. *Gregory of Nazianzus*. London: Taylor & Francis, 2006.

Dalton, Polly, and Robert W. Hughes. "Auditory Attentional Capture: Implicit and Explicit Approaches." *Psychological Research* 78 (2014): 313–20.

Dandelion, Pink. *A Sociological Analysis of the Theology of Quakers: The Silent Revolution*. Lewiston, NY: Edwin Mellen Press, 1996.

Daniels III, David D. " 'Gotta Moan Sometime': A Sonic Exploration of Earwitnesses to Early Pentecostal Sound in North America." *Pneuma* 30 (2008): 5–32.

Dauenhauer, Bernard P. *Silence: The Phenomenon and Its Ontological Significance*. Bloomington: Indiana University Press, 1980.

Davey, Nicholas. "On the Polity of Experience: Towards a Hermeneutics of Attentiveness." *Renascence* 56, no. 4 (2004): 217–34.

Davies, Oliver. "Reading the Burning Bush: Voice, World and Holiness." *Modern Theology* 22, no. 3 (2006): 439–48.

Day, Juliette. *Reading the Liturgy: An Exploration of Texts in Christian Worship*. London: Bloomsbury/T&T Clark, 2014.

Day, Juliette. "The Status and Role of Doorkeepers in the Early Medieval West." *Studies in Late Antiquity* 6, no. 1 (2022): 148–73.

De Blaauw, Sible, and Klára Dolzalová. "Constructing Liminal Space? Curtains in Late Antique and Early Medieval Churches." *Convivium Supplementum* (2019): 46–67.

De Boer, Wietse, and Christine Göttler, eds. *Religion and the Senses Early Modern Europe*. Intersections 26. Leiden: Brill, 2012.

Debby, Nirit Ben-Aryeh. *The Renaissance Pulpit: Art and Preaching in Tuscany, 1400–1550*. Turnhout: Brepols, 2007.

Del modo che si die tenire in chiexia. In Daniel Bornstein, "How to Behave in Church and How to Become a Priest." In *Medieval Christianity in Practice*, edited by Miri Rubin, 110–11. Princeton, NJ: Princeton University Press, 2009.

Desarnaulds, Victor. "De l'acoustique des églises en Suisse—une approche pluridisciplinaire." PhD diss. École Polytechnique Fédérale de Lausanne, 2002.

Desarnaulds, Victor, António P. O. Carvalho, and Gilbert Monay. "Church Acoustics and the Influence of Occupancy." *Building Acoustics* 9, no. 1 (2002): 29–47.

Dhomont, Francis. "Schaeffer, Pierre." In *Grove Music Online*. New York: Oxford University Press, 2001.

DiCenso, Daniel J., and Rebecca Maloy, eds. *Chant, Liturgy, and the Inheritance of Rome: Essays in Honour of Joseph Dyer*. Woodbridge, UK: Boydell & Brewer, Henry Bradshaw Society, 2017.

Didascalia Apostolorum. Translated by Alistair C. Stewart. In *The Didascalia Apostolorum: An English Version*. Studia Traditionis Theologiae 1. Turnhout: Brepols, 2009.

Directions for a devout and decent behaviour in the public worship of God; more particularly in the use of the Common Prayer appointed by the Church of England. London: F. and C. Rivington, 1799.

Douglas, Mary. *Purity and Danger: An Analysis of the Concept of Pollution and Taboo.* London: Routledge, 2003.

Downey, Michael. "Silence, Liturgical Role of." In *The New Dictionary of Sacramental Worship,* edited by Peter E. Fink, 1189–90. Collegeville, MN: Liturgical Press, 1990.

Du Bois, John W. "Ritual Language." In *The International Encyclopedia of Linguistics,* edited by William J. Frawley. New York: Oxford University Press, 2003.

Duranti, Alessandro. "The Audience as Co-Author: An Introduction." *Text* 6, no. 3 (1986): 239–47.

Dyer, Joseph. *Readers and Hearers of the Word: The Cantillation of Scripture in the Middle Ages.* Turnhout: Brepols, 2022.

Egeria. *Itinerarium.* In Paul F. Bradshaw and Anne McGowan. *The Pilgrimage of Egeria.* Collegeville, MN: Liturgical Press, 2018.

The English Hymnal. London: Oxford University Press and A. R. Mowbray, 1906.

Ettin, Andrew Vogel. *Speaking Silences: Stillness and Voice in Modern Jewish Thought.* Charlottesville, VA: University of Virginia Press, 1994.

Evangelical Lutheran Church in America. *Evangelical Lutheran Worship.* Minneapolis: Augsburg Fortress Press, 2006.

Evans, G. R. *The Thought of Gregory the Great.* Cambridge: Cambridge University Press, 1986.

Fennell, Dana. "Explorations of Silence in the Religious Rituals of Buddhists and Quakers." *Religion* 42, no. 4 (2012): 549–74.

Fisher, Alexander J. *Music, Piety, and Propaganda: The Soundscapes of Counter-Reformation Bavaria.* Oxford: Oxford University Press, 2014.

Foletti, Ivan, and Katarína Kravciková. "Closed Doors as Bearers and Constructors of Images." *Convivium Supplementum* (2019): 24–45.

Foxley, George. *The Groanes of the Spirit or the Triall of the Truth of Prayer.* Oxford, 1639.

Furniss, Graham. *Orality: The Power of the Spoken Word.* Basingstoke, UK: Palgrave Macmillan, 2004.

Gardner, Johann von. *Russian Church Singing: Orthodox Worship and Hymnography.* Vol. 1, *Russian Church Singing,* translated by Vladimir Morosan. Crestwood, NY: St. Vladimir's Seminary Press, 1980.

Gavrilyuk, Paul L., and Sarah Coakley, eds. *The Spiritual Senses: Perceiving God in Western Christianity.* Cambridge: Cambridge University Press, 2011.

Gaylin, Ann. *Eavesdropping in the Novel from Austen to Proust*. Cambridge: Cambridge University Press, 2002.

Gehl, Paul F. "*Competens silentium*: Varieties of Monastic Silence in the Medieval West." *Viator* 18 (1987): 125–60.

Gelston, Anthony. "The Meaning of Theodore of Mopsuestia's Sixteenth Catechetical Lecture and the Silent Recitation of the Eucharistic Prayer." *Journal of Theological Studies* 60, no. 1 (2009): 191–92.

Girón Sara, Lidia Álvarez-Morales, and Teófilo Zamarreño. "Church Acoustics: A State-of-the-Art Review after Several Decades of Research." *Journal of Sound and Vibration* 411 (2017): 378–408.

Goffman, Erving. *Frame Analysis: An Essay on the Organization of Experience*. Boston: Northeastern University Press, 1974.

Gravier, Inbar. "The Paradoxical Effects of Attentiveness." *Journal of Early Christian Studies* 24, no. 2 (2016): 199–227.

Greek-English Lexicon. Edited by Henry G. Liddell and Robert Scott. Oxford: Oxford University Press, 1996.

Gregory Nazianzen. *Orations*. Translated by Brian Daley. *Gregory of Nazianzus*. London: Taylor & Francis, 2006.

Griffiths, Paul. "Varèse, Edgard [Edgar]." In *Grove Music Online*. New York: Oxford University Press, 2001.

Grimlaicus. *Regula solitariorum* (*Rule for Solitaries*). Translated by Andrew L. Thornton. Collegeville, MN: Cistercian Publications, 2011.

Grimshaw-Aagaard, Mark, Mads Walther-Hansen, and Martin Knakkergaard, eds. *The Oxford Handbook of Sound and Imagination*. Vol. 1. Oxford: Oxford University Press, 2019.

Grisbroke, Jardine W. "Silent Prayer." In *The New SCM Dictionary of Liturgy*, edited by Paul Bradshaw, 442–43. London: SCM Press, 2002.

Guardini, Romano. *Meditations before Mass*. Translated by Elinor Castendyk Briefs. Westminster, MD: Newman Press, 1957.

Hachmeister, Jorge. "An Abbreviated History of the Ear: From Renaissance to Present." *Yale Journal of Biology and Medicine* 76, no. 2 (2003): 81–86.

Halton, Thomas P., trans. *Theodoret of Cyrus: A Cure for Pagan Maladies*. Ancient Christian Writers, vol. 67. New York: Newman Press, 2013.

Hammond, Carolyn J.-B., trans. *Augustine: Confessions*. Vol. 27 of the Loeb Classical Library. Cambridge, MA: Harvard University Press, 2016.

Handelman, Don. "Framing." In *Theorizing Rituals, Volume 1: Issues, Topics, Approaches, Concepts*, edited by Jens Kreinath, J. A. M. Snoek, and Michael Stausberg, 571–82. Leiden: Brill, 2018.

Harris, Charles. "Liturgical Silence." In *Liturgy and Worship*, edited by Lowther Clarke, 774–84. London: SPCK, 1954.

Harrison, Carol. *The Art of Listening in the Early Church*. Oxford: Oxford University Press, 2013.

Hayes, Mary. *Divine Ventriloquism in Medieval English Literature: Power, Anxiety, Subversion*. New York: Palgrave Macmillan, 2011.

Heath, Edwin, and Laura Moffat. *Contemporary Church Architecture*. London: Wiley, 2007.

Heath, Malcolm. "Codifications of Rhetoric." In *The Cambridge Companion to Ancient Rhetoric*, edited by Erik Gunderson, 59–74. Cambridge: Cambridge University Press, 2009.

Heidegger, Martin. "*Logos* (Heraclitus, Fragment B 50)." In *Early Greek Thinking: The Dawn of Western Philosophy*, translated by David Farell Krell and Frank A. Capuzzi, 59–78. San Francisco: Harper & Row, 1984.

Heine, Ronald E. *Origen: Homilies on Genesis and Exodus*. Vol. 71 of Fathers of the Church. Washington, DC: Catholic University of America Press, 2002.

Heron, Benedict M. "Silence during the Celebration of Mass and Other Rites." *Notitiae* 8 (1972): 180–81.

Hill, Robert C., trans. *St. John Chrysostom: Commentary on the Psalms*. Brookline, MA: Holy Cross Orthodox Press, 1998.

Hirschkind, Charles. "Religion." In *Keywords in Sound*, edited by David Novak and Matt Sakakeeny, 165–74. Durham, NC: Duke University Press, 2015.

Horst, Pieter W. van der. "Silent Prayer in Antiquity." *Numen* 41, no. 1 (1994): 1–25.

Howlett, John Henry. *Instructions in Reading the Liturgy of the United Church of England and Ireland; Offered to the Attention of the Younger Clergy and Candidates for Holy Orders: With an Appendix on Pronunciation*. England: C. & J. Rivington, 1826.

Hudspeth, A. James. "Where Listening Begins: The Inner Ear." In *What Now? The Politics of Listening*, edited by Anne Barlow, 9–15. London: Black Dog Publishing, 2016.

Hunt, Arnold. *The Art of Hearing: English Preachers and their Audiences, 1590–1640*. Cambridge: Cambridge University Press, 2010.

Ihde, Don. *Listening and Voice: Phenomenologies of Sound*. Albany, NY: State University of New York Press, 2007.

Inter-Lutheran Commission on Worship. *Lutheran Book of Worship*. Minneapolis: Augsburg Fortress Press, 1978.

Iser, Wolfgang. "Indeterminacy and the Reader's Response in Prose Fiction." In *Aspects of Narrative*, edited by J. Hillis Miller, 2–45. New York: Columbia University Press, 1971.

Isidore of Seville. *De ecclesiasticis Officiis*. Translated by Thomas L. Knoebel. New York: Newman Press, 2008.

Isidore of Seville. *The Etymologies of Isidore of Seville*. Translated by Stephen A. Barney, W. J. Lewis, J. A. Beach, and Oliver Berghof. Cambridge: Cambridge University Press, 2006.

Jerome. *Letters*. Translated by W. H. Freemantle and G. Lewis. Nicene and Post-Nicene Fathers 2nd series. Vol. 6. New York, Oxford: Parker & Co., 1893.

John Cassian. *Collations (Conlationes)*. In Boniface Ramsey, *John Cassian: The Conferences*. New York: Paulist Press, 1997.

John Chrysostom. *Hom. on 1 Timothy*. Translated by J. P. Tweed. In *The Homilies of St. John Chrysostom, Archbishop of Constantinople, on the Epistles of St. Paul the Apostle to Timothy, Titus, and Philemon*. England: Rivington, 1853.

John of Apamea. *On Prayer*. In "John the Solitary, On Prayer," translated by Sebastian Brock. *Journal of Theological Studies* 30, no. 1 (1979).

Joncas, Jan Michael. *From Sacred Song to Ritual Music: Twentieth-Century Understandings of Roman Catholic Worship Music*. Collegeville, MN: Liturgical Press, 1997.

Jones, Christopher A., trans. *Ælfric's Letter to the Monks of Eynsham*. Cambridge: Cambridge University Press, 1999.

Juslin, Patrik N., and John A. Sloboda. *Music and Emotion: Theory and Research*. Oxford: Oxford University Press, 2001.

Juslin, Patrik N., and Petri Laukka. "Expression, Perception, and Induction of Musical Emotions: A Review and a Questionnaire Study of Everyday Listening." *Journal of New Music Research* 33, no. 3 (2004): 217–38.

Justinian. *Novella*. In *The Novels of Justinian: A Complete Annotated English Translation*, translated by David Miller and Peter Sarris. Cambridge: Cambridge University Press, 2018.

Jütte, Robert. *A History of the Senses: From Antiquity to Cyberspace*. Translated by James Lynn. Cambridge, UK: Polity, 2005.

Kane, Brian. "Jean-Luc Nancy and the Listening Subject." *Contemporary Music Review* 31, nos. 5–6 (2012): 439–47.

Kane, Brian. *Sound Unseen: Acousmatic Sound in Theory and Practice*. New York: Oxford University Press, 2014.

Karant-Nunn, Susan C. *The Reformation of Feeling: Shaping the Religious Emotions in Early Modern Germany*. New York: Oxford University Press, 2010.

Karant-Nunn, Susan C., and Ute Lotz-Heumann, eds. *The Cultural History of the Reformations: Theories and Applications*. Wiesbaden: Harrassowitz Verlag, 2021.

Kelman, Ari Y. "Rethinking the Soundscape: A Critical Genealogy of a Key Term in Sound Studies." *Senses and Society* 5, no. 2 (2010): 212–34.

Kempe, Margery. *The Book of Margery Kempe*. Translated by Anthony Bale. Oxford: Oxford University Press, 2016.

Khrushkova, Liudmila G. "What Is a Solea? The Solea in Rome, Constantinople and Other Places." *Hortus Artium Medievalium* 25, no. 2 (2019): 263–82.

Kierkegaard, Søren. *For a Self-Examination*. Translated by Howard V. Hong and Edna H. Hong. Princeton, NJ: Princeton University Press, 1876.

Kilde, Jeanne Halgren. *Sacred Power, Sacred Space*. New York: Oxford University Press, 2008.

Kilde, Jeanne Halgren. *When Church Became Theatre: The Transformation of Evangelical Architecture and Worship in Nineteenth-Century America*. New York: Oxford University Press, 2002.

Kleiner, Mendel, David Lloyd Klepper, and Rendell R. Torres. *Worship Space Acoustics*. Fort Lauderdale, FL: Ross Publishing, 2010.

Klomp, Mirella. *The Sound of Worship: Liturgical Performance by Surinamese Lutherans and Ghanaian Methodists in Amsterdam*. Vol. 26. of Liturgia Condenda. Leuven: Peeters, 2011.

Knight, Frances. "Preaching in Britain's 'Parish Church': Sermons at London's St. Paul's Cathedral in the Eighteenth and Nineteenth Centuries." *Sermon Studies* 3, no. 2 (2019).

Knoebel, Thomas L., trans. Isidore of Seville. *De ecclesiasticis Officiis*. New York: Newman Press, 2008.

Kurzon, Dennis. "Towards a Typology of Silence." *Journal of Pragmatics* 39 (2007): 1673–88.

Le Huray, Peter, and John Harper. "Anglican Chant." In *Grove Music Online*. New York: Oxford University Press, 2001.

Leaver, Robin A. *Luther's Liturgical Music: Principles and Implications*. Grand Rapids, MI: Eerdmans, 2007.

Levy, Kenneth, John A. Emerson, Jane Bellingham, David Hiley, and Bennett Mitchell Zon. "Plainchant." In *Grove Music Online*. New York: Oxford University Press, 2001.

Lewers, T. H., and J. S. Anderson. "Some Acoustical Properties of St. Paul's Cathedral, London." *Journal of Sound and Vibration* 92, no. 2 (1984): 285–97.

Lingas, Alexander. "From Earth to Heaven: The Changing Musical Soundscape of Byzantine Liturgy." In *Experiencing Byzantium: Papers from the 44th Spring Symposium of Byzantine Studies*, edited by Claire Nesbitt and Mark Jackson, 311–358. Farnham, UK: Ashgate, 2013.

Locher, Gottfried W. *Zwingli's Thought: New Perspectives*. Leiden: Brill, 1981.

Locke, John L. *Eavesdropping: An Intimate History*. Oxford: Oxford University Press, 2010.

Loetz, Francisca. "Giving the Reformation a Voice: The Practice of Psalm Singing in Zurich." In *The Cultural History of the Reformations: Theories and Applications*, edited by Susan C. Karant-Nunn and Ute Lotz-Heumann, 105–131. Wiesbaden: Harrassowitz Verlag, 2021.

Lutheran Church in America. *Lutheran Book of Worship*. Minneapolis: Augsburg Fortress Press, 1978.

Mark the Monk. *A Monastic Superior's Disputation with an Attorney*. In *Counsels on the Spiritual Life: Mark the Monk*. Translated by Tim Vivian and Augustine Casiday. Crestwood, NY: St. Vladimir's Seminary Press, 2009.

Mason, Henry. *Hearing and Doing the Ready Way to Blessednesse: With an Appendix Containing Rules of Right Hearing Gods Word*. London: John Clark, 1656.

Mateos, Juan. *La célébration de la parole dans la liturgie byzantine: étude historique*. Vol. 191 of Orientalia Christiana Analecta. Rome: Pont. Institutum Studiorum Orientalium, 1971.

Maximus the Confessor. *Mystagogia*. In *Maximus Confessor: Selected Writings*, translated by George C. Berthold, 181–226. New York: Paulist Press, 1985.

Mayer, Wendy. "John Chrysostom: Extraordinary Preacher, Ordinary Audience." In *Preacher and Audience: Studies in Early Christian and Byzantine Homiletics*, edited by Mary Cunningham and Pauline Allen, 105–37. Leiden: Brill, 1998.

Mazouji, Rojin, and Mohammad Raayat Jahromi. "'Silence' as a Language of Faith and Being: A Comparative Study of Kierkegaard's and Heidegger's Uses of 'Silence.'" *Heythrop Journal* 62, no. 1 (2021): 39–52.

McDermott, Jennifer Rae. "'The Melodie of Heaven': Sermonizing the Open Ear in Early Modern England." In *Religion and the Senses Early Modern Europe*, edited by Wietse De Boer and Christine Göttler, 177–97. Leiden: Brill, 2012.

McInroy, Mark J. "Origen of Alexandria." In *The Spiritual Senses: Perceiving God in Western Christianity*, edited by Paul L. Gavrilyuk and Sarah Coakley, 20–35. Cambridge: Cambridge University Press, 2011.

McInroy, Mark. *Balthasar on the Spiritual Senses: Perceiving Splendour*. Oxford: Oxford University Press, 2014.

Mellas, Andrew. *Liturgy and the Emotions in Byzantium: Compunction and Hymnody*. Cambridge: Cambridge University Press, 2020.

Merleau-Ponty, Maurice. *The Prose of the World*. Translated by John O'Neill. Evanston, IL: Northwestern University Press, 1973.

Moberg, Marcus. *Faster for the Master!: Exploring Issues of Religious Expression and Alternative Christian Identity within the Finnish Christian Metal Music Scene*. Åbo: Åbo Akademi University Press, 2009.

"More Noise at Lumb Church: Police Called into Porch. Protestors' Open-Air Service." *Manchester Guardian*, December 23, 1929.

Mudry, Albert. *The History of Otology: A Tribute to Adam Politzer*. Amsterdam: Wayenborgh Publishing, 2015.

Mueller, Mary Magdeleine, trans. *Caesarius: Sermons, Volume 1 (1–80)*. Vol. 31 of Fathers of the Church. Washington, DC: Catholic University of America Press, 1956.

Muers, Rachel. *Keeping God's Silence: Towards a Theological Ethics of Communication*. Oxford: Blackwell, 2004.

Nancy, Jean Luc. *Listening*. Translated by Charlotte Mandell. New York: Fordham University Press, 2007.

Nancy, Mandeville Caciola. *Discerning Spirits: Divine and Demonic Possession in the Middle Ages*. Ithaca, NY: Cornell University Press, 2015.

Nekola, Anna. "'More Than Just a Music': Conservative Christian Anti-Rock Discourse and the U.S. Culture Wars." *Popular Music* 32 (2013): 407–26.

Origen. *Homilies on Exodus*. Translated by Ronald E. Heine. Vol. 71 of Fathers of the Church. Washington, DC: Catholic University of America Press, 2002.

Oxford English Dictionary. Oxford: Oxford University Press, 2023. https://www.oed.com/.

Oxford Latin Dictionary. Edited by Charlton T. Lewis and Charles Short. Oxford: Oxford University Press, 1969.

Page, Christopher. "To Chant in a Vale of Tears." In *Chant, Liturgy, and the Inheritance of Rome: Essays in Honour of Joseph Dyer*, edited by Daniel J. DiCenso and Rebecca Maloy, 431–40. Woodbridge, UK: Boydell & Brewer, Henry Bradshaw Society, 2017.

Patel, Aniruddh D. *Music, Language, and the Brain*. Oxford: Oxford University Press, 2008.

Pearce, Eiluned, Jacques Launay, and Robin I. M. Dunbar. "The Ice-Breaker Effect: Singing Mediates Fast Social Bonding." *Royal Society Open Science* 2 (2015): 150221.

Pearce, Marcus T., and Geraint A. Wiggins. "Auditory Expectation: The Information Dynamics of Music Perception and Cognition." *Topics in Cognitive Science* 4 (2012): 625–52.

Pedrero, Antonio, Rogelio Ruiz, Alexander Díaz-Chyla, and César Díaz. "Acoustical Study of Toledo Cathedral according to its Liturgical Uses." *Applied Acoustics* 85 (2014): 23–33.

Pentcheva, Bissera V. "Aesthetics and Acoustics of Hagia Sophia, Istanbul." *Icons of Sound*. Accessed January 19, 2018. http://iconsofsound.stanford.edu/index.html.

Pentcheva, Bissera V. *Hagia Sophia: Sound, Space, and Spirit in Byzantium*. University Park, PA: Penn State University Press, 2017.

Pfatteicher, Philip H., and Carlos R. Messerli. *Manual on the Liturgy*. Minneapolis: Augsburg Fortress Press, 1979.

Philostorgius. *Philostorgius: Church History*. Translated by Philip R. Amidon. Atlanta: Society of Biblical Literature, 2007.

Picard, Max. *The World of Silence*. Translated by Stanley Godman. London: Harvill, 1948.

Pike, Mark A. "From Personal to Social Transaction: A Model of Aesthetic Reading in the Classroom." *Journal of Aesthetic Education* 37, no. 3 (2003): 61–72.

Politzer, Adam. *Geschichte der Ohrenheilkunde*. Stuttgart: Verlag von Ferdinand Enke, 1907–13.

Ramsey, Boniface. *Ambrose*. London: Routledge, 1997.

Ramsey, Boniface. *John Cassian: The Conferences*. New York: Paulist Press, 1997.

Ramshaw, Gail. *Reviving Sacred Speech: The Meaning of Liturgical Language; Second Thoughts on Christ in Sacred Speech*. Franklin, NJ: OSL Publications, 2000.

Rappaport, Roy A. *Ritual and Religion in the Making of Humanity*. Cambridge: Cambridge University Press, 1999.

Rappaport, Roy A. "Ritual, Time, and Eternity." *Zygon* 27 (1992): 5–30.

Raveh, Dana, and Nilli Lavie. "Load-Induced Inattentional Deafness." *Attention, Perception, & Psychophysics* 77, no. 2 (2015): 483–92.

Remez, Robert E. "Perceptual Organization of Speech." In *The Handbook of Speech Perception*, edited by David B. Pisoni and Robert E. Remez, 28–50. Malden, MA: Blackwell, 2005.

Reynolds, Simon. "Noise." Chap. 10 in *Audio Culture: Readings in Modern Music*, edited by Christoph Cox and Daniel Warner. New York: Continuum, 2006.

Reznikoff, Iegor. "The Evidence of the Use of Sound Resonance from Paleolithic to Medieval Times." In *Archaeoacoustics*, edited by Christopher Scarre and Graeme Lawson, 77–84. Cambridge, UK: McDonald Institute for Archaeology, 2006.

Roman Catholic Church. *Paschale Solemnitatis (On Preparing and Celebrating the Paschal Feasts)*, 1988.

Rupert of Deutz. *De divinis officiis*. In *Readers and Hearers of the Word: The Cantillation of Scripture in the Middle Ages*, translated by Joseph Dyer, Ritus Et Artes 10. Turnhout: Brepols, 2022.

Russo, Francis. "Sonic Piety in Early New England." *The New England Quarterly* 95, no. 4 (2022): 610–44.

Russolo, Luigi. *The Art of Noises (L'arte dei Rumori)*. In *Audio Culture: Readings in Modern Music*, edited by Christoph Cox and Daniel Warner, 10–15. New York: Continuum, 2006.

Sartore, Domenico. "Silenzo." In *Liturgia*, edited by Domenico Sartore, Achille M. Triacca, and Carlo Cibien, 1864–73. Milan: Edizioni San Paolo, 2001.

Schaeffer, Pierre. *Traité des objets musicaux: essai interdisciplines*. Paris: Éditions du Seuil, 1966.

Schafer, R. Murray. *The Soundscape: Our Sonic Environment and the Tuning of the World*. Rochester, VT: Destiny Books, 1994.

Schmidt, Charles W. "Noise That Annoys: Regulating Unwanted Sound." *Environmental Health Perspectives* 113, no. 1 (2005): A42–44.

Schmidt, Gary D. *The Iconography of the Mouth of Hell: Eighth-Century Britain to the Fifteenth Century*. London: Susquehanna University Press, 1995.

Schwartz, Hillel. *Making Noise: From Babel to the Big Bang & Beyond*. New York: MIT Press, 2011.

Searl, Stanford J. *The Meanings of Silence in Quaker Worship*. Lewiston, NY: Edwin Mellen Press, 2005.

Searle, John R. *Expression and Meaning: Studies in the Theory of Speech Acts*. Cambridge: Cambridge University Press, 1979.

Sharrock, Roger, and Ted L. Underwood, eds. *The Miscellaneous Works of John Bunyan*. Vol. 1. Oxford: Clarendon Press, 2014.

Sheingorn, Pamela. "'Who Can Open the Doors of His Face?' The Iconography of Hell Mouth." In *The Iconography of Hell*, edited by Clifford Davidson and T. H. Seiler, 1–19. Kalamazoo, MI: Medieval Institute, 1992.

Shelemay, Kay Kaufman. *Soundscapes: Exploring Music in a Changing World*. New York: W. W. Norton, 2006.

Shinn-Cunningham, Barbara. "Auditory Selective Attention." In *The Handbook of Attention*, edited by Jonathan Fawcett, Evan Risko, and Alan Kingstone, 99–117. Cambridge, MA: MIT Press, 2015.

Sieben, Gary. "The Soundscape of Worship." In *Worship Space Acoustics: 3 Decades of Design*, edited by David T. Bradley, Lauren Ronsse, and Erica Ryherd, 7–9. New York: Springer, 2016.

Simmons, Thomas F., trans. *The Lay Folks Mass Book; Or, The Manner of Hearing Mass: With Rubrics and Devotions for the People, in Four Texts, and Office in English According to the Use of York, from Manuscripts of the Xth to the XVth Century*. England: Early English Text Society, 1879.

Smith, Barry C. "Speech Sounds and the Direct Meeting of Minds." In *Sounds and Perception: New Philosophical Essays*, edited by Matthew Nudds and Casey O'Callaghan, 183–210. Oxford: Oxford Academic, 2009.

Smith, T. Roger. *A Rudimentary Treatise on the Acoustics of Public Buildings; Or, The Principles of the Science of Sound Applied to the Purposes of the Architect and Builder*. England: J. Weale, 1861.

Socrates Scholasticus. *Ecclesiastical History*. Translated by A. C. Zenos. Nicene and Post-Nicene Fathers 2nd series. Vol. 2. Edited by Philip Schaff and Henry Wallace. Edinburgh: T&T Clark, 1890.

Springsted, Eric O. *Simone Weil for the Twenty-First Century*. South Bend, IN: University of Notre Dame Press, 2021.

Spurgeon, Charles. *C. H. Spurgeon's Autobiography: Compiled from His Diary, Letters, and Records*. Vol. 2. Cincinnati: Curts and Jennings, 1899.

Stewart, Alistair C. *The Didascalia Apostolorum: An English Version*. Vol. 1 of Studia Traditionis Theologiae. Turnhout: Brepols, 2009.

Straus, Erwin. "The Forms of Spatiality." In *Phenomenological Psychology*, translated by Erling Eng, 3–37. New York: Basic Books, 1966.

Styles, Elizabeth. *The Psychology of Attention*. New York: Psychologists Press, 2006.

Suárez, Rafael, Juan J. Sendra, and Alicia Alonso. "Acoustics, Liturgy and Architecture in the Early Christian Church: From the *Domus Ecclesiae* to the Basilica." *Acta Acustica united with Acustica* 99 (2013): 292–301.

Szuchewycz, Bohdan. "Evidentiality in Ritual Discourse: The Social Construction of Religious Meaning." *Language in Society* 23 (1994): 389–410.

Taft, Robert F. "How Liturgies Grow: The Evolution of the Byzantine 'Divine Liturgy.'" *Orientalia Christiana Periodica* 53 (1977): 8–30.

Taft, Robert F. "Little Entrance." In *The Oxford Dictionary of Byzantium*, edited by Alexander P. Kazhdan. Oxford: Oxford University Press, 1991.

Taft, Robert F. *Through Their Own Eyes: Liturgy as the Byzantines Saw It*. Berkeley, CA: Interorthodox Press, 2006.

Tavares, Menino A. S. M. P., S. Rajagopalan, Satish J. Sharma, and António P. O. Carvalho. "Prediction of Acoustic Comfort and Acoustic Silence in Goan Catholic Churches." *Inter-Noise* (2009).

Thornton, Andrew L. *Grimlaicus. Rule for Solitaries*. Collegeville, MN: Cistercian Publications, 2011.

Tovey, Phillip. *Inculturation of Christian Worship: Exploring the Eucharist*. Aldershot, UK: Ashgate, 2004.

Trousdale, Ann, Jacqueline Bach, and Elizabeth Willis. "Freedom, Physicality, Friendship and Feeling: Aspects of Children's Spirituality Expressed through the Choral Reading of Poetry." *International Journal of Children's Spirituality* 15, no. 4 (2010): 317–29.

Truax, Barry. *Acoustic Communication*. Westport, CT: Ablex Publishing, 2001.

Trutt, Gordon E. "Cantillation." In *Worship Music: A Concise Dictionary*, edited by Edward Foley, 53. Collegeville, MN: Liturgical Press, 2000.

Tsumura, David Toshio. "Chaos and Chaoskampf in the Bible: Is 'Chaos' a Suitable Term to Describe Creation or Conflict in the Bible?" In *Conversations on Canaanite and Biblical Themes: Creation, Chaos and Monotheism*, edited by Rebecca S. Watson and Adrian H. W. Curtis, 253–82. Berlin: De Gruyter, 2022.

Tweed, J. P. *The Homilies of S. John Chrysostom, Archbishop of Constantinople, on the Epistles of St. Paul the Apostle to Timothy, Titus, and Philemon*. England: Rivington, 1853.

U.S. Episcopal Church. *Book of Common Prayer*. New York: Seabury Press, 1979.

Vaissière, Jacqueline. "Perception of Intonation." In *The Handbook of Speech Perception*, edited by David B. Pisoni and Robert E. Remez, 236–63. Malden, MA: Blackwell, 2005.

Valière, Jean-Christophe, Benedicte Bertholon-Palazzo, and Nadia Barone. "An Example of the Restoration of a Monastic Church with Acoustic Pots: L'Abbaye des Anges of L'Aber-Wrach (Brittany)." *The Journal of the Acoustical Society of America* 141, no. 5 (2017): 3774.

Van Leersum-Bekebrede, Lydia, Martijn Oosterbaan, Ronelle Sonnenberg, Jos de Kock, and Marcel Barnard. "Sounds of Children in Worship: Materiality and Liturgical-Ritual Spaces." *Material Religion* 17, no. 5 (2021): 557–79.

Vanden Bosch der Nederlanden, Christina M., Marc F. Joanisse, and Jessica A. Grahn. "Music as a Scaffold for Listening to Speech: Better Neural Phase-Locking to Song than Speech." *NeuroImage* 214 (2020): 116767.

Vivian, Tim, and Augustine Casiday, trans. *Counsels on the Spiritual Life: Mark the Monk*. Crestwood, NY: St. Vladimir's Seminary Press, 2009.

Voegelin, Salomé. *Listening to Noise and Silence: Towards a Philosophy of Sound Art*. New York: Continuum, 2010.

Wacker, Grant. *Heaven Below: Early Pentecostals and American Culture*. Cambridge, MA: Harvard University Press, 2001.

Walsh, Philip J. "The Sound of Silence: Merleau-Ponty on Conscious Thought." *European Journal of Philosophy* 25, no. 2 (2017): 312–35.

Watson, Rebecca S., and Adrian H. W. Curtis, eds. *Conversations on Canaanite and Biblical Themes: Creation, Chaos and Monotheism*. Berlin: De Gruyter, 2022.

Weigert, Laura. *Weaving Sacred Stories: French Choir Tapestries and the Performance of Clerical Identity*. Ithaca, NY: Cornell University Press, 2004.

Weil, Simone. *Gravity and Grace*. New York: Putnam, 1952.

Wellesz, Egon. *A History of Byzantine Music and Hymnography*. Oxford: Oxford University Press, 1961.

Wheelock, Wade T. "The Problem of Ritual Language: From Information to Situation." *Journal of the American Academy of Religion* 50, no. 1 (1982): 49–72.

Whytock, Jack C. "The Reformation of Space for Public Worship: Past and Present—Continuing the Discussion." *Die Skriflig/In Luce* 52, no. 3 (2018): a2307.

Wilcox, Helen. "Puritans, George Herbert and 'Nose-Twange.'" *Notes and Queries* 26 (1979): 152–53.

Wood, Julia T. "Foreword." In *Dialogue: Theorizing Difference in Communication Studies*, edited by Rob Anderson, Leslie A. Baxter, and Kenneth N. Cissna, xv–xxiv. Thousand Oaks, CA: SAGE Publications, 2003.

Wood, Simon P. *Clement of Alexandria: Christ the Educator*. Vol. 23 of Fathers of the Church. Washington, DC: Catholic University of America Press, 1954.

World Health Organization Occupational and Environmental Health Team. *Guidelines for Community Noise*. 1999.

Wren, Christopher. *Parentalia*. London, 1750. In T. Roger Smith, *A Rudimentary Treatise on the Acoustics of Public Buildings; Or, The Principles of the Science of Sound Applied to the Purposes of the Architect and Builder*. England: J. Weale, 1861.

Yarnold, SJ, Edward J. *Cyril of Jerusalem*. London: Taylor & Francis, 2000.

Yelle, Robert A. "Ritual and Religious Language." In *The Encyclopedia of Language & Linguistics*, edited by E. K. Brown and Anne Anderson, 633–40. Amsterdam: Elsevier, 2006.

Index

Aber-Wrach, Brittany, France, church of, 176
acclamation(s), 61, 62, 65, 70
acoustic boundaries, 14
acoustic design, 16, 17, 192
acoustic environment, 7, 13, 18, 94, 158, 174
acoustic horizon, 49
acoustic pots, 175–6
acoustic(al) community, 11, 14, 15, 159, 160
acoustic(al) measurement, 16, 168
acoustical science, 163, 179
acoustics, of worship spaces, 160, 163, 165, 166–82, 188; dry, 166; wet, 17, 166
Admonition to Parliament (1572), 132
Advent, 23, 89
Ælfric, 51–2
aisle(s), 170
Alain, Claude, 144
Albrecht, Daniel, 68, 70
Alexander of Hales, 39–40
Algargoosh, Alaa, 166, 174
alleluia, 16, 81
Allen, Pauline, 50
Alonso, Alicia, 160n7, 175
altar, 26, 49, 52, 104, 124, 132, 161, 162, 170–71, 174–75, 177–79, 180, 191

Alternative Service Book, 97
Álvarez-Morales, Lidia, 168n29, 171, 173
ambient sound or noise, 4, 16, 19, 25–6, 28, 56, 86, 143, 185
ambo, 65, 160, 176–78
Ambrose of Milan, 85, 92, 150
Amen, 43, 70
amplification, of sound, 86, 124, 168, 176, 192; electronic, 124, 176, 192
anamnesis, 46
Anderson, Michael A., 63–4
Andreas, Johannes, 100
anechoic chamber, 111, 166
Angela of Foligno, 135
Anglican Chant, 81
Anglican liturgy/worship, 21, 28, 65–6, 71, 74, 97, 103–4, 133, 169
anointing of the ears, 40
anticipation, 11, 53, 94
anxiety, 92, 94
apse, 160, 170–71
Aristotle, 44
Arius, Arian(s), 85 and 85n33, 95
Aruza Street Revival, 19–20
ascetic movement, 98–99, 116, 126, 147, 148, 150
Athanasius, 85, 124, 150
atonement, 92

213

Attali, Jacques, 119, 121
Attende Domine, hymn, 33
attendo, 34
attendre, 147
attention, attentiveness, 6, 13, 18, 33, 36, 63, 69, 75, 80, 132, 138, 139–57, 184–85
audibility, 161, 176–77
audience, 43–6, 69, 71, 109
audire, 33
auditorium, 163, 179
auditory landscape, 12
Augustine of Hippo, 3, 44–5, 92, 99, 125–26, 150
aural architecture, 158–82, esp. 158–60
aural framework, 27
aural punctuation, 80
auscultare, 33, 36
Austin, John L., 58, 74n4
auto-communication, 56

Babel, 125, 133
Bach, Jacqueline, 78
Bach, Johann Sebastian, 89
Backer, Kristina, 144
Bacon, Francis, 163, 178
Bader, Günter, 148–9
Bailey, Peter, 118, 120
Balthasar, Hans Urs von, 41–2, 103–4
baptism, 40, 48, 51, 99n11, 128; of Christ, 38
Bard, Delphine, 176n55
baroque church architecture, 162, 175
basilica, 160–61, 167–68, 170–72, 174
Bastable, Richard, 105n23
Bateson, Gregory, 57
Baumann, Dorothea, 168, 170, 173
BCP. *See* Book of Common Prayer (1662)

Bede, Saint, 126–27
behavior, in church, 6, 67, 109, 128, 130, 132–33, 140, 149–52, 154, 188, 190
bell(s), 11, 14, 18, 25, 131, 152
Bellamo, Tiffany, 124
bema, 160, 176–77
Bendixen, Alexandra, 141
Berkaak, Odd Are, 121–22
Bhattacharji, Santha, 134
Bijsterveld, Karen, 118, 121, 123
bishop(s), 44, 171
Bitton-Ashkelony, Brouria, 98–9
Blackburn, John, 181
Blesser, Barry, 158–60, 165–66
blessing, liturgical, 63, 65, 79; of palms 51–2;
Bloch, Maurice, 57
Body of Christ (the Church), 2, 27, 137
body, mystical, 40; physical, 92, 99, 101, 111, 145, 155, 157. *See also* embody, embodiment.
Bonaventure, 39–40
Book of Common Prayer, (1549), 81, 97, 101n1; (1662), 21, 33, 63, 75, 77
Book of Common Prayer (1979), 105
Book of Homilies, 131
boundary, boundaries, 48–9, 52, 95, 113, 115, 159
Bourdieu, Pierre, 145
Bownde, Nicholas, 66
Bradley, David T., 174
brain, and audition, 31–2, 83, 141, 155–56, 183
Bregman, Albert S., 143n9
Bressler, Scott, 142n5
Broadbent, Donald E., 141
Broadway Tabernacle, 163, 164
Bronkhorst, Alfred W., 141n2
Brown, Laura Feitzinger, 132–33

Brownrig, Ralph, 40
Bruneau, Thomas, 108–9
Buckland, Ralph, 133
Buddhist worship, 101–2
Bunyan, John, 127
Burgos Cathedral, 174n50
burial, 50
Byzantine chant, 16–17, 172
Byzantine liturgy, 15–17, 24, 27, 69, 81, 86, 92, 149, 151, 161, 172, 177. *See also* Divine Liturgy; Orthodox worship.

Caciola, Nancy Mandeville, 129
Caesarius of Arles, 130, 150
Cage, John, 122
Calvin, John, 74, 76, 84, 88, 178
Camilleri, Sylvain, 113
Canon (of the Mass), 63, 97, 100
canon(s), canon law, Church of England, 130–31, 190
canticle(s), 77, 92, 106
cantillation, 5, 79–82, 84, 167, 171
cantor, 17, 52, 64, 79–80, 159
Carside, Charles, 84
Carter, Tim, 82
Cartledge, Mark, 70
Carvalho, António P. O., 169
Caryl, Joseph, 153–55
Cassian, John, 98–9, 150–51
catechesis, 48, 85
catechumen(s), 1, 49
ceiling (of church building), 52, 159–60, 167–68, 174, 176, 179
chancel, 168, 178
chant, chanting, 5, 7, 18, 22, 65, 73–4, 77, 84, 91, 93–6, 160, 167–69, 171, 176, 188, 191; listening to, 79–83. *See also* Byzantine chant; Gregorian chant; melismatic chant.

chaos, 125
Chase, Nathan P., 47n49
Chatham Theatre, Manhattan, 163
chatter (during worship), 20, 24, 97, 130 and 130n40, 133, 136, 139, 149, 190
Cherry, Colin, 141
children, 135–36, 190
choir (in church building), 170, 176, 177
choir, 16–17, 19, 51–2, 64, 81, 136, 159; heavenly, 20
choral recitation, 59, 77–8, 103, 188
Christ Church, Attercliffe, Church of, 181
church building(s), 26, 28, 49, 79, 124, 128, 158–82
Church of England, 65, 97, 103–4, 130–32, 140, 156, 169, 171
Cicero, 44
Cioni, Francesca, 132
Cirillo, Ettore, 167, 168, 169, 170
Clement of Alexandria, 86–7, 98–9
Coakley, Sarah, 39,
cochlea, 32
cocktail party effect, 141–2
cognition, cognitive process(es) 58, 90, 141, 145–46, 148, 183
cognitive science, 5, 90, 140, 191
collaborative listening, 63
collect, 51, 62, 67, 79, 103, 106
Common Worship, 65
communication, 2, 14, 18, 25, 42, 44, 53, 62, 75, 109, 111, 120, 157
communication studies, 13–15, 119
comprehension, 72, 83, 90, 101, 188
comprendre, 34, 36
compunction, 72, 82–4, 92
concealment of sound source, 51–2
confession of sins, liturgical, 106
confirmation, 50
Confiteor, 152

Constantinople, 15–17, 27, 95, 149
contemplation, 24, 147–48, 155
contrition, 67, 82
conversation with God, 49–50, 98;
    between worshippers, 73, 101
Coolman, Boyd Taylor, 40
Corbin, Alain, 12
Corpus Christi, feast of, 18–19
corpus mysticum, 40
Corradi Fiumara, Gemma, 2, 4–5,
    35, 37, 111, 186
Craig John, 134–35
Cranmer, Thomas, 81
creatio ex nihilo, 124
creation, the, 115, 124–25
Creed, the, 59, 77, 151, 152
Csordas, Thomas J., 68–9, 145–46
Cunningham, Mary, 50, 69
curtains (in church building), 167,
    174, 191. See also textiles.
Cyprian of Carthage, 98–9
Cyril of Jerusalem, 1, 48

daily prayer, 43, 103. See also Divine
    Office; Liturgy of the Hours;
    Evensong; Matins.
Dalby, Sweden, church of, 176
Dandelion, Pink, 101n16
Daniels, David D., III, 19–20, 71,
    133–34
Dauenhauer, Bernard P., 103n20,
    112, 114–15
Davey, Nicholas, 146–47
Davies, Oliver, 115
Day, Juliette, 49n56, 150n29
deacon, 1, 51, 61, 67, 149, 150, 159
Debby, Nirit Ben-Aryeh, 178
De Blaauw, Sible, 174n48
Del modo che si die tenire in chiexia, 152
demonic possession, 128–29
Desarnaulds, Victor, 1, 22, 159–62,
    168–69, 176, 181

Deutsche Messe, 80–1
dialogue, homiletic, 69; liturgical,
    62–3, 187; ordinary, 57, 107, 122
Didascalia Apsotolorum, 149–50
di Lasso, Orlando, 18
din, 117–8, 126
Directions for a devout and decent
    behaviour in the public worship
    of God, 139
Directory of Public Worship, 140
dirt, 118–9, 136
Diruta, Girolamo, 89
disposition, 67, 99, 110, 140, 141,
    146, 148, 150–51, 153, 155, 156,
    184, 191
distract, distraction, 26, 66, 129, 137,
    139, 142, 144, 148, 150, 155, 156,
    184, 189, 191
disturbance, 117–8
Divine Liturgy, the, 61
Divine Office, the, 43
Dix, Gregory, 100
dog-whipper, 135
dogs, in church, 135
Dolzalová, Klárá, 174n48
dome, 160–1, 168–71
door (of church building), 48–9,
    159, 174
doorkeeper, 48, 150, 159
Douglas, Mary, 118–19
Downey, Michael, 98
Dryhthelm, 126–7
Du Bois, John W., 60–1
Dunbar, Robin I. M., 95–6
Dunstan, Saint, 127
Duranti, Alessandro, 44–5, 69
Dyer, Joseph, 79–80

earcon, 164–5
ears, operation of the, 6–7, 31–2
earwitness, 46–8
Easter Vigil, 46, 66–7

Index   217

eavesdrop, eavesdropping, 20, 33, 36; eavesdropper, 47–51
ecclesial community, 6, 12, 94–5
ecclesiology, 136
echo, 166–67, 172
echoic memory, 143
écouter, 34, 36
edify, edification, 23, 25, 89, 99n11
Egeria, 174
Egerton, Stephen, 141, 155
elocution, 75
embody, embodiment, 5, 48, 56, 91–2, 145
emotion(s), 23–4, 44, 47, 67, 75–77, 82, 85, 90, 92
endorphins, 96
English Hymnal, the, 33–4
entendre, 34, 36
Environmental Protection Agency, 124
environmental sound, 10, 123; noise, 118, 123
epistle, 79, 80
escuchar, 34
ethics, 6, 110–112, 146–47, 184, 191
Ettin, Andrew Vogel, 107
Eucharist, 49, 62, 104, 161, 171. See also Mass; Divine Liturgy.
eucharistic prayer, 46, 50, 66, 71, 76, 97, 102–4, 108
Eustachian tube, 41
Eustochium, 150
Evangelical Lutheran Worship, 106
Evans, G. R., 125
Evensong, Anglican, 66, 74
exorcism, 128–9
Exsultet, 66

faith, and hearing, 38–40, 74, 147, 186, 188, 191
Fall, the, 125–26, 190
Fennell, Dana, 101–2, 109–10

filter, filtering, of sound, 141, 143, 156, 183
Finney, Charles Grandison, 163–64, 179
Fisher, Alexander J., 17–19, 28
floor (of church building), 159, 163, 168, 176–77, 179
Foletti, Ivan, 49
Fosse, Edward, 132
Foxley, George, 134–35
fraction, the, 26, 104
Furniss, Graham, 41, 45–6

Gadamer, Hans-Georg, 37
gallery (in church building), 179
gap, in meaning, 78
Gardner, E. C., 172
Gardner, Johan von, 24
Garrick, David, 75
Gavrilyuk, Paul, 39
Gaylin, Anne, 47
Gehl, Paul, 126
Gelston, Anthony, 99n11
General Instruction on the Liturgy of the Hours, 106
General Instruction on the Roman Missal, 62, 64–6, 103
Girolamo da Siena, 152
glossolalia, 19, 23
Goa, India, churches in, 165, 169
Goffman, Erving, 55
Good Friday, 102
gospel, reading of, 18, 26, 51, 63–7, 80, 144, 151–52, 187
gothic church architecture, 160, 169, 179
Gramsci, Antonio, 44
Gravier, Inbar, 147–48
Gregorian chant, 80, 156, 171
Gregory Nazianzen, 44–5
Gregory of Nyssa, 86
Gregory the Great, 100, 125

Grimlaicus, 82–3
Grisbroke, Jardine, 97–98
groan, groaning, 19–20, 120, 133–35, 150
Guardini, Romano, 105

habitus, 145
Hachmeister, Jorge, 31n1
Hagia Sophia, Church of, 15–17, 27, 161, 166, 168–69, 177
Halgren-Kilde, Jeanne, 163
Harris, Charles, 98
Harrison, Carol, 44–5, 49–50
Hayes, Mary, 49–51, 100
hear, hearing, definitions of, 32–4
hearken, 33, 35–6, 53, 186
hearkening attunement, 35–6
Heath, Edwin, 163n14
Heidegger, Martin, 35–7, 113
hell, mouth of, 127–8; noise of 126–27
Heron, Benedict, 105–6
hesychia, 99, 189. *See also* stillness.
Hirschkind, Charles, 137
Hogarth, William, 28–30, 156, 163
Holy Sepulchre, Jerusalem, Church of the, 174
Holy Spirit, 20, 48
Holy Week, 23–4
homily. *See* preach.
Horst, Pieter van der, 98
Howlett, John Henry, 75
Hudspeth, A. James, 32
Hunt, Arnold, 67, 93
hymn(s), hymnody, 3, 5, 18–19, 22–3, 43, 73, 81, 84–5, 92–3, 95, 156–57, 172, 185, 188

iconostasis, 48
Icons of Sound project, 17
Idhe, Don, 89–90
idol, idolatry, 38, 86, 87

inattention, inattentiveness, 6, 13, 34, 113, 140, 144, 149–56, 190–91
inattentional deafness, 141, 143, 145
incarnation, the, 115, 137
incense, 65, 88
inculturation, liturgical, 21
information exchange, 13–14, 26, 57, 59, 62, 71, 76, 193
institution narrative, 51, 76, 103
instrumental music, in worship, 23–4, 85–91, 167, 188
instruments, musical, 16, 20, 23–4, 74, 86–9
intellect, 40, 147
intelligibility, 17, 79–80, 160–61, 165, 167–76, 182, 188, 191–92
intended hearer/listener, 47, 50, 58, 71, 85
intentional sound(s), 4, 5–7, 14, 16, 20–6, 56, 72, 91–2, 100, 105, 107–8, 112, 167, 182, 185, 188–89, 191–2
interaural time difference, 144
intercession(s), intercessory prayer, 1, 63, 76, 103
Inter-Lutheran Commission on Worship, 106
interval, silent, 103–8, 189
intonation, 74, 76–8, 188
introductory rites, 62
Iser, Wolfgang, 78
Isidore of Seville, 72, 80–1, 84, 151
Italy, churches in, 169, 173

Jahromi, Mohammad Raayat, 112–13
Jerome, 150
Jesus, 38–9, 80, 115
Jewish worship, 24, 86–7
John Chrysostom, 86–7, 95, 129–30, 149–50

John of Apamea, 99
John, Gospel of, 38
Juslin, Patrick N., 93
Justinian, emperor, 99–100

Kane, Brian, 34, 52
Kant, Immanuel, 148–49
Karant-Nunn, Susan, 92–3
Kelman, Ari, 11–13, 26, 28, 185
Kempe, Margery, 134
kenosis, 147
keynote sound, 10–11, 13, 17–19, 26
Kierkegaard, Søren, 112–13
Kleiner, Mendel, 165
Klepper, David, 165
Klomp, Mirella, 136
Knight, Frances, 169
Koch, Iring, 141
Kravčíková, Katarína, 49
Kurzon, Dennis, 108–9
Kyrie eleison, 62

laity, 1, 19, 51, 66, 100–2, 105–6, 130, 150–51, 153, 156, 163
lamentation, 72, 80, 126–27
laugh, laughter in church, 20, 50, 120, 131, 133, 149
Launay, Jacques, 95–6
Lavie, Nilli, 145
Lay Folks Mass Book, 151–52
lectern, 178
lector, 72, 80
legein, 35, 37
legislation, for noise, 27, 137
Lent, 23, 48, 89
Leviathan, 128
Liddon, Henry Parry, 169
liminal, liminality, 47, 49
Lingas, Alexander, 15–17, 27, 81
listen, listening, definitions of, 2, 4, 13–14, 32–4, 36–8; modes of, 42–53

litany, 1, 33, 62, 64
Litany of the Saints, 64
Little Entrance, 61–2
liturgical assembly, 1, 64, 73, 102
liturgical book(s), 1, 63, 105, 106, 128, 185
liturgical listening, 183–93
Liturgy of the Hours, 63, 106
load-induced deafness, 145
Lord's Prayer, the, 3, 49, 77
loudness, 77, 118, 123, 142, 176
Low Mass, 74, 98, 104
Lumb-in-Rossendale, church of, 136–37
Lunde, Ingunn, 69
Luther, Martin, 80, 85, 88, 148
Lutheran Book of Worship, 105–6
Lutheran Church, 17–19, 23, 89, 136

Manchester Guardian, 136
Manual on the Liturgy (Lutheran), 106
marble, acoustic properties of, 167, 174
Marie d'Oignies, 134
Mark the Monk, 148
Martellotta, Francesco, 167–71, 174–75
Mason, Henry, 155
Mass, 18–9, 22, 47, 51, 54–5, 59, 62–3, 74, 79–80, 100, 103, 105–6, 134, 138, 151–52, 156, 171
Mass for the Dead, 23, 89
Mather, Cotton, 155
Matins, 136
Maximus the Confessor, 100
Mazouji, Rojin, 112–13
McDermott, Jennifer Rae, 41
McInroy, Mark, 41
meditative listening, 64
melismatic chant, 16, 80–1, 167, 172
memory, 13, 46, 67, 85, 94, 107–8, 142–44, 166, 184

men and behavior in church, 130–31, 159
mendicant orders, 161, 178
Merbecke, John, 81
Merleau-Ponty, Maurice, 35, 114, 145
Methodist worship, 28–30, 163
Metropolitan Tabernacle, London, 172–3
minister(s), 1, 22, 63, 64, 67–9, 73, 93, 97, 101, 106, 131, 137, 140, 159, 161, 163n14, 177, 187, 190
monastic prayer, 78–9, 82, 98–9, 102, 130, 147–50, 153, 160
Monica, Saint, 126
mosaic(s), 169, 174
movement, in worship, 19, 25, 59, 87, 101, 110, 130, 152, 155
Muers, Ruth, 110–12, 115–16
Murdoch, Iris, 146–47
music, 5, 7, 9–10, 12, 15–20, 25, 71, 72–3, 91–6, 103, 117, 119, 122, 165, 167–68, 170, 184, 188, 191–92
Musicam Sacrum (Roman Catholic Instruction on Music in the Liturgy), 23, 89
Myrc, John, 151
mystic, mysticism, 52, 108, 113, 116

Nancy, Jean-Luc, 36
Narsai (bishop of Edessa), 99n11
Nativity, Bethlehem, Church of the, 174
nausea, 117
nave, 19, 65, 159, 167–68, 170, 177–9
Neisser, Ulrich, 143
New Testament, 38, 66, 115, 186
Niederstätter, Christina, 168, 173
noise, 6, 10–13, 16, 18–20, 26–28, 74, 86, 97, 101, 109, 111, 117–38, 140, 142, 157, 159, 185–86, 189–91

non-intentional sound, 4, 21, 25, 27, 56, 185
non-semantic sound, 23, 120

Odo of Cluny, 127
oír, 34
Old Testament, 38, 66, 115, 125
On Preparing and Celebrating the Paschal Feasts, 66–7
Ong, Walter, 3
ordination, 50, 97n1, 101
organ music, 23–4, 86–9, 95, 105, 167, 169
organ of Corti, 32
organ sermon, 88–9
Origen, 39, 99, 130n40
Orthodox Church, 24, 61, 64, 86, 97, 104, 135
oüir, 34

pagan worship (in antiquity), 24, 86, 133
Page, Christopher, 82–3
Palm Sunday, 51
parabolic reflector, 181
passion of Christ, 92, 104
passivity, in worship, 1, 36, 45, 50, 146, 187, 191, 193
Patel, Aniruddh D., 90
Paul the Silentiary, 177
Paul, the Apostle, 2, 39, 40, 42, 74, 88, 129
pause, silent, 103–5, 107–8, 189
Pearce, Eiluned, 95
Pearce, Marcus, 92, 94
Pedrero, Antonio, 169–70
penitent(s), 49, 159
Penrose, Thomas, 132
Pentcheva, Bissera V., 17, 161, 169
Pentecost, feast of, 16
Pentecostal/Charismatic worship, 19–20, 23, 68–70, 133–34

perception, sensory, 34, 35–6, 40, 46, 65, 145
Perrissin, Jean, 162
Peter Lombard, 40
phenome, 83
phenomenology, 35, 90, 114, 186
Philo, 98
philosophy of listening, 4, 35–7
Philostorgius, 85n33
physiology, 5–6, 31, 55, 74, 90, 92, 123, 124, 166
Picard, Max, 114
Pike, Mark A., 78
pilgrimage, 134
pillar(s), also columns (in church building), 159, 160, 170, 174, 175
pitch, 77, 79, 83, 90, 118, 120, 142
plainchant, 80–1
Politzer, Adam, 31n1
Polwhele, John, 133
polyphony, 18–19, 79, 81, 167–69, 172
Portugal, churches in, 169
Praetorius, 89
prayer, communal, 43, 49, 77, 159; improvised, 19, 68; mystical, 113; private, 43, 107, 152; silent, 97–101, 102, 109, 189; wordless, 134–5
preach, preacher(s), 6, 18, 19, 22, 39–42, 44–5, 49–50, 67, 69–70, 93, 101, 129, 133, 149, 156, 161, 163, 167, 169, 172, 178–79, 191–2
presbytery (in church building), 170, 177
priest, 19, 25, 42–3, 49–51, 98–100, 103, 108, 151–53, 170–71. *See also* minister.
private devotion(s), during Mass, 130, 134, 151, 153, 156

procession, 16, 18, 25, 51–2, 61, 65, 86, 144,
Proclus (philosopher), 98
prophecy, 68–70
Protestant(s), 40–1, 55, 66, 134, 161, 163; church buildings, 161n10, 163, 169, 172, 175; worship, 129, 153, 161, 178
psalmist, *psalmista*, 72, 84
psalm(s), psalmody, 22, 67, 72, 77, 81–3, 84–5, 95, 103, 106–7, 148; metrical, 84; responsorial, 66
Psalms, the, 9, 38, 87, 88, 115
Psalter, the, 16, 84, 128–29
psychology, psychological, 90, 124, 191
pulpit, 7, 28, 132, 161, 162, 173, 176–81
Puritan(s), 52, 133, 135

Quaker worship, 101–2, 109–10
Quintilian, 44

race, 20, 120, 134
Rahner, Karl, 41
Ramshaw, Gail, 73
Rappaport, Roy A., 55–8, 68, 107
Raveh, Dana, 145
recitation, silent, 50, 97–100
Reformation (Protestant), 76, 84, 88, 100, 153; liturgical consequences of the, 81, 138, 153, 191
Reformation churches, the, 92–3, 101, 126, 130
Reformed Church, the 1, 22, 81, 136, 168
relics, 128, 160
Remez, Robert, 76
repetition, 58, 74, 110, 157
resonance, acoustic, 166, 179; bodily, 43, 77, 91, 111
revelation of God, 42, 113

Revelation, Book of, 128
reverberation, 17, 38, 160–61, 165–67, 167–72, 173–76, 178, 181–82, 191–92. *See also* resonance, acoustic.
Reynolds, Simon, 120
Reznikoff, Iegor, 171
rhetoric, 44–5, 69, 129
rhythm(s), of speech, 76–7, 79–80, 83
Ricoeur, Paul, 2
right hearing, 40–1, 67, 154, 182, 193
ritual frame, 54–5, 73, 105, 187
ritual gesture, 77, 85–6, 94, 129, 185, 187, 189
ritual hiatus, 73, 108, 189
ritual language, 56–61
ritual listening, 54–71, 112, 187
ritual objects, 51
ritual sound(s), 25–6, 71, 103, 107, 159, 185
ritual theory, 15, 55–6, 107
Ritualists, 156
ritualized listening, 61–71
Roman Catholic Church, 64, 67, 71, 88–9, 102, 104, 156, 161, 171, 174
Romanesque church architecture, 160
Ronsse, Lauren, 174
Rorty, Richard, 37
rosary, 156
rubric(s), 1, 23, 65, 97, 104–5
Rupert of Deutz, 63
Russo, Francis, 40
Russolo, Luigi, 122
Ryherd, Erica, 174

sacrament(s), 71, 102, 146, 161, 185
Sacrosanctum Concilium (Constitution on Sacred Liturgy), 23, 43, 89

Salter, Linda-Ruth, 159–60, 164–5
salvation history, 46, 66–7, 92
San Clemente, Rome, Church of, 177–78
sanctuary (in church building), 26, 61, 65, 100, 153, 159, 170, 177
Sanctus, 81, 87, 151
Santi Domenico e Sisto, Rome, convent of, 52
Sartore, Domenico, 102–3
Satan, 128
Sauvo, Finland, church of, 161, 179–80
Schaeffer, Pierre, 34, 122
Schafer, R. Murray, 10–12, 28
Schmidt, Gary D., 127–28
Schwartz, Hillel, 120, 125–26
screen(s), 49, 51, 159, 161–2, 178. *See also* iconostasis.
Scripture, reading of, 19, 22–3, 45, 62, 66–7, 76, 81, 101, 103, 149, 153, 185, 188, 191
Searl, Stanford J., 109
Searle, John, 58
seats, seating (in church building), 132, 135, 161, 163, 167–68, 173, 175, 178–79
segregation (of sound), 142
selective auditory attention, 140
self-examination, 154
senses, physical, 31–2, 35, 38, 42, 55, 80, 98, 145–46, 148, 186; spiritual, 39–42, 186
Service of the Word (Lutheran), 106
Seville Cathedral, 175
Shelemay, Kay Kaufman, 11–12, 16–17, 28
Shinn-Cunningham, Barbara, 141, 143
shout, shouting in worship, 70, 118, 128, 129, 134, 136

Sieben, Gary, 159
silence, 5–6, 20, 22, 37, 62, 66, 71, 97–116, 121, 124–25, 130, 150, 152, 165, 189; of Christ, 103, 115; and death, 103, 114, 115; experience of, 112–15; of God, 99, 112–13, 115–16, 126; hearing/listening to, 111–12; liturgical, length of, 105–8; ritual performance of, 51, 98, 103–4, 108–11, 131; typologies of, 98–9, 102, 103–4, 108–9. *See also* interval, silent; pause, silent.
sin(s), 6, 82, 87, 125, 127, 135, 152, 157, 190
sing, singing, 5, 9–10, 18, 23, 43, 66, 72, 74, 79, 84, 92–3, 95–6, 156, 169, 171, 188, 192
singer(s), 16, 42, 51, 81–2, 161, 169
situational speech, 59
sleep, sleeping (during worship), 28–9, 139–40, 154–56
Sloboda, John A., 93
Smart, Benjamin Humphrey, 75
Smith, Barry C., 120
Smith, Henry, 41
Smith, Roger T., 181
social bonding, 95–6
social identity, 18, 94–6, 134, 192
solea, 117–8
Solesmes, abbey of, 80
somatic modes of attention, 145
song(s), 19, 23, 73, 83–4, 95, 185
sonic identity, 73
sonic personality (of a space), 159, 161, 192
sonic piety, 40
sonic stimuli, 92
sound, authorized, 13, 23; background/ambient, 19, 26; hierarchy of, 22, 27, 117–22, 129–30, 135–38, 185, 190; processing of, 31–2, 35–7, 76–7, 83–4, 90–2, 123, 141–46, 156–57, 158–59, 183–84, 191
sound absorption, 159, 167–68, 173–75
sound reflection, 156, 160–62, 166–72, 177–78, 182. *See also* reverberation.
sound signal, 7, 11, 14, 25, 140, 157, 183, 192
sound source(s), 32, 43, 51–2, 76, 111, 120, 142–3, 158–59, 163, 166, 184, 187, 191
sounding board, 179–81
soundmark, 10–11, 14, 17–18
soundscape, 4, 6, 9–28, 56, 94–5, 123, 184–86, 189; personal, 111
space(s), liturgical/ worship, 6–7, 17, 48, 52, 158–82; and music, 90–1
Spain, churches in, 173
speaker, position of, 42, 159, 168, 171–73, 176–81
speech, listening to/hearing, 2–4, 7, 36–7, 44–5, 73–7, 83, 107, 112, 142–44, 187; cessation of, 99, 113
speech act(s), 58, 74n4
speech intelligibility. *See* intelligibility.
spiritual, spirituality, 6, 40, 69, 78, 82, 99, 112, 116, 140, 147–49, 151–52, 155, 166, 182, 184, 189–90, 192. *See also* senses, spiritual.
spiritual gifts, 20
Springsted, Eric O., 147
Spurgeon, Charles, 156, 172–73, 179
St. John Lateran, Rome, Church of, 171

St. Paul's Cathedral, London, 168–69
St. Thomas on Fifth Avenue, Church of, 169
stillness 99, 101–2, 105, 108, 110, 116, 148, 189
Stonehenge, 121
Straus, Erwin, 119
streaming (of sound), 142
Styles Elizabeth, 142–3, 145, 157
Suárez, Rafael, 171
sub-deacon, 159
subjective, subjectivity, 6, 24, 27, 113, 123, 137
subjectivism, 147
Suffrages, the, 63
Sunday, permitted activities on, 137
Sursum corda, 63
Switzerland, churches in, 1, 22, 168–69, 181
syllable, 79–81, 83, 143, 188
syntax, 19, 75
synthronon, 170
Szuchewycz, Bohdan, 68

Taft, Robert F., 85, 104, 149
tears, 67, 82, 92–3, 134, 150
temptation, 148–49, 151
Tertullian, 86, 98–9
tester. *See* sounding board.
text, liturgical, 2–3, 12, 19, 21–2, 25, 27–8, 43, 63, 72, 74, 77, 79–82, 84–5, 93, 104–5, 128, 144, 151, 188–89
textiles, 174–75, 191–92
theatre, 78, 86, 163, 175, 179
Theodore of Mopsuestia, 99n11
Theodoret of Cyrus, 87
Thomas Aquinas, 125
Thomas Gallus, 39
timbre, 16, 90, 142
Toledo Cathedral, 170, 177

Torres, Rendell, 165
tranquility, 121, 125–26
transcendence, 169, 174
transept, 160, 170, 177–78
Trent, Council of, 17, 52, 162
Triduum, 23, 89, 104
Trinity, the, 59, 112
Trousdale, Ann, 78
Truax, Barry, 13–15, 18–19, 25, 28
Tsumura, David Toshio, 125

United States of America, churches in, 86, 163, 174

Vaissière, Jacqueline, 76–7
Valière, Jean-Christophe, 176
Van Leersum-Bekebrede, Lydia, 135–36
Vanden Bosch der Nederlanden, Christina, 83, 91
Varèse, Edgard, 122
vault, vaulted ceiling, 160, 167–68, 170–71, 175–76, 179
ventriloquism, 51, 76, 100
versicle and response, 62–4. *See also* dialogue, liturgical.
violence, 95, 119
visibility, 164, 177
Vitruvius, 175
vocal gesturing, 77
Voegelin, Salomé, 111

Wacker, Grant, 20, 133
Walsh, Philip J., 114
Weil, Simone, 147
Wesley, John, 163
Wheelock, Wade T., 57–60
whisper, whispering (during worship), 132, 139, 140, 149
Wiggins, Geraint, 92, 94
Wilcox, Helen, 133
Wilkinson, Robert, 41, 155

Willis, Elizabeth, 78
Willis, G. G., 100
women and noise, 130; and silence, 109, 121, 129–30; position in church, 159, 170
Wood, Julia T., 62
Word, Liturgy or Service of, 62, 65, 106
Word, the (Christ as), 3, 38, 42, 74, 103–4, 112, 115
Word of God/ of the Lord, the, 1, 41–2, 62, 69, 112–13, 126, 129, 153–54, 178, 182, 186–88, 191, 193
World Health Organization, 118, 123
Wren, Christoper, 179

Zbikowski, Lawrence M., 90
Zwingli, Ulrich, 74, 76, 88

Milton Keynes UK
Ingram Content Group UK Ltd.
UKHW021831210424
441470UK00012B/631